D1254169

WHAT OTHERS AR
ABOUT THIS BOOK:

"This is a wonderful manuscript that surely will be **a must for all who have interest, personal or professional, in Little People**. A wealth of experience and wisdom are made animatedly realistic, personal, revealing and at times humorous. Parents of Little People as well as Little People themselves will discover that it is remarkable, insightful, as well as practical. 'When your Down and Out,' as the song goes, read this book for a lift."

Charles I. Scott, Jr., M.D.
Director, Department of Genetics, Alfred I. duPont Institute
Chairman, Medical Advisory Board, Little People of America, Inc.

"I loved this manuscript and consider it a privilege to have shared so much of Angela's personal life. I enjoyed her wonderful wit and wept over some of the sadness and thoughtfulness she has experienced. **This book has certainly heightened my awareness!** I thought I knew a great deal about what it was like to be a short-statured person but like so many others, I was not realistically seeing life as a Little Person experiences it. I am much better informed as a result of this wonderful experience."

Elizabeth R. Elder, M.S.
Parent of short-statured adult.

"Every human is born a dwarf. Perhaps this is why most of us find the topic so intriguing. Because Van Etten's style encourages empathy without sympathy, it **provides a keen insight into the dwarf experience** while holding up a mirror to the 'little person' we each carry inside. You may learn more than you bargained for. I did."

Leonard P. Sawisch, PH.D.,
Dwarf and parent of a dwarf.

i

"Angela Muir Van Etten's remarkably detailed, poignant yet humorous, and instructive autobiographical account provides **a rare window into the life experiences of a dwarf** child, teen-ager, and young adult growing up in New Zealand. Ms Van Etten's autobiographical account is complemented by **wide-ranging discussions of contemporary issues** such as mobility and access, education, employment and prejudices that dwarfs confront more vulnerably and problematically than do others in our society. This book is **a unique and valuable resource** for those who wish to better understand the life experiences and concerns of Little People and others with conditions of physical difference."

Joan Ablon, PH.D.
Professor of Medical Anthropology
Author, *"Little People in America: the Social Dimensions of Dwarfism,"*
Praeger Publishers (1984).

"The author describes the real struggle for acceptance that a dwarf faces daily; however, the positive approach to life, emphasizing ability rather disability serves as **a model for all persons of short stature.** Such a positive outlook should help other dwarfs to come to terms with his/her own identity. **I recommend this honest, realistic reflection by Angela to all dwarfs, their parents, educators and interested persons.** The book handles issues in a forthright manner that presents information, sparks interest and includes a refreshing bit of humor."

R. Helen Ference, PH.D., RN
National Parent Coordinator, Little People of America, Inc
Mother of adult dwarf

DWARFS DON'T LIVE IN DOLL HOUSES

Angela Muir Van Etten, LLB., JD

Cover design: Hy and Tracy Roth

Cover photograph: Robert Van Etten

Adaptive Living

Dwarfs Don't Live in Doll Houses

Angela Muir Van Etten, LLB., JD

Published by:

Adaptive Living
P.O. Box 60857
Rochester, NY 14606
(716) 458-5455

Printed in the United States of America

Library of Congress Catalog Card Number: **88-70331**

ISBN: **0-945727-80-1** Softcover

WHY PEOPLE SHOULD READ THIS BOOK:

DWARFS WILL IDENTIFY with the experiences of the author and will be encouraged to accept themselves as individuals of value and to defend their right to a place alongside, not beneath, others in the community.

PARENTS WILL OVERCOME their disappointment and despair at the birth of a dwarf child, and will understand that in return for loving, disciplining, and developing independence and self-esteem in their child, they will be rewarded with a truly whole person fully prepared to meet the world's challenges.

RELATIVES WILL APPRECIATE their role in relating to both the parents and the dwarf in the family.

EDUCATORS WILL LEARN that dwarf children are denied an equal education unless they are integrated into regular classrooms, and are treated according to their age, not their size.

PROFESSIONALS WILL SEE the dynamics of the life experience and expectations of the dwarfs and families they counsel.

DISABLED PEOPLE WILL RECOGNIZE the similarity between the dwarf experience and their own in maintaining self-respect in the face of public ridicule and rejection, and in achieving a positive public reaction through education and integration.

ALL PEOPLE WILL ACCEPT the reality and equality of dwarfs in society by breaking through the barriers which prevent meaningful interaction.

ACKNOWLEDGMENTS

This book would not have been possible without:

BARBARA MUIR, my loving mother, whose influence in my life will never be forgotten and can never be replaced;

NEIL MUIR, my loving father, whose influence in my life is still being exercised and will always be cherished;

ROBERT VAN ETTEN, my loving husband, whose emotional support and technical ability enabled me to carry this project through to its conclusion;

The opportunity I was given by the Internal Affairs Department of New Zealand, as a **WINSTON CHURCHILL FELLOWSHIP** recipient in 1981, to travel to America and meet so many members of the Disability Movement in the United States, including members of the Little People of America, Inc.

The moral support and valuable insight of my FRIENDS and FAMILY who were willing to read and critique this manuscript and contributed to the book in its various stages of development.

In particular, I acknowledge the contributions of:

Joan Ablon	Wayne Foster	Leonard Sawisch
Barbara Aring	Beverly Jacklin	Nan Scarlett
Ed Aring	Craig McCulloh	Charles I. Scott, Jr.
Evelyn Asplin	Carol McDonald	Joel Smith
Tammy Benton	Harry McDonald	Marguerite Smith
Deborah Muir Coote	David Minneman	Norman Smith
Betty Elder	Neil Muir	Rodger Smith
Karen Ellmore	Gregory Muir	Harriet Stickney
Helen Ference	Merrin Parker	Joan Teshima

TABLE OF CONTENTS

Dwarfs Don't Live In Doll Houses

Chapter One

UNDERSTOOD

"This is one that should never have been born!" The exclamation was whispered by the Director of Nursing in the corner of the delivery room on August 3rd, 1953. My mother was only told about my beautiful head of blond hair. However, my aunt got the full story and expressed her anguish in one word. *"Why?"*

A nurse explained, *"It's like a packet of one hundred seeds that are planted; ninety-nine grow as expected, one will be different."* Why this should happen was not the only question asked. Hanging in the balance was the question of whether I was going to live. Things certainly looked grim. I was a suspected blue baby and I was not expected to survive, let alone walk. Almost every bone in my body was dislocated; I was so tiny that I had to be fed with an eye-dropper. If there was to be any hope for my future, extensive surgery would be necessary.

A hospital Chaplain was rushed in for the Christening so embarrassment would be avoided if I died on the operating table. Too many times babies died without being christened and all hell would break loose because no clergyman could be found to bury the unchristened child! No chances would be taken with me. I was christened and given an opportunity to fight for life by an eminent surgeon who undertook a series of operations over the next two years. He soon discovered and related to my mother, *"She's as strong as an ox."* Doubts about my survival were soon put to rest. There was no way this baby was going to die; I was determined to live. I not only survived the surgeries, but proved their success by walking before I was one-year old!

Years later, my aunt found her answer to the *"why?"* question. She wrote me this poem as a birthday gift:

"Twenty-two years ago today,
A little angel made her way - to earth,
To all who've known her through the years,
her courage, laughter and her tears,
they've proved her worth,
Her family here on earth this day,
all love her much and join to say
please stay."

Early years

Before long, the first words of the Director of Nursing in the delivery room were forgotten and I won my way into the hearts of many people who were glad about my birth and very reluctant to see their 'lovely blond doll' leave the hospital. One nursing sister went so far as to try to prevent my transfer to a rehabilitation facility by hiding me in the linen closet so the doctor would not find me.

Even though the staff wanted me to stay, after two years of surgery and rehabilitation, I was discharged from the Wilson Home for Crippled Children and returned to my family to begin my initial experience in family life. My arrival totally bamboozled the neighbors.

My parents had just moved into the area with my brother, Gregory a new-born infant; I arrived soon after; then Janet who was six months younger than I was came along. Janet and I were both calling my mother 'mummy' and the neighbors were asking, *"How can they have so many children so close in age, and where are they all coming from?"*

I'm sure the mystery was soon solved when they learned Janet was my mother's youngest sister and was living with us much of the time because my grandmother was dying of cancer and I had just been released from the Wilson Home. Two years later, there was no doubt about the origin of Deborah, the fourth child. Mom was obviously pregnant.

My addition to the family merely added to a life already full and hectic. There were regular trips to visit my sick grandmother; dad worked long hours in his newly formed bricklaying business while mom had to care for three children under the age of three years. The birth of my sister Deborah two years later meant mom had the care of four children under the age of five!

My parents were surprised to learn I was coming home. No one had prepared them that one day I would leave the convalescent home. None of us were ready for it.

As the Home was too far away for my parents to visit regularly, we saw little of each other. When they came to visit, I would have nothing to do with them and would scream during their entire visit. It was so embarrassing; when they came they would take me somewhere quiet to try and calm me down; but I only stopped screaming when someone else took me in their arms. Even total strangers had better luck with me than my parents did. It was particularly painful for my mother since I wouldn't even talk to her.

The Home attempted to ease my transition by arranging occasional weekend visits, but I would not cooperate. Even though able to speak fluently, when released into their custody for the weekend, I refused to talk. One day while mom was bending over doing the vacuuming, I came up behind her and asked, *"What are you doing nur?"* She looked up amazed to hear me speak! However, as soon as she lifted her head, I realized that she wasn't a nurse, and clammed up instantly. It was not the beginning of our communication.

Regardless of my attitude toward my parents, and the desire of the nursing staff to have me stay, the powers that be decided I should go home. It was said, *"It is high time Angela experienced a family environment."*

Although the news took my parents by surprise, they rose to the occasion and agreed I should come home. They were given the option of placing me in foster care, but refused it. As far as they were concerned, I was their child and they would be the ones to care for me. The emotional trauma experienced at my birth was dealt with long before and my parents were willing to accept me as just another one of their children. Maybe it was because there was no time for anything else, but I credit them with more than that. I believe they saw the differences between me and the other children, but chose not to treat me differently.

My parents were as proud of me as they were of my brother and sister. I believe it was their ability to come to terms with their own grief and disappointment after my birth which enabled me to adapt to my size and the limitations associated with short-stature.[1]

Their willingness to take photos and place them in the family album reveals their acceptance and pride. I am forever grateful for their attitude, especially when I hear the horror stories of some Little People. One woman tells with great pain, how she was deliberately sent out on an errand, so she would be out of sight whenever family photos were being taken. A dwarf wasn't wanted in the picture!

I was never made to feel that I didn't belong and was included in as many activities as the rest of the family.[2] Their expectations of me were the same as those expected of my siblings; no special allowances were made. Even so, my parents understanding did not eliminate our time of adjustment after my release from the Wilson Home.

I had been greatly loved in the Home and was used to being pampered by the staff. This made things doubly difficult for mom and dad, who did not have the time to give me such attention. Besides, it was the last thing I needed.

I increased my mother's daily washing pile by wetting the bed most nights. Not so unusual for a two year old child, especially after such a big change in living arrangements. However, mom and dad were told I did not wet the bed and was fully toilet-trained.

My father suspected I was doing it deliberately. His judgment seemed harsh to mom who could accept it was taking time for me to settle down, or because of being in a strange room was having trouble finding my way to the bathroom in the dark. Dad came to his conclusion after many nights of trying to anticipate my toilet needs by taking me to the bathroom during the night. He noticed that even in the early hours of the morning, there were still no signs of wetting. It was

1   Diane L. Rotnem, *"Size Versus Age: Ambiguities in Parenting Short-Statured Children"* (1984) printed in *"Slow Grows the Child: the Psychosocial Aspects of Growth Delay,"* Lawrence Ehrlbaum Associates, Publisher.

2   Studies show that the familial environment may be an important contributing factor to the social adjustment of short-statured children, according to Deborah Young-Hyman, *"Effects of Short Stature on Social Competence,"* (1984) printed in *"Slow Grows the Child: the Psychosocial Aspects of Growth Delay,"* Lawrence Erlbaum Associates, Publisher.

his theory that I would wet the bed after I was awake. Determined to catch me, he got up extra early one morning to check. He found me lying wide awake and the bed warmly wet!

He was absolutely right. I was old enough to know exactly what I was doing and had been wetting the bed on purpose. He decided I was also old enough to learn that bed-wetting was not acceptable, and he gave me a good spanking. The result? I never wet the bed again.

My parents recognized from the outset that I needed discipline in the same way any child does. I probably needed even more because of my experience in the hospital where so many had been at my beck and call. Unfortunately, not everybody understood this.

My mother clearly recalls the day she was shopping with my brother and me. We were sharing a stroller and were told to stay put while she went into the store. I was four years old and fully capable of obeying instructions. Like typical children, we were not worthy of our mother's trust and as soon as she turned her back, we both climbed out.

Mom came back to find us running around and promptly spanked us both. An elderly gentleman on the street proceeded to reprimand mom for disciplining me. How dare she hit a child so small? Fortunately my mother was a strong minded young woman and was able to ignore his advice. However, before storming off down the road she retorted, *"The child is old enough to know exactly what she's doing!"* His protection was the last thing I needed.

My mother knew that I was more in need of discipline than my brother. After all, I was two years older and knew better than he did. Although mom knew not to treat me differently, at times she was willing to make allowances for my physical limitations. This was not one of those occasions and she was not about to limit my understanding of appropriate behavior. I was going to be taught the same things that other children are taught --- and that day, it was learning to do what I was told. My physical handicap was no excuse for disobedience.

Many people were like the old man and tried to compensate for my physical differences. I was constantly being spoiled by relatives. Some would even growl at my parents for being too harsh on 'poor little Angela.' Perfect strangers would even approach us, wanting to give me money. They would completely ignore my brother and sister standing close by.

At a young age, I was ready to take their money not realizing why they were making the gift. Mom regularly tried to refuse the offer but my response often interfered with her efforts. One time I remember well.

We were at the local fair-grounds when an elderly man reeking of liquor fumes offered me a quarter. I wasn't concerned about who he was or why he was giving it. All I could see, was that it translated into a ride on the merry-go-round. I wanted the ride and gladly accepted the money. Mom could not persuade me to give the money back; the man disappeared into the crowd and I got my ride.

I was too young to know and other people were too ignorant to see the long term effects of such charitable gestures. Consequently, it fell to my parents to try and off-set these incidents. Mom had to keep especially alert at the home of my elderly aunts.

Frequently the aunts would slip me a quarter when they thought my brother and sister were not looking. However, such moves seldom escaped the eagle eyes of either my mother or sister. On the way home in the car, mom would ask how much I got and insist that I share it with the other two who had either received nothing or a dime in comparison to my quarter.

In spite of my parents attempt to equalize the attention given, I still received benefits that my brother and sister didn't get. There were the special events for crippled children, hosted annually by the New Zealand Crippled Children's Society. Each year, I got a bird's eye view of the Santa parade from the parking lot of the Farmers Trading Company in Auckland. Afterwards, I was spoiled with hundreds of other kids at a fine party and given Christmas presents.

Medical Considerations

Until I was twenty-two years old, there were regular medical check-ups at either Middlemore Hospital in south Auckland, or at the clinic of the New Zealand Crippled Children's Society branch in Auckland. The visits were more to observe my progress than a search for a cure.

I'm grateful that my parents could accept that my dwarfism, known as Larsen's Syndrome, had come to stay. They did not parade me to endless doctors or subject me to the indignities of constant dressing and undressing, poking and prodding; over-expose me to radiation with the taking of countless x-rays for research purposes; force me to take useless remedies such as calcium tablets, or stretching exercises. Offers to take me to faith healers were also declined.

Of course my parents understood the value of routine medical care and advice. I was taken on a regular basis for check-ups. However, they didn't expect the physicians to make the impossible happen. My parents were happy so long as everything possible was being done for me. For a long time, they didn't even know what height I could be expected to reach.

When I was about seven, I remember my mother asking my orthopedic specialist how much more I would grow. It was a legitimate question, since I was much smaller than other kids my age. Just how small, did not hit mom until she saw me perform in a school play next to much bigger class-mates.

The specialist couldn't tell her how tall I would grow. How could he when he didn't know himself? Not that his uncertainty reflected incompetence, rather it showed the rarity of my condition for which there were more questions than answers. It also accounted for the great interest in my case.

At each appointment, the orthopedist had at least one student or visiting doctor observing. He would explain my condition to them and point out its various characteristics. My nose, hands and legs attracted the most attention. They would feel the bridge of my nose, fiddle with my fingers and notice how neither my thumb or knees would bend. There was always a closing number.

I'd be asked to get up from the couch where I'd been lying for the examination, lift my dress and do my walking routine. I knew the number by heart. Walk here a little, there a little, and then just smile a little. Their response was as predictable as an enraptured audience. They would say, *"Do it again, do it again."* I would do my encore and everyone was happy, except me. If I'd been paid for all those performances, I'd be a millionaire today. Instead, I just grew older and wiser.

The students weren't the only ones who learned about my condition at those sessions. I was just as attentive as they were. I learned that at that time there were only six cases of my syndrome recorded in medical literature. Years later, I discovered that the condition is named after the San Francisco orthopedist who diagnosed the first case and that other cases have been sporadically reported.[1]

My specialist had only seen one other person with the syndrome and that was a middle-aged gentleman who had grown to more than five feet and was admitted to the hospital with an unrelated complaint. I have yet to meet someone with Larsen's Syndrome.

My progress was recorded conscientiously by radiographers, photographers, doctors and student doctors. At least, they did their best. In my early years, I was not in the least bit cooperative. I not only refused to do encores, but refused to perform the routine in the first place. The only performing I did was to scream and cry when asked to remove my clothes for photos; wriggle around when x-rays were being taken and refuse to walk across the room for the doctors' observation. Of course, my doctor was much smarter than I and would watch the walk I was very happy to make --- down the corridor in a fast retreat from his office.

When my girlfriend left school, she became a radiographer at Middlemore Hospital, where many of my childhood x-rays and photos were taken and was able to research my medical file. She said it was hilarious. All those early photos showed a child fully expressing the anger of such indignities.

When I was about seven, the doctors decided that my function could be improved by straightening my legs with surgery. There was no urgency, so I was put on a waiting list. The only stipulation was that the procedures be done separately and completed before I began high school. I heard the doctors all talking about surgery and though I knew what was being said, the significance did not sink in. Four years went by before it became a reality.

The experience of surgery was a tremendous shock. Even though it wasn't my first time on the table, the memories of the operations in my first two-years of life were discarded with diapers and baby-talk; I had no recollection of them.

After waking up from the surgery performed on my right leg and discovering how I had to be for two months, I was furious with my

---

1   Ann Radiol, 15:297-328 (March/April 1972), a 1972 review of cases of Larsen's syndrome in medical literature discloses reports of 46 patients.

mother and let her know it. I told her angrily, *"You know I can't sleep on my back."*

I guess she knew what was coming, but thought it best not to tell me. This strikes me clearly as I remember the Sunday morning mom admitted me to the hospital. It was also the morning to announce the results of the Sunday School Union exams. Mom knew this and took me to Sunday School before we went to the hospital. I didn't know why, until I was presented with my diploma and prize for earning honors. We left the class straight afterwards with the best wishes of our church friends. Mom was struggling to hold back the tears as we walked out to the car. No doubt she was even more upset when I vented my anger against her after coming out of surgery a couple of days later.

However, my anger could not change anything and sleep on my back was exactly what I had to do. Turning to the side was impossible, because the splint on my leg was hooked over a post at the end of the bed. It turned out that getting to sleep was not to be my only problem. I soon discovered, I could not get out of bed either!

The bed became my host for night and daytime activities: eating, bathing, toileting, you name it. School, the one activity I would have been glad to escape, was even brought to me in bed. My incapacity could not get me out of that.

Well, I did learn how to sleep on my back and eventually stopped blaming mom for my predicament. She faithfully visited me in the hospital every day for a month. I even got to recognize her footsteps coming down the hall. The daily twelve mile trek to the hospital was hard enough, but I suspect the second month was even more difficult. Mom had to care for me at home.

No special nursing required my continued stay in the hospital and mom was told I could go home. The only qualification needed was a willing hand to bath, pan, feed, and wait on me. Mom got the job. Whenever she went out, she had to find someone to stay with me in the unlikely event the house caught on fire, or in the very likely event I needed to use the bed-pan. Our house was so small that had I been carried into the living room to watch television, as I often wanted to do, there would have been little room for anyone else. I wasn't allowed the luxury of taking up the whole couch and instead had to stay in my bedroom. It didn't seem fair, all I wanted to do was watch television.

After expressing myself long enough, a settlement was finally reached. The solution satisfied everyone. There was a way all of us could watch TV: the rest of the family in the living room and me from the bedroom through a mirror dad rigged up. This was possible, because my bedroom was once an outside verandah and the windows of the living room still faced onto the verandah. By balancing a mirror in one of the windows, I could see the reflection of the television from my bed. It was marvelous. Now I only complained on the days dad was late coming home from work, as he was the only one who could set up the mirror.

Since my bedroom overlooked the street, I could also watch people coming and going. To give me a better view, my bed was even raised on cinder blocks. Friends would drop by on their way home from school to say hello and to deliver and collect my homework.

When I was still in the hospital, one class assignment was for everyone to write to me. I thoroughly enjoyed those letters and kept them for years. Some of us were Bonanza fans and this showed up in our letters. My brother's Little Joe and Adam wrote to me as Hoss, telling about all the antics of Ben Cartwright (our school-teacher) on the war-path. I heard how much everyone was missing me and of the seating change in the classroom.

Two and a half months later, I was glad to take my new seat assignment. According to my school teacher's report at the end of the year, I came through the surgery experience with my education unscathed. He gave credit to the hospital instructor saying, *"Angela seemed to lose nothing by her spell in the hospital; she maintains high standards of achievement. A very good girl."*

The surgery on my left leg was not scheduled until my second year of high school. Someone forgot the earlier advice that my high school education should not be interrupted. However, to complain would not recover the time, so at age fourteen arrangements were made for surgery on my left leg. I was not too thrilled about it. I expected to be in the hospital for three months and gave this notice to my teachers and said goodbye to my friends.

The doctors thoroughly embarrassed me by their week long observations. At fourteen, I did not appreciate topless modeling and parades, certainly not when I was the model. It was little consolation for the medical photographer to tell me that I stood like the Statue of Liberty.

Embarrassment turned to anxiety when I saw traction being rigged on my bed, was refused breakfast, was dressed in a surgery gown, and heard the ward sister phone to tell my mother I was on the way to surgery. However, just before being given the final injection, my surgeon sent word that he wanted to see me in his office before I was taken to surgery. It turned out to be my reprieve.

He decided the risk of surgery was far greater than the value it could potentially offer. There had been little if any functional improvement from the previous surgery on my right leg. (The only noticeable difference to me was the rounder shape of the knee). Since I was doing so well, he didn't want to mess up anything. He called the surgery off, and I was saved from the knife.

Even though it was great news, I felt silly going back to school and telling everyone I wouldn't be in the hospital for three months after all. It seemed like I had made a big thing out of nothing. As silly as I felt, I knew it was better than facing surgery again.

Social Skills

My medical needs were secondary to the additional social skills required to be happy in a world which delights in taunting those who are different. My parents accepted me and taught me to accept myself. Together we had to teach others that I was not an object of ridicule.

My responses to other people were pretty much learned from my parents. When people would stare and make fun of me with teasing and name-calling, my parents would usually walk on and ignore them. Between ourselves, we might comment on how rude they were, but rarely would we demean ourselves by retorting.

I was encouraged to ignore rudeness. Most people would limit themselves to staring, so it was easy to block them out. If any reaction was called for, I was taught,

"It is better to smile than scowl. After all, most people are only acting in ignorance and don't even realize they're being rude. It's only natural for people to look at something or someone different. A positive response will make it easier for people to accept you."

Many years later when our family became involved in the Little People of New Zealand,[1] we met one parent with a different philosophy. This mother encouraged her child to reciprocate the name-calling and teasing. This didn't help her son to be accepted into the community, or to face himself.

Some parents, involved in the Little People of America, Inc.,[2] have suggested preparing the child for name-calling by deliberately using in a loving way in the family circle all the phrases or words that the child is likely to hear others use. In this way the child learns not to attach negative feelings to the name-calling episodes.[3] However, all the teaching in the world does not prepare a child for some situations. People can be so exasperating. A mother who had taught her fourteen-year old son to be polite encouraged him to let it all fly out the window one day. They were at a family wedding and as part of the reception line greeted the guests. Every single person who came by patted him on the head. Mother and son somehow continued to smile and greet the guests. However, after a hundred or more pats, the mother was so frustrated that she turned to her son and said, *"If they insist on patting you on the head like a dog, I give you permission to bite them like one."* Fortunately, the son was so accustomed to dealing with people's infuriating behavior that he was able to withstand that temptation.

Another parent taught her child to be polite, but had reasons other than education. She feared that if her daughter was rude, people would dislike her and might even take a swing at her. The daughter suspects a more dangerous belief accompanied her mother's advice, *"Big people*

---

1   The inaugural meeting was in 1968, at the Tauherenikau Race Course, Wairarapa, New Zealand.

2   Information about the Little People of America, Inc., can be obtained from Post Office Box 633, San Bruno, CA 94066, USA.

3   Wendy Ricker, Report of a Discussion by Parent Members in the Little People of America, Inc.

don't like to be told what to do by Little People, so don't talk back."

Common sense was the source of my parents wisdom. There was no organization for Little People until I was sixteen-years old and so they figured things out for themselves. Today many parents are assisted by associating with an organization for Little People and their families.[1] Mutual sharing of experiences helps parents in their initial time of adjustment and continues to provide a resource, through the years of their child's development.[2]

Though not a part of an organization in the early years, I believe my parents appreciated the understanding of two parents who were members of the Little People of America, Inc. They taught their son to *"treat the public with compassion and to educate them into the ways of a little person. Never be antagnostic towards an uneducated public."*[3]

My parents were not totally lacking guidance. Some advice was given by a Field Officer of the New Zealand Crippled Children's Society. She would try to visit my mother on an annual basis, to answer questions and comment on things she noticed. However when the rough times came, my parents had to deal with them alone.

Sometimes I would come home from school quite distraught and mom would wheedle out of me what had happened. One day a girl in my class predicted that I would not be able to walk when I got older. Her claim convinced me, as she had the word of authority from her mother who was a nurse. I don't remember what answer my mother gave, but it was enough to relieve my fears for the future.

One of the best things my parents did to teach me appreciation of people and responsibility for society was done without their even being conscious of it. Our home was always full of visitors, whether for a cup of tea, a meeting, a party, staying for the weekend, or boarding for the year. Through my parent's hospitality our family was extended far beyond its nucleus. We all participated in hosting our guests from the

1   There is an international network of organizations for short-statured individuals and their families in about twenty countries around the world. For specific information on any one of these organizations write to the International Coordinator, Miss Pam Rutt, 24 Pinchfield, Maple Cross, Rickmansworth, Herts WD2 2TP, England.

2   For further discussion on the advantages of belonging to an organization for Little People, see Chapter 8, *"Shared."*

3   Priscilla P. Strudwick, *"the Story of John Phillips Strudwick as Seen by his Parents"* (1976).

task of simply making conversation to preparing their sleeping quarters.

We never set out to have boarders, they just arrived at times of need: Eric not long after he emigrated from England; mom's brother John when he first left school and needed a place to live and work; mom's sister Janet returned to the family at age fourteen for the last three years of high school when her father and stepmother separated; Sam, a school friend of my brother's and a state ward needed a placement near our high school so that he could take his University qualifying exam; Vagn from Denmark could not speak English and was looking for both work and board; Alan a school teacher friend was trying to save money; and Rodger needed a roof over his head when he came home from work to find his apartment burned out.

Somehow this exposure to many people with their various needs and values helped me to be more open and willing to share with others. Our family environment also reached the many people who walked through our doors for a few hours. They could see that life with a Little Person was not so unusual and rarely deserved special mention.

Treated according to age

It was important to my development as an independent mature person that I be treated according to my age not my size. Most of the public had difficulty doing this, as the following examples demonstrate.

One day when waiting for my mother in a store, the assistant in an effort to make conversation asked me what class I was in at school. I was fourteen and told her I was in grade ten. To my infuriation, she heard me say grade two! I could think of no better response than to ignore her. I decided if she was silly enough to think that the young teenage girl sitting in front of her wearing a bra and lipstick was only seven years old, what use would it be to correct her?

My parents knew I was old enough to make bus trips alone, but bus drivers had a lot to learn. When I was fifteen, I rode the bus every day for a week to attend a vocational assessment course in the city. On my very first morning, an incident occurred which I will never forget.

I knew my destination well and when the bus turned onto the street, I knew it was still three stops away. However, at the first stop, I was mortified when the driver stopped the bus and called out, *"Don't you want to get off here?"* I didn't take any notice of him, as I assumed he was speaking to some little old lady having difficulty getting out of her seat. That was a mistake. He repeated himself and this time his question was obviously directed at me. (He must have taken note of my destination at the time I purchased my ticket).

I was embarrassed to have all attention turned toward me and furious at him for treating me like a young child who did not know one end of the street from the other. Though I was tempted to tell him where to get off, I controlled myself and just told him, *"No, I want to get off at Mount Street."* Two stops later, I did exactly that without any help from the driver.

The driver's mistake was that he not only said the wrong thing, but spoke to me at an age when I was highly indignant if anyone mistook me for a child, let alone treated me like one. But then, he wasn't the only confused driver that week.

Most drivers didn't say anything, they just charged me half fare. Even when I was charged full fare one way and half the other, I didn't let their contradictions disturb me. It was all a part of my learning that although old enough to be independent, others had to be shown I was capable.

Surprisingly, even the professionals had trouble treating me according to my age. This was apparent at age ten when I attended a party for children with disabilities on a ferry in the Auckland harbor. It was during a school vacation, and I was allowed to bring a guest. Janet was staying with us for the vacation and was pleased to join me for the event. When it came time to give out the presents, Janet was quite disgusted when they gave me a book suitable for a child of five or six years old. She grabbed it off me and returned it in disgust, telling my benefactor that I was older than she was. Janet wasted no time correcting their mistake. She wanted to be certain that I received a gift more appropriate for my age.

As neither the public nor the professionals were very proficient at treating me according to my age, the responsibility fell to my parents. They took it very seriously. Much more than I appreciated.

As the eldest child, I was the first to be given regular chores and like most kids complained bitterly. I couldn't wait until my sister was old enough to peel the potatoes; I figured she would succeed to my job.

As a teen-ager, I kept a diary for a couple of years. I read now with great amusement how put upon I felt about having to help out. At fifteen, I wrote:

"I'm becoming a regular housewife, what with washing, ironing, and cooking, I'll be ruining my hands. It seems as though I've been washing up dishes all day. I just get one load cleaned up and there's another to start on."

Even though my parents did their best to treat me according to my age, I didn't always think they were treating me as they should. I used to get so mad with mom when she wouldn't let me stay up later than my brother, even though I was two years older.

My mother was fully aware of who was the eldest, but also realized that I got more tired physically. She kept telling me this was the reason we both had the same bedtime, but I refused to accept this reasoning. The fact that I would get headaches and become nauseous when lacking sleep was irrelevant to me. I was only interested in comparing bedtimes with my girlfriends. From that, I decided I was going to bed much too early.

At age fifteen, I was still vehemently expressing myself about being expected to retire early. I wrote in my diary, *"I went to bed absolutely ropeable (furious), thinking all sorts of horrible things."* As always, my mother had the last word, (only because she was much older than I) and in spite of all my objections, I was still sent to bed early. Strangely enough, my brother now tells me he used to be just as angry at mom for sending him to bed earlier than he thought was appropriate.

Occasionally some relatives would recognize that my small size did not equate with the number of years I had accumulated. I have great pleasure in remembering how at a family wedding my cousin offered me a sherry. I was quick to accept. Mom didn't think that at fourteen I was ready to partake in adult beverages, but she was too late. I was already drinking the sherry he offered.

To my frustration, however, many of the relatives found it impossible to treat me as they would someone else of my age. Their behavior drove me crazy. On one occasion after visiting with the elderly aunts, my teen-age diary states *"It's a wonder I don't have a rash under my chin, because everyone who came into the room grabbed me under the chin and stroked me like a cat."* I dreaded those family visits.

In spite of my frustration, I was able to excuse the aunts because of their advanced years. I was much more flustered by the unwillingess of people to hire me as a baby sitter. It was obvious why they were slow to invite me and at fifteen, I noted my fury in my diary by writing:

" Lately I'm just getting sick of people underestimating me. It annoys me intensely. People I know, talk to me as though I'm only a little girl of two or three. I feel like being really rude. I'd quite like to get a baby-sitting job, but of course that's impossible as no one would think I was responsible enough, just because I'm short."

Two more disappointing years passed after that diary entry, and it wasn't until I reached seventeen that I was finally offered a baby-sitting job. This was exciting; at last, I was recognized as being just as capable as other girls my age. The added financial reward made it even more worthwhile.

The baby-sitting opportunity came from a friend who played badminton with my mother. It was the year her husband was on overseas military service. The kids were always well behaved, knowing their routine and bedtimes. It hardly deserved the title of 'work,' as one of the older children would always make me a hot drink, and they were so good. I could even continue my school homework uninterrupted.

I definitely preferred to sit for older children, at least those old enough to be reasoned with. This decision was made after my experience helping out in the church nursery school. One tortuous afternoon spent in supervising several youngsters, ended up in me being threatened by a five year old. He was convinced he could beat me up in a fight and would have put his strength to the test given the opportunity. Fortunately, I was not the only supervisor and he didn't get me into the ring.

Self-image

As I approached puberty, I began to have trouble with my self-image. Until then, I had never been self-conscious about my appearance. However, at eleven years old it became a very touchy subject. My parents tried their best to be diplomatic and understanding, but their advice didn't always help.

The issue first came up when the girls had to change into sports clothes at school. There was no way I wanted to show off my legs, but wearing shorts was compulsory. The only way out was to bring a note from a parent giving a legitimate reason for an exemption. It seemed like my way out.

I asked mom for the note and was most upset when she refused. I cried and complained how awful shorts made me look and said I didn't care what anyone said, I was not going to wear them. She still wouldn't write the note and called dad into the discussion to see if he could reason with me.

Dad told me to put the shorts on and stand in front of the mirror. I did that and dad asked me, *"Can you see anything wrong with the way they look?"* I could see they looked okay and agreed there was nothing wrong with them. He reinforced my observation and probably thought that was the end of the matter.

The next day, I went off to school without a note, with the shorts in my school-bag and a firm resolve never to wear them. Mom and dad didn't understand that it was easy for us to think I looked okay, we were all used to the way I looked, but the other kids weren't used to seeing me. No way did I want them staring at my legs and I wasn't going to give them the chance.

I decided to try to get by without the note. Already the Principal had told me I didn't have to participate in sports unless I wanted to. Anyway, I reasoned my contribution to the game was minimal. In afternoon soft-ball, I only stood to bat and had someone else run for me. There was absolutely no reason for me to wear shorts.

I was almost positive no teacher would have the nerve to tell me to put them on. I was right. In the next two years, not one teacher asked me for a note or told me to go and change. I succeeded in never wearing shorts in school.

My father never knew that our session in front of the mirror did not resolve the shorts crisis (at least I didn't tell him), but he realized my image crisis was not over. A couple of years later, a similar issue came up on our annual summer beach vacation.

All the family would go down to the beach for the day to relax, sun and swim. I would go too, but instead of sitting with everyone else, I began secluding myself in the sand-hills. Getting a suntan was still important, so I was willing to wear my bathing suit. However, I was not prepared for every man and his dog to see me in it. Dad noticed my peculiar behavior and without any discussion told me to come and sit with the rest of the family. He had more nerve than my teachers and I had to obey his command.

It was a hard lesson for me to learn, but without it I would have missed out on so much. Even today, I'm still self-conscious in my bathing suit, but grateful that I was taught to submerge such feelings so that I could be included in all the fun things that can happen on the beach.

I'll never forget the day mom was trying to help me get a good surf ride on a hand held surf board. I stood with the board and she was poised ready to throw me into a wave. The opportunity soon came. Actually three waves piled on top of each other. I wasn't too sure it would be a good experience, especially as the water around us was receding into the approaching triple-decker, but there was no turning back.

From ankle deep water, I was lost in the force of the four-foot wave crashing me onto the sand. My board went flying; my bathing cap was swished off and I got a fast ride in on the bottom of the ocean floor. My feet were the only evidence of my position in the wave. They rode in all the way facing their soles to the sun!

Mom waited for me to surface expecting a barrage of abuse from me. However the situation was so absurd, all we could do was laugh. It was enough excitement for the day and I gladly returned to the safety of my towel and sun-chair on the beach.

I knew who was the better off when years later I met another Little Person who did not even own a bathing suit. Her family joined us on the beach one afternoon and she hardly seemed to enjoy herself. She could only watch us having fun.

Today I rarely go into such vigorous surf. I feel I'm past the age when it's fun to be buffeted about by the elements. It's much more enjoyable to experience the swirling waters of a whirl pool.

Even though I learned to be comfortable with my own body as a teen-ager, I still wanted to look like and be as attractive and up to date as the other girls my age. For a while, I was even reluctant to participate in activities if I was going to stand out as different. Once I refused to attend a concert, because everyone was going to sit on cushions on the floor. That was too uncomfortable for me and I would have been the only one sitting on a chair. Rather than stand out as different, I chose not to go.

For me cosmetics and clothes were the key to looking like the others. Simple things like make-up, stockings, shaving my legs, clothes and hair-styles made the difference between belonging and not belonging. It was very important to feel that I belonged.

At fourteen, it was a thrill to wear lipstick and eye-shadow at last. They were visible signs of my maturity and of course satisfied my desire to do what the other girls were doing. Mom was happy to let me wear lipstick and eye-shadow, but slow about letting me wear stockings. I felt ridiculous wearing socks when all my girlfriends had been in stockings for months.

To make it worse, mom wouldn't even let me shave my legs! Her reason was very practical, as usual, and she tried to tell me, *"Once you start shaving you have the drudge of the job all your life."* I would not be discouraged. It felt very degrading to be the only one with hairy legs.

When I was fourteen, the matter was taken out of both our hands. I went into hospital and in the preparation for surgery my left leg was shaved. When the surgery was canceled, I was released from the hospital with one hairy and one unhairy leg and I was determined not to be seen in public like that. At last, mom agreed to let me shave; finally, I presented myself as smooth as the other girls.

Dressing like the other girls was one way of looking the same, but that was easier said than done. Because of my size, I couldn't buy clothes off-the-rack and that made it more difficult for me to keep up with fashion. However, our family had an excellent dressmaker. It was her ability to sew anything requested and my choice of the latest fabrics and designs that kept me up with the times.

I followed the fads as religiously as everyone else. During my teen-age years, dress lengths reached the two extremes of mini and midi. Some of my dresses were so short, I dared not bend over. If I dropped something, I was truly the damsel in distress and would find some obliging male to pick it up for me.

I ventured into the midi with brightly colored purple shoes to match my dress. For some time, I had to go without boots, even though they were the best combination with the calf length skirts. However, there were none to fit me and the cost prohibited my having any specially made. Fortunately, fashion itself rescued me the following year.

Granny boots came into vogue. They were perfect! Instead of reaching my calf as intended, they came right up to my knees. I was probably the last one among my friends to wear boots, but I was so pleased to have some fit that I didn't worry that at knee length they were last year's model.

Even though concerned about following fashion, I was equally concerned to wear clothes that were flattering. As a dwarf with a very short trunk, I knew not to wear clothes which cut me off in the middle. It didn't matter how fashionable waisted styles were, I never wore them. There was no doubt, they made me look fat and very unattractive.

Independence

It was never assumed, I couldn't do things. If something seemed too difficult, I was encouraged to find my own way of doing it. Stools made lots of things possible, but because of my difficulty getting on and off a stool, I would always look for alternatives.

In the house, I would merely push the doors open when I couldn't reach the handles, but I wasn't the only one doing this. Our dog Sport couldn't reach the handles either, and he used to get in by jumping up against the doors. My brother also confesses to kicking doors open (no doubt he had his own reasons for that). Between the three of us, we wore out the closing mechanism on more than one door in the house, and eventually they would not latch. When the latches were finally replaced, the handles were lowered to within my reach.

A coat-hanger was given many roles: flicking light-switches on and off; pushing off stockings or socks; not to mention for hanging clothes on. In time, my great-grandfather relieved the coat-hanger of one duty. He made me a shoe horn, which I used to both push off my socks and stockings and to ease my feet into shoes. The rail on one side of the wardrobe was lowered for me to hang my clothes up without the need to use a stool. The other side was left at regular height for my sister.

I was never allowed to use my size as an excuse to get out of anything. I could work at the counter standing on a stool, and iron using our board which was easily lowered to my height. A stool in our kitchen was part of the regular decor. It was so much a part of me at the counter, that my brother or sister would frequently slide the stool sideways. If I was standing in front of a cupboard they wanted to get into, they often forgot I was standing on the stool, and that such a surprise move could easily topple me. It was common for me to roar at them and to angrily ask how they would like an equivalent experience of having a rug pulled out from underneath their feet? Yet they were never responsible for me falling off the stool. The day I fell, it was my own fault.

As my legs don't bend, I had developed a habit of lifting myself up onto the stool by resting one hand on the counter and the other on the slide-out cutting board. Unfortunately, the cutting board wore out after such continued abuse and eventually snapped in two underneath my weight. The day it snapped, I went crashing to the floor with such a noise that everyone in the house came running. They found me lying on the floor next to the cracked-off cutting board. The only damage I suffered was a sprained left hand. The crash got me out of the day's dishes, but the experience was too traumatic to use as a way of getting out of dishes on a regular basis.

I'm sure my parents realized how difficult it was for me to get on and off the stool, but they also knew that it would be harder on me in the long run if I didn't learn to be independent. In their wisdom, they chose not to fuss over or do everything for me.

My parents were also concerned that I not be dependent on them to get to and from school. Although I began school with rides in a taxi, I was soon strong enough to walk the distance. Naturally, after such a luxurious beginning, I preferred to be driven and on the mornings my father was working at home I would try to cajole him into giving me a ride.

He regularly withstood my pleas and the imploring looks of my girlfriend, who I had wait with me while I asked, hoping the additional pressure of her presence would be too great for him. He would only succumb on the days when it was raining, otherwise his reply was, *"No, you better get on your way before you're late."* It was too bad that by waiting, we had already made ourselves late! He was too smart to be fooled by that trick. Believe me, he was not too popular with either of us. However, his wisdom did set me on the road to independence.

Being allowed to try things out for myself got me to participate in many things. I even learned to rollerskate. Admittedly, my pace was really slow, and I balanced myself with a cane, but I proved it could be done. The caution used saved me from the many spills the other kids had and kept me rolling with the crowd.

I was not allowed to try everything, however. Iceskating, for example, was on the 'no' list. I was only young, but well remember my mother telling me I could not ice skate because my ankles would not be able to take the stress. She was right in her assessment that iceskates were more dangerous than rollerskates, but knowing the danger didn't help me accept it. Yet, I had to learn there were some activities not suitable for my participation. It was the first time I remember being left to watch from the side line, but it certainly would not be the last.

My parents also taught me how to be independent of them, by allowing me to go places without them. I attended my first camp with a school friend when I was about eight years old. It was for one week, and we thoroughly enjoyed ourselves. Yet mom wasn't too pleased when we got home. I hadn't bathed in the whole week! She couldn't get me in the bath fast enough and I was most indignant as she scrubbed me clean. Our requests to go back the following year were flatly refused.

Although still concerned about the adequacy of supervision, the one bad experience did not mean mom stopped me from attending other camps. Over the years, I attended quite a few. The ones I enjoyed the most were the Christian camps of my teen-age years. I went to most of these with my own friends; we had a great time together.

It was also fun staying over-night with girlfriends. We would chatter and giggle into the wee hours of the morning. At age fifteen, I wanted to go and stay for a week with a girlfriend who lived about three-hundred miles from our home. I was surprised that mom agreed to let me go. Today I'm told she was reluctant, but was persuaded by dad's advice that I should be given the chance to flap my wings. I felt very grown up, being allowed to make that train trip alone.

My independence was jealously guarded. If anyone tried to take it away or suggested I was dependent on others, I would get really mad. One morning, when walking to school with my friend Raewyn and Janet, we had a terrible argument. Janet said I was dependent on other people and Raewyn and I disputed it. Though the heat of the argument passed, I was ever watchful to be sure Janet could never prove her point.

Mobility

It was not very easy for my family when we all attended a fair or function where there was a lot of walking around. I was too old for a stroller and didn't need a wheelchair on a regular basis. This meant if I went along, someone would end up carrying me before the day was over. Although my father was a bricklayer and pretty strong, as the years went by it got harder and harder for him to carry me. I didn't grow very much, but my weight certainly increased. According to him, carrying me was like carrying dead weight.

He could attest to this, after almost killing himself in his efforts to carry me as a young teen-ager around one of the Waitomo Glow-worm and Limestone Caves. I would never have made it without his help up and down all those stairs. It was a real effort for dad to keep up with the guide, but somehow we made it through the whole cave. The glow of the worms only just surpassed the glow of perspiration from dad's face. (Today he tells me, his knees have never been the same since).

The annual Easter Show, much like the annual county fair in the United States, was something we all enjoyed. Mom and dad enjoyed the exhibits and we kids couldn't wait to get to the side-shows. One year, I remember well. The entire family went to the show and we kids had a wonderful time save for one scary moment.

The three of us had squeezed into one carriage for a ride on the ghost train. We were all frightened in the dark rocky tunnels watching the skeletons, hearing eerie noises, and feeling unknown 'things' brush across our faces. Greg and I tried to put up a brave front for Deborah's sake, but the ghost-like color of our faces showed how relieved we were when the carriage crashed through the doors into the daylight.

Mom stepped forward to help us out. However, she only managed to get Greg and Deb out, when the carriage suddenly took off again. I was left in the carriage by myself! The prospect of going for another ride all alone was more than I could handle. All consciousness of the need to be brave was lost and I screamed blue murder. Little did I know, the carriage was only moving a few feet forward to let the people in the carriages behind us out. I did not calm down until we were well away from that train.

With our excitement over and the money for rides gone, all we kids wanted to do was go home. I trailed behind as always, complaining that I was too tired to walk. It was too much for dad to carry me around the exhibits for the couple more hours they wanted to spend, so I'm sure mom and dad decided to come home much sooner than they wanted to. I might have been tired of walking, but they were just as tired of listening to my complaints.

The next year mom and dad made plans to go to the Show without me. I was most put out to be left with my grandmother and aunt. Probably the answer would have been to have a wheelchair for these occasions, but for some reason we never did. At that time, wheelchairs were not available for hire at a fair and it was too expensive for the family to buy one for such infrequent outings.

Besides, my father tells me, I was always too proud to use a chair anyway and would insist on walking without help. Even so, I do remember agreeing to use a chair on one occasion. Mom and I decided to rent a stroller for our visit to the zoo. It was the only way I would get to see everything. Dad wasn't with us, there was no way mom could carry me and I didn't want to be left at home.

The disadvantage of using a stroller was that it made it even more difficult for people to treat me as a nine year old. They were much more inclined to baby me. However, their behavior was almost excusable when you consider I was using a toddler's chair. How could they know any better?

At age eleven, I was confronted with the challenge of almost a mile between our house and my new school. Obviously that was too far for me to walk comfortably and any suggestion that I stay at home would have been treated as absurd. My parents realized this and determined to find me an independent means of transport. Their solution was to buy me a bike.

Some thinking had to go into how I was going to ride the bike. It was easy to find a child's size learner bike, but how would I rotate the pedals with stiff legs? A full rotation would be impossible. The answer was to remove the brake mechanism on the chain, so that forward propulsion was possible by making continuous half circles, forward with the left foot and reverse with the right foot. It was never anticipated that I would go fast enough to achieve a constant balance, so the additional learner wheels were permanently attached. As I could only go about the speed of the average person walking, all my riding was done on the sidewalk.

A carrier was added to the rear for my books and away I rode to school. Actually I would only ride to my girlfriend's about ten houses from our place, park on the sidewalk and toot my horn to let her know I was there. She would soon come out, place her bag on the carrier with mine and off we would go. It wasn't long before we discovered my riding speed was no faster than her walk and required a lot more exertion. Instead of me riding the bike, Raewyn adopted the practice of pushing it.

This routine lasted for five years and only ended when Raewyn left school. Our going to school together had begun when we were five years old, long before I got the bike. The friendship was established when we began kindergarten at age four.[1] It was clinched by the fact that there were only four days difference in our age.

Riding a bike also allowed me to be just like the hundreds of other kids who rode to school. Every day, I parked my bike in the racks among theirs. My bike was smaller, but that made sense because so was I.

The days when Raewyn wasn't around to push, I could ride by myself, so I did not become totally dependent on her. However, riding was almost as tiring as walking and in my last two years of high school (after Raewyn had left school), I stopped using the bike. I would walk home and my brother Greg was appointed to carry my bag.

Some of those walks were agonizingly painful and slow, especially after a day of walking around at school. I longed for the day when I could have my own car to get around in. Well, that day finally came. My parents surprised me on my eighteenth birthday with a present on wheels. This was no bike. This time they gave me a car![2] It was a great day indeed and applauded by many members of the family who were invited to celebrate the event. The days of waiting for someone to take me places were over. It also gave me the opportunity to change my reputation for being late everywhere, since timing was now in my con-

---

1   Four is the customary age for New Zealanders to begin kindergarten.
2   The purchase of the car was made easier by the availability of an interest
     free loan from the Auckland branch of the New Zealand Crippled
     Children's Society for one third the cost of the car and nominal weekly
     repayments.

trol. Driving lessons,[1] a raised seat, and pedal extensions all followed quickly and I was on the road.

I loved to go when and where I wanted. The only problem was that this car was a machine that had to be fueled, watered, oiled, lubed, aired, and cleaned. I never had to think about such things before. Now, it was my responsibility. It was so much easier to let someone else do it for me, but dad insisted that I look after the car myself. One day our different views on the subject clashed.

Mo, a long time friend of our family, noticed that one of the car tires was low on air and he offered to take it to the garage for me. I was about to let him, when dad butted in and said, *"No Angela, you take it to the garage yourself."* I was furious. What did it have to do with dad anyway? Mo was willing to take it, so why not let him. But there was no chance of that now, dad had said enough for Mo to withdraw his offer. I had no choice but to take the tire in myself.

It didn't take me long to realize that dad was right. It was important that I learn how to look after my own car. Along with the privilege of driving the car, came the responsibility of caring for it. It was the only way to be truly independent.

Family Relationships

My brother Gregory and sister Deborah must have picked up the attitude of my parents, because I'm not aware of them treating me any differently.[2] Our childhood days were pretty typical. We had our times of getting on famously and of fighting furiously.

Even though it wasn't long before Greg and Deborah were both bigger than me, there was no confusion as to who was the oldest. Somewhere along the way, I learned that a voice like a fog-horn and a bossy streak were enough to keep my authority. I must say though, that their spirits were as independent as mine and I had little control over their behavior.

---

1   These lessons were paid for by the Papakura branch of the New Zealand Rotary Club.

2   According to Carol Brazier, Dip. G.T.C. siblings nearly always adopt the parents' attitude toward the dwarf child, as reported in *"Little People in Today's Society: Social Development"* (1975). The article was reprinted with permission in the Little People of Australia Journal.

My cousin, although three years older than me, was not quite so sure how to show his authority. At four years old, I was able to bully my seven year old cousin out of using his own pedal car! Apparently he just gave up the fight when confronted by me sitting in the driver's seat glaring at him over the hood.

Deborah and Gregory were not so easily intimidated. Although I have to admit when Deborah was really young, my brother and I both delighted in teasing her. One thing I did to her was shameful. I would tell her stories about earwigs and alarm her by saying that, if they got into your ears there was no way they could get out, because they couldn't walk backwards. The poor child would go to sleep with her fingers in her ears, just to make sure no earwigs got in. We rarely had physical fights, but whenever we did, I put my finger nails to good use. I got my point across very well that way.

As we got older, my brother would want to demonstrate his strength by lifting me up onto my stool. For years, I would not let him lift me because I wasn't sure he had sufficient strength. Eventually, the day came when he was able to lift me without any effort, but by then he was too old to need to prove himself.

Deborah was four years younger than me and there were the usual frustrations of sharing a room with a younger sister. Yet age was only one of our differences. Deborah would drop things where she finished with them and I would put my things away. Her bed was only made after many reminders and mine would be so neat that I would get mad if anybody sat on it.

It came to a show down when Deborah started piling her things on the foot of my bed. She did this because she knew my feet didn't reach that far and figured she might as well make use of the space. However, what she didn't figure was that I wouldn't be willing to have an unsightly jumble at the end of my bed. Something had to be worked out.

Finally, I agreed not to complain about the way she kept her side of the room as long as she didn't mess up my side. It worked for us, but the room was thrown into the trauma of a split personality. The room never knew whether to call itself tidy or messy; it was both. More important, the relations between Deborah and myself improved. As Deborah reminded me, *"Overall, we got on pretty well - you were always studying in the bedroom, and I was always watching television."*

I often wondered what it was like for Greg and Deb growing up with a dwarf sister. When I was twenty-seven years old, my curiosity finally got the better of me and I decided to ask them how they felt about it. Some of their responses surprised me. I had been oblivious to some of the concerns they had as children.

First, I asked if they felt different about me or sorry for me. Deborah replied this way,

"I do not ever remember feeling embarrassed. I think the only thing was when we went out together, say down to Papakura[1] or something, I may have got a little uncomfortable sometimes at the speed of your walk -- just a little slow, but when I say uncomfortable, I say it in an unembarrassed way, because I have always been proud to be seen with you because my love for you makes up for any handicap."

Greg said,

"I often thought that it wasn't fair that Deborah and I were normal and you weren't, but then again I don't think it could have been too often as I don't remember thinking about your disabilities too often at all. At home you were my older sister and that's how things were -- just that. I can always remember that you were always good -- never doing anything wrong. It used to make me mad when people stared at you. At school, I think I avoided you, probably because I was embarrassed by you, but that was silly because everyone knew we were brother and sister. As I grew out of that stage, I realized that I may have been a little jealous of you, because your academic results were better, you were a prefect etc.[2] At home, we were on equal footing, so there was no need for any petty jealousy."

I was also interested to know how they felt, when mom and dad asked them to do things for me. Deborah had vague recollections of being annoyed at having to take turns to carry my sun-chair down to the beach. Greg mentioned my school bag. He didn't comment about any reluctance to carry it home for me, but did say, *"I can remember you having to carry that huge brief case -- it was probably half your size. That used to make me wince a little."*

Greg answered my next question. I asked if they thought I got more

1   My home-town, a city of about 25,000 people, located 20 miles south of Auckland, New Zealand.

2   Prefects are fourth and fifth year High School students appointed and/or elected to set an example for and to help monitor the activities of other students.

attention than they did and whether they were jealous of me for it. He responded this way,

"It used to annoy me when people fussed over you, knowing that you thought them silly as well. No, I don't think you got more attention from mom and dad, but you probably got more attention from distant relatives and strangers, but that kind of attention I never wanted anyway. I don't ever remember resenting or feeling jealous of you for this. Perhaps, I was spoiled and you were jealous of me."

They both had something to add to the next question. I wanted to know if their friends had asked them about me and how they had answered. I had been totally unaware of one experience Deborah had. She told me this, *"I received my one and only bloody nose at Cosgrave Primary School from Terry for teasing me about you. I'm not sure of the details now, but we had a fight and I came out second best."*

Thank goodness that was not Deb's daily experience and she went on to say,

"I do not remember much about getting to and from school or having any other trouble from smart kids. Because you were four years ahead of me, you had left Primary school[1] and then Intermediate school[2] before I really got there, so there was no connection or embarrassment from anyone. Once I got to high school,[3] as I remember it, no one I associated with said anything nasty about you to me, if anything you were very highly respected among my friends. Whenever someone asked me about my family, I always came right out and told them about you."

Greg had this to say,

"I guess people asked me about you, but I don't think anything out of the ordinary, just like anybody asking about a mate's[4] sister.

---

[1] New Zealand children attend Primary school for six years from ages five through ten.

[2] New Zealand children attend Intermediate school for two years from ages eleven to twelve.

[3] New Zealand children are required by law to attend High School for at least three years or until they reach age fifteen, whichever occurs the earliest. However, students are encouraged to spend at least four years in High School. Those going on to University usually put in five years, leaving school at age eighteen.

[4] *"Mate"* is Australian and New Zealand slang used to describe a person's friend or buddy.

Anyway, even if they had, I doubt whether I would have said much, as I have never spoken a lot about any member of my family to anybody but close friends. I can always remember your ability to speak to anybody and usually some comment would be passed to the effect that you were a great person. Bryan (Greg's best friend) did say that he was a little apprehensive about you before meeting, but once he met you, he felt quite at ease and proud to say he knew you."

I really appreciated Deborah and Gregory sharing their feelings with me and was pleased that my assessment of our relationships - - honest, open and loving -- was accurate. In our adult lives, the three of us continue to be close. We travel thousands of miles to visit each other and pay many dollars in long-distance calls to make contact at special times in the year.

When Greg was living in Brisbane, we spent ten days together traveling the Gold-Coast of Queensland. It intrigued me that he did not tell his landlady that I was a Little Person. I knew she did not know the minute we met because of the total surprise on her face. I was pleased to see Greg handle it this way, as he saw no reason to mention it. I am just like anybody else.

One motel proprietor thought he had us worked out. When checking into his motel, we asked for one room with two single beds. However, the proprietor kidded us about having a lover's tiff. We explained we were brother and sister, but he didn't believe it.

He stepped in to help us make up and gave us a room with a double bed. Even when Greg returned to the office and again asked for single beds, the proprietor only complied reluctantly. He could not accept we were not romantically attached. He overlooked the fact that married couples do not enjoy the monopoly of sharing the same name, brothers and sisters can too.

The four year age difference between Deborah and myself soon became insignificant and the days of worrying about keeping our room tidy have long gone. Today, we share a warm friendship and look forward to the times we can spend vacations together. Regrettably, they are few and far between.

Childhood days have their traumas most of which I'm happy to leave behind, but one aspect can be preserved -- the caring and stability found in a loving family. As adults, we can no longer share the warmth and comfort of a nuclear family, but we can continue to share our love and concern for each other.

Chapter Two

EDUCATED

Opportunity Denied

Lillian was not sent to school until she was nine years old, and then for only six years. Danielle dropped out of school at aged twelve. Both were academically capable of completing a full education program, but because of their short-stature they were denied this opportunity.

Indeed the decision not to advance Danielle from the private elementary school was thought to be in her best interests. It was to protect her from the rigors expected in the public high school environment. The teachers feared the teasing would be too traumatic and worried how she would fit into a standard sized school.

Roberta was also a dwarf and her parents doubted that she could cope in a regular school environment. They feared she would be knocked down by the big doors. To protect her, she was sent to a special school for children with handicaps. Her parents succeeded in saving her from the heavy doors, but sadly the segregation from average-sized kids denied her the opportunity to prepare for life in the real world. Roberta believes that her eight years in the special school seriously impaired her personal development. It didn't take too much digging to unearth a part of that experience. This is what Roberta told me: *"The school was for both handicapped and non-handicapped children, yet we were always kept very separate. We never crossed paths in the course of the day; our classes were on the bottom floor and theirs were on the top. We were even scheduled to use the bathroom at different times!"*

"The only event when we were in the same place at the same time was the morning assembly; even then we sat in a special section and entered the hall after everyone else was seated. We were always made to feel extremely different. The focus on our differences made us feel there was nothing the same about us."

"*Right through to aged fourteen, we were expected to take a half hour nap everyday. I would lay down not sleeping and listen to the playing noise of the non-handicapped kids. It bothered me to hear them playing while were expected to sleep! I didn't like being so confined, especially since we never got a play-time.*"

"*We were regularly on exhibit to various doctors and nurses. Our sense of modesty was ignored. One time a doctor expected me to undress for him; I was infuriated when one of the boys in my class saw my nakedness. I hated the boy and the doctor for that.*"

"*To my despair, private things often became public. We were even expected to use bathroom cubicles without doors. The only exception came the week a girl got her period. Then she was allowed to use the toilet. Yet even this created a problem. Although actual use of the bathroom was private, because the bathroom was accessed directly from the classroom, it was still public knowledge who used it and when. I never used the teacher's toilet and so everyone knew I hadn't gotten my period. I couldn't figure out which was worse, not having a period, or having everyone know when you had it.*"

"*Even though there were about seventy-five kids in the handicapped school, ranging from age six to seventeen, the loneliness was the greatest problem. Three grades were taught in the same room and there were few people my own age and grade. It was hard to make friends with kids younger or older. We rode to school in a special bus and the trip made the day so long. It was probably only forty-five minutes or so, but I remember it as being hours. When I got home, I was too tired to play with anyone. Besides, even if I had the energy there wasn't anybody to play with; no one from the school lived in my neighborhood and life was very boring for me.*"

"*At age thirteen, I had a girl come to my house to visit. She was much bigger than me and although a year and a half younger was showing signs of pubic development. My father perceived her to be much older than I and at a certain time in the evening sent my sister and me to bed. The girl stayed on visiting with my father. I was so mad, I didn't ask her to come again.*"

In retrospect, Roberta accepts that her parents believed they were doing the best for her. However, she believes it would have been better if she had been allowed to attend a school that focused on her abilities rather than her disabilities. The segregation meant that she later had to learn what most people take for granted -- how to socialize and make friends. That long slow process in adolescence and early adult years is not something she wants other Little People to experience.

I am grateful that my educational experience was totally different than Lillian's, Danielle's and Roberta's. My parents did not try to protect me. I was not kept out of school or sent to a school for children with handicaps. At age four, I began regular kindergarten[1] with other kids my age. There was no reason not to. My size did not affect my ability or intelligence.[2] Physical limitations could easily be accommodated and dealing with the teasing of other children was something I would have to learn sooner or later.

Peer Acceptance

Starting school was certainly traumatic and learning how to deal with teasing and taunting came much sooner than I would have liked. I was already conscious of being different and accustomed to people staring, but at school I had to learn how to handle a whole group of on-lookers by myself.

The day is still clear in my mind, when a group of kids saw me walking onto the school grounds. I was alone and there were about six or seven of them. One child noticed me and made sure the rest didn't miss seeing me. She pointed at me, and they all jumped up and down laughing and making fun of me in their excitement. Most times, I would have just ignored them, but this day it was impossible. Their message was loud and clear -- I looked funny. I couldn't take it and the tears spilled out as I walked passed them and heard their jeers behind me.

Afterwards, one of the children of my mother's friend saw me and

---

1   The customary age for New Zealand children to begin kindergarten is four years.

2   According to Deborah Young-Hyman, there is general agreement among the experts that the IQs of short-statured children, regardless of the cause of dwarfism, approximate those of the general population and are independent of height, *"Effects of Short Stature on Social Competence"* (1984), printed in *"Slow Grows the Child: Psychosocial Aspects of Growth Delay,"* (1984) Lawrence Erlbaum Associates, Publisher.

asked what was wrong. I told her it was nothing, but my tears spoke much louder than any mask of bravery. She duly reported the incident to her mother, who in turn told my mother. Mom asked me about the incident.

I don't remember exactly what mom said to console me, but I imagine it went something like this:

"Just ignore them; they don't know any better than to make fun of people who are different. They're only tough when they're together in a group. You are much braver because you don't need a crowd to make you strong. Besides, it's not nice to go around hurting people. If you fight back you only reduce yourself to their level and you certainly don't want to be like them. Don't worry, once they get used to you they will get tired of teasing and will leave you alone."

Her advice served me well. I heard the story of a ten year old girl, who did not get this kind of support from her family. The result, she was not doing well in school and the principal was about to suggest she be sent to a school for retarded children. There was nothing wrong with her mentally; she just felt so different that she developed a mental block to learning.

Fortunately, the principal did not have to carry out his intention. Over the course of one weekend, the girls' outlook transformed from clouds to sunshine. It all happened, because she had an opportunity to visit with a family of dwarfs. Somewhere in that interchange, she found a positive identity for herself and discovered a new courage and the ability to face her life with optimism.

The child returned to school so radiant that her parents, the principal and her teachers could not believe the transformation. The principal later reported that she surged ahead so much in her school work that it became necessary to advance her a class.[1]

David Hornstein was initially rejected by his peers and worked out his own way to get back into the group. He tells it like this:

"When I was about eight years old I stopped growing -- I experienced unhappiness for a few years -- all of my contemporaries rejected me. I was abandoned. It wasn't my doing. I wanted to belong. They wouldn't let me. Every day they dinned into my sensitive ears,

---

1   Brazier, *"Little People in Today's Society, Part 4, Social Development,"* reprinted in the Little People of Australia Journal (1975).

'Go home and tell your mother she wants you.' I did go home because there was nothing else for me to do. I hoped that I was not going to stay rejected. Maybe I could figure out a way to get back with the crowd. I didn't get sore. I didn't become cynical. I didn't get smart-alecky. And I didn't become a cry-baby. I just went on being nicer than the rest of them. Patience and confidence that I was as good as they, brought me back into the gang." [1]

I was not only lucky to have a supportive family, but through circumstances was saved the repeated trauma of going as a stranger into a whole new school. Our family always lived in the same house in the same neighborhood. This meant even when I advanced from kindergarten to elementary to junior high to high school, the schools were in the same neighborhood and I always had friends making the changes with me.

It made the transition that much easier as there were already a group of kids well adjusted to having me around. After years of being together in the same schools, they didn't see me as different. In fact, they would even stand with me against new kids who tried to have fun at my expense.

After the first few weeks of the new school year passed, the new kids would settle down and I'd have very few problems with them. In fact, many took pride in finding out what my name was. Endless numbers of kids would walk by me and say, *"Hello Angela."* It became quite embarrassing, as I couldn't acknowledge them by name. I simply didn't know who most of them were. Yet a friendly nod was enough to gain their acceptance.

The kids seemed to like me. Some even admired me for being able to do very ordinary things. I remember being in line with a group of husky young boys all waiting for our tuberculosis injection. When I emerged after my shot, they no doubt expected to see me crying. In-

---

1   David Hornstein is four feet seven inches and an attorney in Washington D.C. This is an excerpt taken from a 1967 letter of encouragement that he wrote to a young girl called Cathy who was also a Little Person.

stead, I was smiling. Immediately, I was acclaimed as very brave. After that, even the tough ones looked up to me.

Physical Concerns

Sadly, some elementary schools, contrary to the view of experts,[1] have made the mistake of holding a Little Person back a class waiting for the child to grow closer in size to their peers and taller to reach the facilities. Indeed, one child I heard of recently is not going to be advanced to the next grade until she can reach the lock on the toilet door! How ridiculous. In another year, she still won't be able to reach the door and the prospect of her catching up to the height of her peers will diminish more as each year passes. The most significant growth will be the number of inches which separate the child from her peers, not the number of inches she will add to her height.

Many dwarf children are not only short, but also have small hands and fingers. This means a teacher needs to consider the ability of the child to hold a pencil and to remember the child may write at a slower pace. Often a child learns to write late or flunks a written test, because the teacher doesn't appreciate that the child needs guidance in pencil holding techniques and perhaps some extra time to finish written work.

Accommodations

The answer is not holding the child back until he or she grows taller, nor to give the child an F on a test which isn't finished. The better solution is to make accommodations to overcome the physical limitations, to keep the child with their peer group and to promote the child's independent use of facilities.

In the case of the child having difficulty with writing, all he or she needs is extra time and occasionally an oral test substituted for the written one. Not to allow the extra time is as absurd as expecting a child who is blind to visually identify objects drawn on a test paper.

When a child can't reach an object there is no need for the teacher

---

1   Diane L. Rotnem, *"Size Versus Age: Ambiguities in Parenting Short-Statured Children"* (1984), printed in *"Slow Grows the Child: Psychosocial Aspects of Growth Delay,"* Lawrence Erlbaum Associates, Publisher.

or another child to lift the Little Person. Instead, a stool in an appropriate place allows the child to reach the item without assistance.

Parents strive to teach their short-statured child basic skills of independence in preparation for school. Teachers need to encourage the short-statured child to exercise that independence. However, to the frustration of some parents, they have discovered that the child's teacher proceeds to undo all their hard work. One mother had trained her daughter to go to the toilet alone and to tie her own shoe laces. When the child started school, the mother found that the teacher had been carrying her daughter to the toilet, tying her shoe laces and lifting her up when she wanted a drink. This was not the sort of help the child needed. The teacher's actions were returning the child to babyhood, not helping her to reach maturity.[1]

In addition to allowing the child to be independent, accommodations should not stand out in a way that separates the child from other kids. One dean of students understood this when she made steps around a drinking fountain on both the girls and boys side. This saved the female Little Person from thinking all the special effort was for her benefit.[2]

The teachers at the school Thomas attended weren't so thoughtful. In supplying Thomas with a special table and chair so that he didn't have to sit at the regular sized lunch table with his nose at table top level, they succeeded in making it easier for him to reach his food, but completely isolated him from his friends. He hated to eat lunch, because it meant sitting alone in the corner. The solution would have been to boost Thomas' height with a cushion at the regular sized table. With this easy remedy, his appetite for friendship would also have been satisfied.

Actually, this wasn't the only poor choice made for Thomas. When it came time to take the class photo, Thomas was placed alone in the front now giving the impression that he was some kid's younger brother trying to get in the act. Yes, his proper place was in the front

---

1   Brazier, *"Little People in Today's Society, Part 4, Social Development,"* reprinted in the Little People of Australia Journal (1975).

2   ibid.

row, but not alone in the front looking like the class mascot.

Even though as a youngster, I would be infuriated when I was placed in the front row on the far left or far right of the school photo, I didn't know how lucky I was. At least I was being placed alongside my school mates and not made to sit separately.

When I first started school, I was ferried to and fro in a taxi as it was too far for me to walk.[1] Although I appreciated and needed the ride, I didn't like being separated from my friends who had to walk home from school. I would try and persuade the driver to let at least one girlfriend ride home with me. My success depended on who the driver was. Some were more willing than others. After a year or so, it was decided I could walk the distance and the taxi rides stopped. This pleased me greatly as now I could play with my pals on the way home.

This desire not to be separated from the group is something that lasts a lifetime. Many years later when I was in law school and the Dean offered to reserve a special desk for me in the library, I refused. My reasoning was no different from my days in elementary school. I didn't want to stand out from or be treated differently from the other students. It was important to be part of the group and that meant combing the library for a seat just like everyone else. Also, the desk the Dean offered to reserve was situated in a part of the library separated from other students.

Some children are naturally independent and will even refuse to use accommodations provided and apparently needed. Valerie was one such child. Her school had built steps up one side of her chair, but rather than use the steps she would deliberately climb up the side without steps.[2]

More often than not, a child will resolve their own dilemma. Ed worked with his classmates to overcome his difficulty climbing stairs. He arranged for one person to get on each side and to hoist him to the top. He evened the score by always beating them to the bottom of the stairs -- he slid down the banister. His mother was the only one to complain about this as she had to wash his dirty clothes.

On my grade twelve geography field trip, we had to find a way for

---

1   Discussed in Chapter 1, *"Understood."*

2   Brazier, *"Little People in Today's Society, Part 4, Social Development,"* reprinted in the Little People of Australia Journal (1975).

me to get around the farm where our research was being conducted. Our teacher first considered a farm horse as my transport, but decided it would be too much for the horse! I was the envy of every kid in the class, especially those who had to hike up into the high country of the farm-land to get their soil samples, when Alan, a boy in my class, was co-opted to ride me around the farm on his trail bike.

In my years of education after high school, I discovered that the university campus was no access euphoria. There were the usual hassles with parking, stairs, doors, counters, and elevators.[1] But for each and every barrier, an accommodation was soon worked out. Parking was the first obstacle to overcome.

The easiest way for me to get to the campus was to drive.[2] However, once I arrived there was nowhere close I could park all day at a reasonable price. The solution was to apply for a special parking permit, which would allow me to park within a stone's throw of the law library building. My application was approved and I was extremely fortunate to only pay a nominal annual parking fee. Not even all the staff had the privilege of parking on campus.

Once parked, I would make my way to the law school building. The law library was on the fifth floor and the lecture rooms were on the sixth. However, the highest button I could reach on the elevator was number four! On the days when I was feeling energetic, I would walk the extra one or two floors, but that wasn't very often. Otherwise, I would wait for someone to come or use an object such as my pencil case or umbrella to reach the button.

Only once in my whole five years at law school did I use the stairway to exit the building and that wasn't by choice. I was studying in the library when a bell rang. It did not mean it was time to go home, (those bells never ring for law students). No, it was the fire alarm!

The bell kept ringing and ringing. No one considered the pos-

---

1   For a discussion of access obstacles, see Chapter 5, *"At Your Physical Pleasure."*

2   As to my ability to drive, see Chapter 1, *"Understood;"* and as to driving adaptations see Chapter 7, *"Doing Things Differently."*

sibility of a real fire. The bell only ever rang for drills. However, whether drill or fire, we were all expected to vacate the building. The prevailing sense of unreality at least ensured an absence of panic and everyone walked out in a quiet and orderly fashion.

My concern mounted when I realized that my exit would be by way of the stairs, because the elevator cannot be used when there is a fire. I had to jump[1] down each step of the whole ten flights. As I landed at the bottom I discovered that it was neither a drill or a fire. It was a false alarm caused by some student prank. I was not in the least bit amused.

Most of the stairways on the campus were railed; the few that were lacking rails I learned to avoid by walking around the long way. I learned to do this after unsuccessfully negotiating some steep steps without a rail. The experience of falling flat on your face is not one you're anxious to repeat.

In the lecture theaters, my two difficulties were easily overcome. To see the black-board, I would choose a seat with an uninterrupted view near the front or on the aisle; to overcome the difficulty of taking notes on a desk almost level with my chin, I brought a hard-backed clip-board to lean my paper on. The only draw-back came at exam times, when it was against the rules to bring anything but writing materials into the room.

My history tutor asked how I would write my exams if I couldn't reach the desk. Not one to stir up trouble and walk off, he also offered a solution. He suggested I take a cushion to the exam and a note from the administrative office authorizing its use.

I followed his advice the first year, but no supervisor ever asked to see the note. It was obvious to anybody that I needed the cushion. In subsequent years, I continued to bring a cushion but didn't bother getting a note. No one ever asked to see one.

In the law library, the desks were too high, but instead of using a cushion I would just grab the closest and thickest case book from the shelf. My stature was increased by these nineteenth century volumes, chosen as least likely to be in demand by other students. Looking back, I wonder why I didn't just bring a cushion to the library. It would have

---

1   Refer to Chapter 5, *"At Your Physical Pleasure,"* for an explanation of my jumping descent of stairs.

been more comfortable and no one would have minded.

Reaching and finding books on shelves, extending from floor to ceiling, was a task too steep for me to tackle. At least half the books were out of reach and those on the very top shelves, couldn't be identified without binoculars. As my knees don't bend, climbing onto a chair was difficult. Even when prepared to make the effort, it was total frustration to make the climb and find the book I needed was three paces further along the shelf. To dismount, move the chair and climb up again was more trouble than it was worth. Besides this, the chair cluttered the passage and other people looking for books could not get past. The solution was to ask someone to reach books for me. If no one was walking in the vicinity, I would stroll around until I found someone day-dreaming at their desk. Then, I had no qualms about disturbing them, as my interruption was welcome.

The catalogue files in the general library were the hardest to deal with. In that case, it isn't easy to ask someone to look for you, because until you have a chance to browse, you don't know what you're looking for. The drawers were locked in, which precluded pulling them out to rest at a lower level. The only way was to struggle with a chair.

The one time I did know what I wanted, I asked a woman for help. However, she brushed me off like a fly grumping that she was too busy. Her attitude was so pathetic I couldn't even get mad at her; she was the one who needed help. I must say in all my years in law school she was the only person to refuse my request for assistance.

Fortunately, the catalogue files were rarely needed in my law school studies. If regular use was necessary, I'm sure I could have worked something out with the librarian as catalogue drawers can be removed from their cabinets for easier access.

In the changeover between classes, I had to take special care not to be trampled. The middle road in this case was not the safest course. Even though other students knew to look out for me, it was better for me to hold back and wait for the crowd to subside. If I was in a hurry, I would move out carefully, stay close to the wall and watch for swinging satchels.[1]

---

1   Also known as book bags.

Although no physical changes were made for me, the teaching staff of the law school were most accommodating. They were continually concerned about my welfare. Not long after I had been in law school, the Dean approached me in the corridor and expressed concern about how I was managing the heavy swinging doors. He was pleased to learn that other students would usually hold them for me and when necessary I could open them myself. Although he didn't have to take any action, it was encouraging to know that he was willing.

No Special Treatment

My bottle of fizz (soda) was upended and I was drinking as fast as I could. However, it was not fast enough, all but one of the other eight year old girls standing in the row had emptied their bottle and patiently stood waiting for me to finish. Finally, my bottle was empty and I swallowed the last mouthful just ahead of one other girl. I finished second to last.

The contest was the usual advertising gimmick at the annual Easter show and my parents had responded to a request for girl contestants of eight years old whose names began with the letter 'A.' I was lifted onto the stage to join a dozen other girls. After the drinking race was over, the moderator of the contest, in an unprecedented move, announced he would be awarding prizes to those in the positions of first, last and second to last. It was obvious he wanted me to have a prize, whether I earned it or not. I left the stage and proudly presented my parents with a can of Andrews Liver Salts![1]

At the time, I was happy to accept the prize, even though I was suspicious that the sudden shift in awards had been made on my account. I was too young to discern the negative aspect of special treatment; I was too young to see that such elevation meant I was not accepted as an equal.

It was a great temptation for people to treat me differently. Teachers were no exception. However, their favors would only retard my development and acceptance as an equal. They had to learn it was okay for them to notice me, but imperative that I not be given special treatment because I was different. The teacher's expectations of me

---

1   Equivalent American products would be TUMS, or Maalox Plus.

had to be as great as for other children in the class, especially in the area of discipline and independence. There was no need to award me a prize, unless it was for something that I had earned.

Some teachers of children with disabilities let their pupils get away with far too much. I saw the end results of this when I met a fifteen year old disabled girl. She boasted of her exploits at school: being rude to teachers, skipping classes, and various other escapades. From her descriptions, her behavior would have brought grave disciplinary measures to any other girl. Yet according to her, she was rarely censured. What favor had she been given? At fifteen and about ready to leave school,[1] she was ill-equipped academically, socially, and emotionally.

My first grade teacher began on the right path when I started school. The class was in session, but not having adjusted to the routine and discipline of sitting in a classroom for a set period of time, I decided to go out into the playground. I just got out of my seat, left the room without a word and headed toward the field.

I didn't get very far before the teacher realized I was gone. She followed quickly and sternly told me to come back inside. I had no special privilege allowing me to do as I pleased. I would have to wait until play-time like everybody else.

As a young child, I was willing to take advantage of any weakness I could discern in a teacher. It came so naturally. If they were inclined to feel sorry for me, I knew it and played on it. I remember one such occasion in my first year of school.

Each afternoon, we would take a nap curled up on the floor on our rug. This day when it was time to wake up, I pretended to be asleep. My second grade teacher was fooled and stirred everyone except me. Darrel knew I was awake, because he saw me open one eye. (I had been looking to see how far I could go with this teacher). Darrel tried to tell the teacher I was awake, but she wouldn't believe it and told him to leave me alone.

Like any mischievous kid who knew better, he took matters into his own hands. He shook me so hard that if I didn't stir they would have

---

1   Fifteen is the earliest age a New Zealand student can leave school.

feared me dead. I had to give up my plan. I aroused myself sleepily, (not willing to let Darrel give my pretense away) and reluctantly returned to the afternoon lessons with the other children. Darrel was not so lucky. He was disciplined for waking me. (My clear recollection of the event probably accounts for the guilt I've harbored all these years for getting him into trouble).

Fortunately, most of my teachers weren't so easily fooled. Though as the years went by, I would occasionally get special consideration from a temporary teacher. I was no longer looking for it, but the teacher not knowing how to treat me would let things slide if I stepped out of line.

I remember an incident with a temporary teacher very well. She had given me a field assignment with a group of other children. They raced outside ahead of me. Not wanting to be left behind, I stood at the door and called out after them at the top of my voice, *"Hey, wait for me."* The teacher was astonished at such playground noise in her quiet classroom and looked up ready to throttle the culprit. When she found out it was me, her anger subsided immediately and I was allowed to follow my group without even a reprimand.

I was not always in a position to reject favors and maybe I was pleased to get out of being disciplined, but by the age of ten I was ready to reject any favors given to me because of my size. I clearly recall one incident which occurred at the end of a week long camp I attended with my younger aunt, Janet. We roomed in a cabin with several other girls and participated in most of the activities: games, cook-outs, and study groups.

The week had its up and down times for both of us. One afternoon when it was pouring rain and all the other girls had gone on a hike, Janet and I stayed in the bunk-house. Instead of reading as planned, I spent my time trying to dissuade Janet from calling her father to come and take us home. I knew we had to stick it out. Mom would be furious if we left early.

We were both pleased when the end of the week brought with it the end of the camp. However, before the camp was officially over, we had to sit through closing ceremonies at which an award was to be given to honor the camper of the week. Guess whose name was called --- Angela Muir. I was both surprised and annoyed. It was the last thing I expected and I immediately became suspicious that I had been picked and promoted by the leaders as a special favor. I did not appreciate the tribute and believed other girls were far more deserving. I was too young to know how to buck the system and not accept the award, but on principle, I never used the prize privilege. To attend the next camp free held no attraction for me and I refused to go.

Most of my teachers were sensible enough to treat me the same as the other kids in the class. No special favors were given. Some would have, but fortunately for me I was spared having them as a class teacher. I knew this for sure when by chance one day, I saw the raw mark of my exam paper on my class teacher's desk.

The exam had been taken by all the grade seven students and had been circulated among a number of teachers for marking. As a policy, no teacher marked the papers of their own students. Our marked papers had been returned to our class teacher and were lying on his desk.

My raw mark was lower than expected, but it had been crossed out and substituted with one much higher. In explanation of the change was a note from the teacher who marked my paper, *"I increased the mark, when I realized who belonged to this paper."* My class teacher chose to ignore the increase and only told me of the lower mark earned, even though it was a disappointing result. He knew there was no reason to give me a handicap on an academic level and made sure I only got the mark I had earned. The help he gave me was not to inflate the mark, but to show me how to improve it with my own effort on the next test.

Teachers were conscious of my size, especially in the early days when the class ritual was to measure everyone against the giraffe image pinned to the wall. Even though I always marked the tail end, I was never made to feel inadequate. The measurements taken regularly were used to compare with the last etching, to show our growth progress, rather than used competitively to show the tallest as the most successful.

My small stature turned to my advantage when my fourth grade teacher was casting pupils in various plays. I was chosen as Puss, in the play Puss in Boots, because I was small enough to wear an outfit from the local kindergarten. To keep me from getting too big for my boots, however, I was only given a bit part in the next play. I was cast as the baby in Sleeping Beauty. The grown-up heroine was played by someone else.

Even so, I was not to be type-cast in roles demanding short stature. In the Highwayman, I played the part of a tree; and in the Three Pigs, I was one of the pigs. The pig role earned me the nickname Piggy for years to come.

By the time I reached University, you would think I would have the rejection of special treatment down pat. However, it's not always so straightforward. You can't always tell whether the person is offering special service because you're a Little Person, because they like you, or because you're the lucky person to walk through the door at the right time of the day.

For this reason, when I'm not sure of a person's motivation, I usually accept the offer being made. To refuse would only reveal paranoia and cause the person making the offer to feel bad. I've found it's best just to play it by ear. At least, this is what I did as a university student when traveling with friends in the South Island of New Zealand.

We not only had a great time, but were able to afford the trip by using Youth Hostel accommodations which in New Zealand are both cheap and clean. However, at the busy times of year, the hostels are so popular they have to turn people away. My friends and I learned from experience to check in as soon as we hit town. At Mount Cook, the highest point in the Southern Alps, towering to 12,349 feet (3,764 meters), we nearly missed getting a bed in the hostel because we did some sight-seeing before checking in. It would have been a hard lesson, because the only other cheap accommodation in town was the free camping ground in the frozen valley. We did not take our bed for granted after that.

However, because of the number of travelers and popularity of many of these resorts, even if you check in early you may miss out on a bed. One summer, my friend and I arrived early at the Queenstown Youth Hostel to discover that the warden was turning everyone away in the line ahead of us. The only place available for them to sleep was the bare wooden boards of the local school house.

We were preparing ourselves for the prospect, but waited in line to get directions to the school house. When we presented ourselves at the counter, the hostel warden suddenly made two beds available. We were very surprised. However, we couldn't be sure it was favoritism, because all those he had turned away before us were male and couldn't have taken the beds we were offered in the girl's dormitory. At the time, we were so desperate and tired we didn't spend long pondering his motives and were pleased to have a mattress to roll our sleeping bags out on. Besides, I'm sure the hostel view of Lake Wakatipu, one of the South Island's most spectacular glacial lakes, could not be paralleled at the school house.

Having said all this about the need to reject special treatment, there are times when it might look like I have caved in to the pressure. On occasion, I will deliberately accept what appears to be special treatment when the extra service being offered makes it possible for me to be included in an activity from which I would otherwise be excluded.

In the Youth Hostel situation, for example, because of my difficulty climbing up and down from a top bunk, I have no problem accepting the assignment of a lower bunk, even though for everyone else it is first come, first served. I will also request light work to fulfill my obligation in the Hostel morning work scheme, even though other people get the job they are given. I do not see this as being contradictory. Rather, to request a job I can do, means that my difference is recognized but is not used as an excuse for treating me differently. On the other hand, it would be inappropriate special treatment for me to be excused from a morning chore altogether.

Sport and Recreation

One of our favorite elementary school games was French skipping. The game could be compared to jump rope, but the only similarity is the jumping skill needed. Instead of holding the rope in the hands, the rope is held around the four ankles of two people standing opposite each other. Unlike jump rope, where the rope is swung over the head and under the feet, the rope is not swung at all, but rather is elasticized and stretched into the shape of an oblong.

A player jumps the rope by jumping in and out of the oblong shape marked by the rope. A player begins with a series of steps with the rope at ankle level; once those jumps are successfully completed, more difficult jumps are attempted with the rope inched further up the legs of those holding the rope. A player will continue jumping until a jump is missed. The winner of the game is the one who jumps the highest.

The only way I could play was for the girls to give me a

'handicap.' The rope would be placed as low as possible and when I made the jumps it would be raised by minute fractions. I had the pleasure of not only holding the the rope around my legs for other players, but also of participating at my own level of competence. I was no competition or threat to the other girls and they were happy to change the rules so I was included. Mainstreaming taught the kids to see me as their friend, someone they wanted to join in. There were no awkward moments when I approached the group; I was part of it.

In official elementary school sports, I was given a 'handicap' so that I could participate. In the running races, I was allowed to start half way up the field, and occasionally even got to break the tape first. Even then no one pretended, I was the best runner. On the day the race was a qualifier for inter-school competition, it was carefully explained to me that even if I crossed the line first this did not mean I was fast enough to compete against runners from other schools. At a young age, I didn't care about that; it was enough to just be in the race.

As I grew older, such concessions no longer held a thrill. In fact, sporting 'handicaps' were rarely offered. The maxim, *"it doesn't matter whether you win or lose, it's how you play the game"* was lost somewhere along the way. Sport was no longer a game designed to include everybody and it mattered very much if you won or lost. There was no longer a place for me. My presence on the team was a handicap they couldn't afford. With the rare exception of the afternoon sport activity in grades seven and eight, where I would play softball by batting and having someone run for me and in the swimming sports at high school where I was the drowning person in a rescue-race, my sporting days were over.

That's not to say Little People, in general, don't participate in sports. Many are very active. However, when competing with average-sized players most choose options not dependent on physical prowess. For example, Little People make ideal coxswains in the sport of rowing. I know of at least three Little People who have been coxswains. One absolutely loved it, though I'm not sure which he enjoyed most, the rowing or the female company of his rowing team.

Others prefer to be involved in the more traditional sports such as football, basketball and baseball. They participate as photographers, sports-writers and commentators, referees, linesmen, umpires, team managers, and coaches.[1] This way they are as much part of the game as the people on the field. However, with the advent of the annual East-West Softball game of the Little People of America, Inc.,[2] and the Dwarf Athletic Association of America (DAA) [3] Little People in the United States are finding opportunities to compete in an even competition against other Little People. In 1986, at the first International Dwarf Games, organized by the DAA to coincide with the annual convention of the Little People of America, Inc., many Little People participated in events such as golf, power-lifting, track, shot-put, discus, swimming, table-tennis, and basketball.

Although my family were all involved in sports: badminton, golf, basketball, fencing, and rugby, I found greater satisfaction in other activities. It was no great hardship for me to end my sporting days. Instead of coming home with sports trophies, I won awards in literature. In High School, I was encouraged in front of the whole assembly with a check presentation for some poetry I had written.

In my leisure time, I would occupy myself writing letters to overseas pen pals in England, Malaysia, and Sweden. At the end of every day, I would enjoy recording the days events in my diary. However, I eventually gave that up when I discovered how vulnerable the diary was to prying eyes. I realized it was safer to keep personal thoughts and comments to myself.

Writing to pen pals helped out in another hobby I had -- saving stamps. I collected stamps from all over the world, and received a great selection from the letters of my pen pals. My mother encouraged all of us in this pastime, as she had her own collection. I am the only one

---

1   For the story of Donald Davidson, a Little Person of four feet who was Assistant to the President and traveling Secretary of the Atlanta Braves, see *"Caught Short"* by Bob Hertzel and Jesse Outlar.

2   Scheduled each year at the annual national convention of the Little People of America, Inc., (LPA). For more information on LPA write to Post Office Box 633, San Bruno, CA 94066.

3   The Dwarf Athletic Association of America (DAA) was founded in 1985. For more information, write to the President, Nancy Stewart, 611 William Ave, Monroeville, Alabama 36460.

who continues to collect. Today I specialize in stamps showing birds, butterflies, flowers, and ironically enough, sports events. Maybe that is my way of participating.

I learned how to crochet in a hobby class in High School, and thoroughly enjoyed being able to make blankets like my great-grandmother did. While relaxing in front of television, I put several blankets together. It was very rewarding to see a finished product used on one of the family beds, or as a furniture cover.

I was about nine years old when our family bought a television. As a result, my brother and I were put to bed as young children with books to read. We never fell asleep with square eyes. My mother truly instilled both of us with a love of books and reading. This was much better preparation for the class-room than watching television.

I participated in most extra-curricular school events that interested me. However, at times, this was made possible with help from my friends. At the end of grade eleven, our class celebrated with a party on a farm near the beach. To reach the beach, we had to trek across the hills. It wasn't long before I began to trail far behind. It became very obvious I wasn't going to make it alone. Rather than leave me behind, the boys got together, and took turns carrying me the rest of the way. Their exhaustion made it an easy decision for me to be ferried back after the party in the boat borrowed from someone's father.

In the following year, I joined our class on a ski-trip camp. I didn't plan to ski; I just wanted to go up the mountain and watch. I enjoyed the ride on the mountain buggy and ski-lift, but soon heard that other people weren't too happy about it.

It was impossible for me to get on the chair-lift without assistance, because the chair was too high and did not stop for you to get on. People were expected to jump on as it went by. The controller saw my predicament and stopped the chair's motion while he lifted me on. Riders screamed up and down the valley fearing they were stranded with no way off but to drop hundreds of feet. Their consolation came when I was securely in place and the controller started the chairs moving again.

At the other end, instead of stopping the chairs, I was instructed to just open the chair's gate, and let the attendant grab me as I floated by. He landed me safely on the mountain slopes and I set off with my poles to watch the other kids skiing down the learner slope. Like iceskating, skiing was on my no list. At age seventeen, I was now old enough to decide for myself what I could and couldn't do. The decision was easy -- stay on the side-line. It would be asking for trouble for me to ski with dislocated hips, weak ankles, and no movement in my knees.

With my box-brownie camera, there was still the potential for me to be at the center of the action. Yet, somehow my over-sized gloves muffed that up. At the end of each finger was a one inch extension of glove. It didn't bother me until I saw some of the kids fooling around. I snapped the shot and was very pleased with myself. However, the pleasure didn't last long. One of the boys noticed the end of my glove was across the lens! There went my reputation as a photographer. We tried to pose the scene again, but somehow the candid shot could not be re-staged.

I did make one attempt to ski. I stood on the back of Andrew's skis, and held onto his legs while he moved ahead with his poles. We couldn't get up too much speed on the flat, so he suggested going onto the slope. However, I was too nervous to try.

It wasn't long before I got tired and cold standing around and after a while I sought shelter in the hut beside the chair-lift. There was no view because the mountain was covered with mist, so I was ready to join friends when they wanted to go back down the mountain.

When the weather was so bad that we couldn't go up the mountain for the rest of the week, I was quietly pleased. It would have been a betrayal of everyone's hopes for me to express how glad I was, so I kept such thoughts to myself. Instead of skiing, we spent our time at the hot pools, and playing cards. I could join in these activities with just as much energy.

I had already shown my ability playing cards in the car rally we had two years earlier. Each day of the camp, we rode with different people. One day, I was assigned with three boys. I had started the day, both excited and shy. I was pleased to be with just boys, but was worried about how we would get along. Would they talk to me? How would I tell them when I wanted to use the toilet?

My worry was for nothing. We had a very enjoyable day. My role was to make sure they followed the rules, and in particular to see that they drove within the speed limit. Impossible! My presence may have slowed them down a little bit, but nowhere near the speed recommended by our teacher, or the police on highway patrol.

They were not satisfied to just drive and were looking for entertainment. They were delighted that I not only played five hundred, but could actually play a mean game. However, at the end of the day, it was time to report and they were nervous that I would tell everything. I felt awkward about not being entirely truthful, but was strangely loyal to my card and car companions.

Ski trips and car rallies were only two of the school activities I had the opportunity to participate in. However, not all activities held the same attraction. My ninth grade teacher gave me the chance to be a science monitor. I tried it out for a few weeks, but decided there were other things I would rather do.

As a music student, I was expected to play an instrument besides the piano. I chose the flute. My preference was for either the cello, or the clarinet. However, the clarinet was impossible. I could not place my fingers over the holes, and at the same time put the reed to my mouth. As for the cello, I could only have played it in the style of a double bass. Given the chance, I might have tried it, but there were no cellos available.

I settled on the flute and although I took lessons for a year, I never really mastered it. My primary difficulty was the breathing (though I know I could have done better with more practice). The instrument belonged to the school and when I gave notice of going into the hospital for three months,[1] the teacher assigned the flute to someone else. I was more relieved than anything else.

All throughout my high school years, I was active in a christian group called Crusaders. In my senior year, I was appointed the Junior Crusader leader. This meant being responsible to encourage other people to attend meetings and on occasion, taking the lesson. I was also liaison between our community leaders and the school staff. At the end of the year, my final duty was to report the year's activities in the school magazine.

Attitude towards school

I enjoyed my school years. So much so, that during elementary

---

1   This experience is described in Chapter 1, *"Understood."*

school days, I wished there were no weekends so that I could go to school everyday. Amazing. I grew out of that and later though I still enjoyed school, I looked forward to the freedom of weekends.

My parents often pointed out that I would not be able to do everything that other kids did and stressed the need for me to concentrate on my education. I responded to this and although not brilliant, I worked hard in school and a couple of times attained academic awards. At the end of grade eight, I had the distinction of being among the top thirteen students of more than two hundred. In high school, I received prizes for excellence in German and Music.

My eleventh and twelfth grade years were the best. Although in many ways they were the toughest academically and socially, I thrived on the increased responsibility and respect given to seniors. Much of this came as a result of my being elected a prefect. It was not only an honor, but brought lots of duties: supervising students on detention, standing on duty at the school-gates to check the passes of those returning from lunch, keeping everyone in line at the lunch canteen and sometimes breaking up fights on the way home from school.

The job didn't go without its perks. Prefects had the prestige of their own uniform and a separate lunch room with lockers. The room provided a great social arena, especially as the boy prefects room was visible through the hole in the wall!

In my last year in high school, I left my mark in the school magazine with a statement I submitted to the section called *"Meet Some Pupils."* I wrote something of what it had been like for me as a Little Person in the school. It's interesting to look back and see how I felt about myself at age eighteen.

My insecurities were obvious. I kept qualifying my account, by telling the reader such things as,

"with my limited ability I will not attempt to describe myself ... I won't bore you by giving long lists of irrelevant material ... and I think I'll sign off now before you all go to sleep."

Yet inspite of a flagging confidence, I did relate my story with some humor and a positive outlook. Indeed, some of what I said then is still true today:

"It is only when I look in the mirror that I think of myself as any different from the rest of you. I guess lots of people are dissatisfied with their reflection. I won't say that I never get annoyed when I look

in the mirror, but 'I've learned in whatsoever state I am, there with to be content.'" [1]

The magazine editor included a page of pictures captioned: *"Our twelfth grade comes in all sizes, by all means of transport, works, plays, enjoys spring, and wears nine different uniforms."* Guess which caption my photo matched? You got it, *"comes in all sizes."* The two photos shown were myself at three feet four inches, and Lyall at six feet ten inches. The editor's closing question was: *"Who says we turn out a stereotyped product?"* It was true; we certainly were a motley bunch. I was sad when the day came to leave. Our years together had been good ones.

Parent-Teacher-Pupil Relations

I'm sure the secret to the happiness of my school days was in *"the good communication between home and school, the good rapport I developed with my teachers, and my classmates acceptance of me."* [2] My mother always attended the school interviews with teachers, arranged three times a year to discuss my progress in school. There she would learn how all her children were doing. It was also the opportunity for her to find out if I had any special needs.

However, in elementary school there was no need to wait for formal interviews. Through the Parent-Teacher's Association, my parents attended some social functions where they got to know my teachers personally. I was amazed to find a photo my parents brought home from one of these parties. There was my teacher dressed like a fairy, magic wand and all.

In the first year interviews at high school, my teacher told mom that when he saw me among his students he anticipated having problems. Yet in spite of his years of experience, he admitted to being wrong. He said there were no difficulties at all. He even told her, that in the change over between classes certain students would always wait back and walk with me. He could report that I was accepted by my class-mates. It was a different story for Roberta, who after eight years

1   New American Standard Bible, Phillipians 4:11.
2   Marjorie King, excerpt from a letter *"To Whom it May Concern"* describing her experience teaching a dwarf child named Jimmy (August, 1977).

in the special school for children with handicaps, was suddenly plunged into a high school with regular sized kids. She knew no one and felt very awkward about making friends.

The school building was five stories high, occupied a whole city block and had a thousand students in each graduating class. Accommodations were necessary to prevent Roberta from being crushed in the corridors between classes and to make easy access to the five levels of the building. She was given a key to use the elevator (otherwise used by staff only) and was let out of classes five minutes early. The problem was, she could not reach the key hole. The Dean of girl students realized this right away, but thought it best if Roberta find a friend to help her. That was well and good in theory; however, the Dean over-looked the fact that Roberta was new in the school and had no friends to ask.

For the first two weeks, Roberta struggled with the stairs instead of using the elevator. Finally, the Dean noticed what was going on and appointed someone to help Roberta. The helper was glad to get out of class early with Roberta, but after performing the duty would run right back to her own friends and walk to class with them. That was painful for Roberta who needed friendship as much as she needed help with the elevator key. In the school for children with handicaps, socialization had not even been considered. Roberta did not even feel confident enough to approach the Dean to explain the difficulty she was having.

By contrast, I always had a good rapport with my teachers. I'm sure it was because I had been taught to socialize with adults. To me a teacher was someone to respect and learn from, not a person to fear. No doubt, being conscientious and well-mannered helped teachers to like me.

I consider myself very lucky to have had good teachers through most of my school days. The teacher I remember and loved the best was my grade three and four teacher, Mr. Rae. He made school so much fun. It appeared that every child in the class was special to him. There was always time for any of us to go to him with our concerns and he would make room for us on his lap, sometimes two or three kids at a time.

He involved us in every kind of learning: art, drama, music, and literature without ignoring the basics in reading, writing and arithmetic. Everything was exciting. We learned to increase our reading speed by watching television, at least we pretended it was a television. A script was wrapped inside a screen and he would roll it through picking up speed as we went.

He had myriads of ideas which made learning enjoyable. It would take me the whole two years to tell of everything we did in his class, but I don't need to do that to show you that he was a wonderful teacher. We learned to appreciate him and the path he set us on for our future years in school. He deserved every tear we shed when we parted.

He made the question, what will I be when I grow up a valid one. If anyone did ask me what I was going to be, my standard reply was, *"I don't know."* It seemed such a long way off, I didn't worry about it. Yet, I always knew I would be something and found it frustrating to meet people who had their doubts about my future. One such person was a doctor I met at aged fourteen. He even asked if I went to school? I couldn't believe the question. What did he think I did? He was one of those who didn't expect me to do anything when I grew up.

Academic Choices and Career Planning

The first time I was asked to choose some direction in my education was at the end of grade eight. I had to chose subjects to study in high school, and was conscious that the selections should also be in preparation for future employment. At the time, my only thought was that I would be a secretary of some kind.

Typing seemed to be a sensible thing to include in my schedule. It became one of my six subjects in grade nine. It also became the most painful lesson of the day. I was pleased to learn touch typing, but was bored out of my brain. The way the teacher practically smothered me with her kind concern was enough to finish me off. By the second half of the year, I was nearly climbing the walls. I just had to get out of that class. I asked my parents and teachers for permission to transfer to the German class.

Fortunately, the German teacher agreed to accept me, and another girl as late starters. The whole years work had to be taught to us in the remaining couple of months. He only accepted us into the class on the condition that we do set exercises for him during our summer vacation. The prospect of sharing the summer sun with German audio records and a textbook was infinitely more appealing than facing another four years of typing.

It was worth all the effort and turned out to be a very timely move. If I had continued in the typing class, I would have been lacking a subject of sufficient academic standard for the examination qualifying me for university. My future options would have been severely limited.

The first time I specifically thought of a career choice was when an Employment Officer approached the Dean of my school for permission to release me from classes for one week. As a result, I attended a Vocational Assessment course conducted at the Auckland branch of the New Zealand Crippled Children's Society. I was tested in the many different aspects of clerical work, probably because I was still expressing a vague interest in secretarial work. On the final day, I was assigned to the main reception desk to observe the duties of a receptionist. Instead of stimulating my interest, the experience stifled any thoughts I may have had about seeking a secretarial position. I was totally bored.

The employment officer agreed this was not the job for me, but he had his own reasons. In his report to my parents he wrote:

"Angela was tested in both the theoretical and practical duties of a receptionist. While her intelligence, initiative, manner and speech equip her for this type of work, her voice is not particularly satisfactory on a telephone and as this also involves a great deal of movement this may not be the best type of employment for Angela."

My parents and I were most indignant. What was wrong with my voice and who said I couldn't move around? The employment officer went on to say:

"Angela showed particular ability in the operation of Adding and Bookkeeping Machines and in fact obtained above average rates. There is no doubt that with training she could become a competent business machine operator, but it is doubtful whether she would have the physical strength to cope with this type of work over an extended period."

The force of our indignation strengthened! Where did he get the idea I wasn't strong enough to handle a days work? And why didn't he consider me for employment options outside of closely supervised office positions?

As if that wasn't infuriating enough, he went on to say, *"Angela's weakness is her lack of punctuality."* My mother nearly blew her top with that one. Hadn't he been told why I was late every day? I was dependent on my parents to drive me to the Center, or take me to the bus-stop. What could I do, if dad decided to call at several job-sites on the way, or if mom arrived at the bus-stop in time to see the bus pulling out? He could at least have had the decency to realize who was responsible for my lateness.

Well, the report wasn't all bad. The officer concluded by saying, *"There is no doubt that she (Angela) is vocationally feasible and that many avenues of employment will be open to her, but it is important at this stage that she continue her education to the highest level. Accordingly, it is recommended that she continue with her schooling."* That much of his advice we did take. I stayed in high school until grade twelve and made the decision to attend university.

At this point, I also had to decide what I was going to study at University. I preferred to pursue a course with a specific employment goal. The only practical use I could see for a Bachelor of Arts was in school-teaching. (Though I now know there are other options). However, the school vocational guidance teacher tried to dissuade me from considering teaching, because of her anticipated fear that I would have difficulty disciplining the class. She believed that the ability to physically dominate a child is a major factor in keeping control in the classroom. That may have been right as a general rule, but if I had wanted to be a teacher, her advice would not have been enough to stop me. I know for sure that she would have been challenged by the many Little People who have successfully entered the teaching profession. However, that is where our debate ended, because I did not want to be a teacher.

It wasn't difficult deciding not to be a scientist, mathematician, engineer, geologist, artist, or accountant as I had no aptitude or interest in any of these subjects. It almost seemed as though my chosen degree program would be by a process of elimination.

Law was one option that had not been foreclosed. However, studying law never occurred to me until an aunt suggested it. I had been considering journalism as a career and decided that law would serve as fine preparation. I was admitted to law school in 1972.

My years in law school at the University of Auckland were exciting and demanding. I knew they would be, when one professor announced that only half of the two hundred students sitting in the auditorium would complete the degree program. I was determined to be in the graduating half, but worried about how much there was to learn. It was even an art learning how to balance leisure and study time.

Paying for higher education

Fortunately, I did not have to juggle my time for friends and study with a job. My parents supported me with free board, and by keeping my car on the road. In addition, a small government scholarship gave me pocket money to cover books, stationery, clothes and entertainment expenses.[1] At thirteen dollars a week in my first year, you couldn't pretend it was any more than pocket money. Even though the amount increased each year, I still needed to get work in the summer vacation to keep me going through the year. However, that was easier said than done.

It was hard for me to get work. Casual summer jobs like waitressing, fruit or crop picking, attending in a shop, or working in a factory, were mainly physically oriented. I wasn't cut-out for any of that because of the limited amount of time I could be on my feet. For a few years, I stuck it out assembling clothes-pins for my uncle. However, it was impossible to make big money doing this and quite lonely clicking away on the days no one else worked.

To my delight, the Auckland Branch of the New Zealand Crippled Children's Society recognized my difficulty in finding summer employment and gave me a grant of five hundred dollars to assist with my education expenses. In the same year, I received two hundred dollars from the June Opie Rose Trust Fund, for being an individual with a disability striving to help myself.

Although these two financial awards were a great boost and much appreciated, I was just as excited at the end of my second year in law school to get a summer job in the office of a large department store.

---

1   The New Zealand government pays about a ninety percent subsidy for the tuition fees of New Zealand citizens.

Yet even here, I was a beneficiary. I got the job because of the influence my uncle had with the manager of the store. However, it was the kind of benefit I could handle, especially when it gave me the opportunity to both prove my ability and to be financially independent.

I thoroughly enjoyed that summer. There was regular money and experience. I made lots of friends and learned so much. I returned to law school with a broader perspective on life and a greater assurance of myself as an independent woman.

Law School Graduation

When it was time for me to graduate four years later,[1] I was determined to be a part of the entire ceremony. It was customary for a procession of graduates to proceed along the street temporarily closed to traffic from the clock-tower building of Auckland University, to the town hall. I had no chance of walking all that distance, but was determined not to miss out completely. Arrangements were made for me to join the procession at the half way point. I waited for the black stream of robed graduates to flow down the hill and eagerly joined my law school peers at the bottom. However, our walk together was short lived.

The rain had caused the parade to begin late and so as not to delay traffic any longer than necessary, the procession moved much faster than usual. I couldn't speed up and they couldn't slow down. However, instead of dropping out altogether, I continued walking at my own pace at the side of the procession. All I needed, was a new color for my hood to match those of the architects, engineers, and doctors that I marched a few minutes with. As one group passed me, I joined the graduates of the school behind them. In less than a half hour, I had the total professional experience!

In the actual ceremony, the Dean arranged for two fellow law students to wait at the bottom of the stairs on both sides of the stage to help me up and down. As we were called in alphabetical order, it was two students whom I already knew well. (When your last name begins

---

1   No undergraduate degree is required as a prerequisite to law school
     admission in New Zealand, and the degree takes four years to complete.
     An additional year of study is required of those preparing for bar
     admission.

with the same letter, it's amazing how many classes you have scheduled together).

On that graduation day, I was donned with the degree of a Bachelor of Law. After seventeen years in school, my formal education was complete. Now all I had to do was learn how to put my knowledge to use in the working world.[1]

---

1   For a discussion of my first job experience as an attorney refer to Chapter 3, *"At the Bar."*

Chapter Three

AT THE BAR

My presence in the bar has been challenged more than once, but exchange the bouncer for the court-crier and you'll find me unchallenged, at the bar of the local court. Eligibility for this bar is based on a certificate of admission to the High Court of New Zealand,[1] not a certificate of birth. On the first day of February 1977, the order of admission was made. Indeed, the day actually carried an air of fantasy. It began with a parallel to *"Goldilocks and the Three Bears."* I felt like big daddy bear robbed of chair, porridge, and bed! When I came to sign the Roll of Barristers and Solicitors,[2] somebody had signed on the line reserved for my name. In all the excitement, one of my peers had signed her name in my space. There was nowhere for me to sign.

The story took a different turn when the Deputy Registrar stepped into the picture. As though a fairy godmother waving her wand, she took out an eraser and removed all traces of the error. With it she also wiped out any suggestions of fantasy. In reality, I was standing there at

---

[1] I was actually admitted to the Supreme Court of New Zealand, now known as the High Court of New Zealand, the equivalent of a United States Federal Court of Appeals.

[2] A barrister and solicitor is known in the United States as an attorney and counselor at law.

the age of twenty-three[1] ready to enter my name on the roll and to begin my career as a Barrister and Solicitor in law.

I stood with pride alongside my fellow class-mates also taking the oaths of admission. As predicted only half of those who began the five year law program stood with us on this day. We were at the end of a long road and were finally entitled to speak before the court.

The occasion called for traditional dress: a white horse-hair wig, and an expensively pleated heavy black legal gown. I couldn't help thinking how much we all looked like over-dressed penguins. However, the apparel was a pre-requisite to appearance and the right to speak as counsel in court. It was no time to voice objections. Instead we all robed meekly and took the oaths put to us. We hoped other people understood that appearances aren't the most important thing in the world.

That hope was put to a severe test when I discovered that prospective employers were very interested in appearances. My admission to the bar was not an automatic entry into the work force. Indeed my prospects of employment were gloomy as the supply of law graduates far exceeded the demand. Only ten jobs were advertised, and almost one hundred applicants were in competition for them. My chances of success were minimal.

There wasn't just the shortage of positions to contend with, but also my shortage of inches and to many employers this fact was over-whelming because they just could not cope with the idea of someone my height representing their clients. Only certain types of people were likely to get a job easily. You had a better chance if you were from a private school, your father or uncle was a lawyer, you were male, and of average height and appearance; I did not qualify on any of these counts. I attended a public school; no members of the family were in the legal profession; I am female, and I am not just less than average

---

1   It is customary for a New Zealander to qualify as an attorney at about age 23, as students may enter the four year law degree program at age eighteen years, without being required to complete an undergraduate degree. However, a first year of general studies, known as pre-law, must be successfully completed before a decision as to law school admission is made. A fifth year of part time study, while working as a clerk in a law office, is spent qualifying for admission to the bar.

height, but am shorter than most short people. It wasn't enough to have a pretty face.

Prospective employers could see and did not question my academic qualifications, but they had difficulty matching them with an ability to function as a lawyer. Many excuses were offered. One person ruled me out saying, *"you won't be able to appear in Court because the legal gown will be too long!"* [1] The mental picture of his legal gown trailing on the ground behind me was too much for him. It was also unnecessary, as I had my own gown tailor made.

The same interviewer was concerned about my inability to run. It never occurred to me that lawyers were expected to move quickly. If anything, I thought they were known for how slow they move! Anyway this interviewer suggested that a judge may request, pronto, that I attend to a client held in custody downstairs in the cells and would not wait the extra time it would take me to go up and down the stairs.

I knew from my observation of court practice that this was ridiculous! If an attorney needs to see a client during a court session, the judge doesn't sit around and wait for the lawyers return. There is always other work to keep the court busy during such an absence. However, at that stage in my career, I lacked the experience of appearing in a court room to refute his concern, but my instinct told me that the interviewer was just throwing up a smoke-screen.

When I later found employment, I learned that the judges before whom I appeared were much more reasonable than my interviewer. They never demanded high speeds up and down the stairs, and were always too busy to even notice that I took a little longer. In fact, the only people I ever saw running around at court were those who were late, disorganized, or both.

Some employers could not even discuss the possibility of my joining their staff. Their total shock at my appearance prevented them even

1 Counsel must wear a legal gown and wig when appearing before the High Court, Court of Appeals, and the Privy Council. However, no gown or wig needs to be worn for District Court hearings.

giving me a hearing.[1] I clearly recall a *"so-called"* interview with one person. He did no more than invite me into his room and offer a seat. He immediately accepted a phone call and throughout that lengthy phone conversation (I suspect protracted deliberately), he *"eyed"* me. When the telephone discussion ended, so did the interview. He had no questions, just one piece of advice. *"You should consider taking a job in a government department, where you can make make use of your academic ability."* I was furious. Every part of me wanted to challenge his rejection, but I had no idea where to begin to break through the barriers in his head. They were cemented long ago. Besides, any outburst would only add to his lack of confidence in me. Then, he would not only see me as physically incapable, but also as emotionally unstable.

What he was suggesting was very disturbing, because it revealed a basic fear he had. He couldn't handle dealing with someone who was different, and projected that inadequacy onto his clients, whom he feared would not have confidence in me either. Of course, that would mean clients would not want me to handle their cases, and the firm would lose business, and most importantly their fat fee. Rather than suggest I wasn't suited to legal employment, which would be a discriminatory act that even his conscience couldn't live with, he suggested government service where I would not be before the public and not dependent on him for a weekly pay-check. I resolved to prove I could function in the private sector and there was no need for me to be safely closeted in government service. He would see for himself, how wrong he was.

It was pleasing to find, however, that there were employers who were not in the least fazed by my size. Some could foresee vacancies in the near future, and were prepared to consider me as a candidate. Even though I wasn't offered a job by any of the prospects, it was encouraging to be given a hearing. At least they considered me.

On occasion, I would be the one to refuse a possible job opportunity, as I could not consider a job if it involved a lot of walking or required the search of property titles and descriptions. At the Land

---

1   For further discussion of the loss of hearing by employers, see Chapter 6, *"Attitudes Disable."*

Transfer Office,[1] I could not reach the drawers with the reference material and knew it would be unprofitable to both the employer and myself to even try. There was no mourning lost opportunity, as it was the type of work regarded by law graduates as temporary. I had no objection to by-passing the first rung on the ladder of legal employment.

All I had to do was find a willing employer with work I could do. Employers with vacancies were few; hopefully, the willing ones were not also far between. I did not speculate on the matter, rather I determined to find out. Days were spent with the yellow pages calling each law office to seek possible vacancies.

I could see no good reason to confront the employer with telephone advice of my height. It wasn't a matter of hiding it, rather a question of timing. Experience has proven it is much better to discuss the matter face to face. That way you have a good chance of persuading the prospective employer that height does not limit ability. To mention my height on the phone was to risk the click of a telephone refusal based on preconceived notions.

My strategy and persistence paid off. After hundreds of calls, I got four interviews; one of these resulted in a job offer. Admittedly my first job was only temporary, but the six weeks promised was extended to ten, and carried me financially while I continued my search for a permanent position.

Once again, I was successful. I was eventually offered a permanent job. The timing was perfect. The job offered was to begin immediately after completion of the temporary job.

I have often reflected on the reason I got a job so quickly, especially when many of my class-mates took much longer to find a position. People expected me to have difficulty and were surprised to learn that I did not experience one day of unemployment!

Of course there was more than one reason, including being in the right place at the right time, and knowing the right people to put in the right word. For one, I began my job search six months before I was ready to start work. Also, the employer who offered me a permanent position, had received high commendations about me from a mutual

---

1   The United States equivalent is known as a Title Deed Registry.

friend. In addition, she got to see the quality of my work, when I was hired on a contract basis to do some process serving.

I gladly accepted the opportunity to earn some money with process serving, and to view 'actual court documents' which to date had only been text book reprints. It never occurred to me that if the person violently objected to the content of the document being served, they might direct that violence at me.

Besides, the first assignment I was given my employer blithely described as 'simplicity.' I followed her directions, attended at the given address, identified the person for whom the papers were intended, and handed them over. It was a piece of cake. However, the second assignment proved to be anything but simple.

The person to be served was in prison,[1] so that's where I went. I had been there before (not as a guest of the government, rather with my criminology class), so I knew to describe my mission at the first gate. I was directed to the barred iron door. It didn't seem possible that my knock would be heard, but amazingly the little peep hole opened in response. After describing my mission again, the door opened long enough for me to enter. It closed heavily behind me. Obediently, I entered my name in the visitors book and noted the time of arrival.

The guard's finger pointed me toward the visitor's waiting room, where I declared my mission for the third time. I explained to another officer which prisoner I wanted to see and why. To be sure he called the right person, I showed him the papers I was going to serve. He appeared to peruse the papers carefully, and suggested I take a seat in the waiting room while he called the prisoner. I followed his instruction and sat down.

It was a room where many other people had also waited. The graffiti on the wall showed how they had spent their time. I decided that in this forum it was better to read than write, so I chose to read. One writing stood out as more official looking. It was actually a warning given under the Penal Act, prohibiting visitors from passing anything across the counter to prisoners. I wondered how this related to the document I planned to pass across. However, before I could give the matter any further thought, I was interrupted by the officer's return. He announced

---

1   A medium security prison for prisoners on remand and those serving
      short term sentences.

the arrival of the prisoner, and pointed me in his direction.

I walked toward him and took a seat opposite. The glass barrier between us made quiet conversation difficult. I had to be sure to serve the right person, so my questions getting him to acknowledge his identity and familiarity with the contents of the papers had to be shouted. Once satisfied that he was the person the papers were meant for, I passed them over the glass barrier.

I realized immediately that my earlier dismissal of the warning under the Penal Act had been a big mistake. The officer's finger tapping on my shoulder and angry scowl made that very clear. He told me I had broken the law and was liable for imprisonment. I had a graphic mental picture of becoming the cell-mate of the person just served! Fortunately for me, I was let off with a warning.

I couldn't believe it. How many times did I have to say what I was planning to do? Where did I go wrong? My intention was hardly kept a secret. However, it had certainly been misunderstood.

Still not knowing where I had gone wrong, I reported the whole incident to my employer. She explained what I should have done at the prison. It appears that inspite of my care in explaining my purpose I had been directed to the wrong place. I should have clearly announced myself as a process-server. Then I wouldn't have been treated as a visitor, and would have been directed to a place where it was not an offense to act in the course of duty.

When I was in her permanent employ a few months later, she told me that she was impressed with my ability to laugh the incident off as a joke: *"the day I nearly didn't get out of jail."* My reaction helped persuade her that I had the right temperament to handle the many sticky situations which arise in the practice of law.

After six months of occasional process serving assignments, my employer was ready to hire someone on a full-time basis. I was a natural candidate for the job. In this case, discrimination even worked in my favor. My employer preferred to employ a woman and that bias eliminated two thirds of the prospective applicants: the males. An interesting reversal, since most employers were only looking to hire males.

Also to my advantage was my employer's unwillingness to advertise and interview dozens of people. Instead she chose me, someone recommended by a person she knew and trusted, and someone who had served her well on a part-time contract basis. She did not regard my short-stature as an impediment to my ability to practice law. Perhaps this was explained by the fact that one of her closest school friends was blind. Through that friendship, I'm sure she had learned that a person's abilities are not canceled out by their disability.

At last I could say, things were going my way. I had a law degree, admission to the bar, and a job. Now all I had to do was make a good impression on the judges and the clients. I had to begin by winning their confidence.

My first meeting with a client shatters all of the stereotypes people have of how lawyers should look. In the crowded court foyer people watch me weaving around people's legs and whisper among themselves, *"Is she really a lawyer?"* In the office, I introduce myself and invite them to come and take a seat in my room. Often they hesitate not sure whether to follow, or to wait for the *"real"* lawyer to come in. Parents' faces brighten with embarrassment, when their curious child crawls under my desk and exclaims in the midst of the interview, *"Mummy her feet don't touch the floor!"*

After the initial surprise, I soon discovered it wasn't hard to win the client's confidence. At the court, peoples' questions are soon answered. They see me working with clients, negotiating with other lawyers, and speaking for clients before a judge. It becomes very obvious that I am indeed a lawyer.

If anything, my ability to break free from the lawyer stereotype is helpful. My distinctive appearance makes it easy for clients to identify and find me. People have come into my office and before agreeing to make an appointment will ask the secretary, *"Is this the office of 'the little lady lawyer'?"* They may even gesture with their hand at waist level to make absolutely sure they will be seeing me.

In the office, I don't get into a discussion about my size. If the client asks whether I'm the lawyer, I just tell them *"Yes"* and ask how I can help them. The goal is to turn their mind back to the reason they came to see a lawyer. The interview begins, and in the process they relax and realize, that so long as I talk and sound like a lawyer it really doesn't matter how many inches I measure.

To relieve those who need more persuasion, I display my law degree certificate on the wall. I assure parents perturbed by the expressions of their children (sounding more like an echo of their own thoughts), that this is a common occurrence, which doesn't bother me a bit. However, I do make an attempt to divert the child's attention to the set of trains laid in a strategic position on the office floor. Invariably they are left idle.

Some long-standing clients have informed me, that they don't even consider my size in our professional relationship. They admit it was a surprise initially, but after the first interview were satisfied I was competent to deal with their legal problem. Judging by the size of my caseload, I would say their response was fairly typical. I had enough clients to keep me busy for many more than the eight hours in the working day.

After gaining a client's respect, I strive for respect from the Bench. However, before this is possible, I must first catch the Judge's attention. This was brought home to me loud and clear on my second court appearance. However, the story makes no sense unless I first explain what happens when a person makes a first appearance on a criminal charge in a New Zealand district court.

The first thing the Judge wants to know, is whether the person charged is represented. The judge usually gets his answer when a lawyer stands up at the same time their client's name is called. However, my standing up doesn't give the Judge any signal. If anything, standing up gives me less chance of being seen, as when I stand my head only levels the shoulders of the other lawyers seated at the bar.

I realized my predicament on a day when the court room was filled to capacity with both lawyers and members of the public. My case was a simple one. All I had to do was enter a not guilty plea, apply for bail, and get the hearing remanded to a later date.

The large crowd worried me because I was very nervous, and knew it could mean waiting all morning for my case to be called. I was delighted after only about half an hour to hear my client's name called. I stood immediately.

My client took some time to make his way to the dock, as he was seated in the middle of the row at the back of the court-room, and had to scramble over everyone's legs to get out. Instead of my stepping out to a position where the Judge could see me, I waited for my client to reach the dock. That was a mistake. What was supposed to be a routine matter suddenly became very complicated. To my horror and in the presence of all these people, the Judge did not wait for my client to get to the dock. He simply saw no appearance of a lawyer, and concluded the defendant was unrepresented. The Judge assigned my client's case to the Duty Solicitor![1]

I wanted to shout out, *"Your Honor, the defendant is represented, I appear for him."* But how could I? It wasn't polite to shout at a Judge. I knew that better than anyone. I also knew it was the only way to get his attention now, as he was looking down at the papers in front of him. I couldn't bear the thought of having to wait all morning for the case to be called again, so I decided to take a chance.

I stood in the aisle where the Judge would see me when he raised his head and shouted out, *"May it please your Honor, I represent the defendant."* The Judge looked up quite startled, but the courteous choice of words and element of surprise, saved me from his censure. He muttered an apology and asked the clerk to call my client again.

Finally, I was able to get the bail and hearing date. Although extremely embarrassed about the situation, I was quietly pleased that I didn't let the circumstances overwhelm me. Needless to say, the lesson was well learned and I never let it happen again. After that, my appearances in court were much more carefully planned.

People suggested that I should stand on a chair, but that didn't appeal to me at all. I never stood on a chair to get attention before, and I wasn't about to begin in a court-room. A much more dignified and natural approach was for me to move away from the lawyers table, and stand in the aisle. That way I was in direct line with the judge's eye, and in a position to be both seen and heard. Besides, I'm much more effective when I keep both feet on the ground.

A lawyer with clients and the respect of the Bench can practice, but

---

1   New Zealand's equivalent to a Public Defender. However, in New Zealand, Public Defenders do not work for a government corporation, but are attorneys in private practice who agree to represent clients without lawyers in criminal cases. The government supports the program by paying the attorneys an hourly fee for service given. The Duty Solicitor only represents the client on a first court appearance on that particular charge. The Duty Solicitor will advise the client on the plea, enter a not guilty plea on behalf of the client, give a plea in mitigation if the client pleads guilty, or arrange for bail if the matter is to be remanded. If the matter is remanded for a trial date and the client cannot afford to pay for a lawyer, the court will appoint counsel from the private bar, and the government will pay the attorney a nominal fee for representing the defendant.

never very well without the respect and trust of other members of the bar. I have found lawyers have just as many inhibitions in their dealings with me as other people. Some have difficulty accepting me as a colleague. Even so, their attitudes have no effect on me in the court room; the court sees all as equal at the bar. However, in situations outside the court-room, their conduct can impact the results of our dealings.

In this situation, it is the non-accepting lawyer who is clearly disadvantaged. Such lawyers may not see me as a serious opponent. Some may not even bother to prepare for negotiations. Consequently, their revelation of my equality and ability only comes as I proceed to defeat their every unprepared argument. I know that my size does not impair my ability as a lawyer, but those who don't know this have to learn the hard way.

It is rare to get direct feed-back of the reaction another lawyer has to me, but occasionally people make comments about me to someone without realizing the person they are speaking to is a friend of mine. In this way I get to hear some of what is said about me from my friend. One secretary told me that after I had finished a real estate closing with her boss, he came out of his office and said to her, *"That's the smallest lawyer I have ever seen!"* Another one admitted to my para-legal friend, that I took him off guard by tearing every one of his arguments to shreds.

I find the best way of developing trust and respect from my colleagues is to earn it. There are but few who, once given time and exposure to me, will not accept me as their equal at the bar.

Some have no idea I am a Little Person, as our business is conducted over the telephone and through the mail. When letters are the only communication, it takes imagination to even get to know the lawyer you are writing to, let alone worry about their appearance. The most interesting exchange I had was with a lawyer more than a thousand miles from my office. At the bottom of one of his letters, he wrote:

> *"There was a young lady named Muir,*
> *Whose suitors grew fewer and fewer,*
> *They threw not a kiss at her,*
> *For she worked for a solicitor,*
> *And not (as they wished) for a brewer."*

When replying I could not resist penciling a limerick at the bottom of my letter. Mine went like this:

> *"There was a brave man named Andrews,*
> *With Limericks he always bemused,*
> *But the solicitor he wrote to,*
> *Had no time to devote to,*
> *The blokes, the breweries and the booze."*

Such light-hearted exchanges help fire my energy for the many obstacles in the daily routine. To practice law successfully, I not only must gain the confidence of my clients, get the attention of the Court and earn the respect of my colleagues, but I also must overcome numerous physical barriers.

Court practice can even be a matter of endurance. When speaking to witnesses or a judge, you have to stand. In a long trial or hearing, this can be very tiring. On these occasions, I usually seek the court's permission to remain seated. No judge has ever refused me.

Some of my difficulties even cause the level of Court proceedings to be lowered, and by that I don't mean the standard. It happens when an exhibit is being produced. When it is shown to the witness for comment, as the lawyer I should also come forward and examine it. However, it is difficult for me to do this when the exhibit is shown to the witness two feet above my head. In that case, the prosecutor or opposing counsel either lowers the exhibit to my level, or shows it to me where I'm sitting. When I am producing an exhibit through my own client, I am familiar with its' content so do not have the same problem. Some Judges will even save me some steps, and will ask the Court clerk to take the exhibit from me and carry it to my client in the witness box.

Access to judicial buildings is again *"at your physical pleasure."*[1] In the court library, which I frequented regularly, I must climb onto a chair to reach the books I need. As the research often involves looking at several books before the answer is found, rather than climbing up and down, I may even make a row of several chairs so I can walk along the whole shelf. Instead of climbing down to peruse the different volumes, sometimes I will perch on the window sill. This no doubt looks rather amusing to those looking up from the street. On one occasion, the surprise even caused a lawyer coming into the library to take one look at me and walk straight out again.

---

1   See Chapter 5, *"At Your Physical Pleasure."*

Stairs are common to every court facility I use. I can manage where there is a rail, but in order to retain my composure, I refuse to be hassled by the clock or bustling crowds. I prefer to make my way deliberately and at my own pace. On crowded Court days, people will often sit on the stairs and I develop the knack of parting the way as I approach. Some days, I am literally driven up the wall. This happens when there is no rail to assist me, and I have to find support from the flat surface of the building. I only carry as much as I can hold in one arm, as I must keep the other arm free for the hand-rail or the wall.

I'm in a predicament, when I want to know if a hearing in a court-room is finished. Even though a window is placed in many doors for people to see in without interrupting the proceedings, that's of no help to me because the window is way above my head. A possible alternative would be to peer through the key hole, but this is useless because of the difficulty in seeing around corners. Besides, it certainly doesn't enhance my image as a lawyer to be classified with the *"peeping Toms"* of this world. My solution is to either ask someone else to look through the window, or to slip into the room as discreetly as possible. This is not too difficult for me as you recall my presence has gone unnoticed in the Court room before.

Sometimes, a lawyer needs to give evidence on behalf of a client, such as when the client agrees and prefers not to make a personal appearance.[1] When preparing to give evidence for my client once, I noticed the witness box. I immediately realized, that although my evidence would be heard, I would not be seen because my head would not show above the side of the witness box. I did not want to be mistaken for a voice from the dead, so decided to stand alongside the box.

When I came forward to give evidence, I declined the Court clerks' invitation to step into the witness box. However, the clerk became very agitated and tried to insist. I stood my ground beside the box. The clerk wouldn't give in, so I looked to the Judge for approval of my position. The Judge nodded that it was okay for me to stand where I was. I remained standing ready to give my evidence and the clerk totally

---

1   Before the introduction of the New Zealand Family Court in 1982, this was done in cases dealing with divorce.

flustered went and sat down. However, the Judge had to intercede again by saying to the clerk, *"Don't you think it would be a good idea to swear the witness in?"*

It was not important where I stood, but very important that what I said be on oath. Some procedures just cannot be over-looked. The clerk recovered sufficiently to swear me in and my evidence was given. I was pleased; I had stood my ground and was afforded the same dignity as other witnesses: to be both seen and heard.

It is very important not to be late when appearing in Court. If the case is called before your arrival, there is every possibility that the person you are to represent will be dealt with in your absence. Sometimes the court, on learning that you have been instructed, is gracious enough to allow the client time to find out where on earth you are. When you eventually appear in the Court, you need to have very good reasons for not having been there on time. No one likes to get off side with the Court for such matters. I do my best to be early, which means allowing an extra time margin to make up for my slower walk and the time needed to find a parking place.

Some days there is a last minute change of venue by the Court staff. This often means the new venue is in another building and at a distance. Everyone races to the new building, where the Judge is imagined to be waiting anxiously. At one time I would also dash frantically and arrive all hot and bothered. I did not want to experience harsh words from the Judge and begin the hearing on the wrong foot. However, by arriving hot and bothered, I was flustered and still began the hearing on the wrong foot.

It didn't take long for me to decide to walk at my own pace to the changed venue, knowing that my lateness was the result of the Court's failure to notify me of the change ahead of time, not my slow pace. I was never called on to argue the point. A Judge's clerk later told me, the Judge expected me to arrive after the others anyway. All I had to do was catch the attention of one of the people rushing to the new venue, the clerk if possible, and ask that person to inform the Judge I was on my way.

Patience is an important characteristic for a lawyer to have, because dealing with people coming through the courts can be very trying. When serving as Duty Solicitor you have to search the crowded foyers for people making a first appearance on a criminal charge without the assistance of a lawyer. These people are entitled to be represented by the Duty Solicitor, but they often don't realize this service is available to them. As a result, when the Duty Solicitor calls for people making their first appearance to step forward, many will sit back and ignore the calls. This means the Duty Solicitor must systematically speak to everyone milling around in the foyer to be sure to find the people needing service.

When I approach people and suggest that they come and talk to me, they often hesitate. I deal with them the same as I do with those that come to my office the first time. I deal directly with their problem. It only takes a few sentences before the person understands, I really am a lawyer. My credibility is improved when the Court staff and other rostered Duty Solicitors greet me and discuss legal problems with me.

On a very busy day, I have to look out for my safety, not so much because I might happen to be *"in the den of thieves and thugs"* conducting interviews in their cells, but simply because there are so many people pressing in together. I am in real danger of being squashed. It takes very careful strategy to safely cross the foyer. It was on one of these busy days that members of a local gang offered to be my body guard. I could have done with their help a few months earlier when I was alone in the office.

On this occasion, two Pacific Island men came to the office for the appointment I had set up with them the week before. Intially, I was pleased to see them return, as it meant we had communicated well despite a language barrier. I was alone in the office, because the secretary was on sick leave and my employer was delayed in Court. It was my task therefore to conduct the interview. The men both followed me into the interview room; I left the door open to see any clients that might come into the reception area.

The interview was laborious without the assistance of an interpreter, but I eventually got through it. It was time for them to leave, but they turned the discussion to more personal matters. There were no welcome interruptions from the telephone or people walking into the reception room.

Henry, the older male did all the talking in very broken English. He wanted to know how old I was, whether I lived with my parents, was I married and so on. Without too much thought, I simply answered the questions. I had answered them a thousand times before, when questioned by other people.[1] In this instance, I thought the replies might help Henry accept me as a lawyer. I believed his fascination was related to my size. I was wrong.

Great concern was shown by Henry about my marital status, or lack of it; he explained that most of the girls from his Island were married by the time they reached my age. His concern was far more than academic. He resolved to do something about it. Confidentially he told me, he was not married either and that he liked me a lot. In fact from the first time he saw me, which was when I made the appointment the week before, he said he had not been able to stop thinking about me. He went on to say, *"I want to take you out."* He assured me this was possible as he had a car.

How could I accept his invitation? He was the client and I was the legal advisor. To go out with Henry would have been a break down in our professional relationship. I would completely lose my objectivity and would jeopardize the firm's ability to properly represent Henry's cousin. Besides which, after listening to the details about the trouble Henry's cousin was in with the police, and seeing Henry's willingness to white-wash the whole affair, I had absolutely no desire to socialize with him.

When Henry saw that I wasn't accepting his invitation, he decided the presence of his cousin was inhibiting me and asked his cousin to leave us alone! Panic rose in me, but subsided for a moment when the cousin did not move. I fostered the hope that he had not heard, and would not leave despite Henry's suggestion.

I remained silent. I was trying to find a safe way out of the situation. I wanted to refuse, but was afraid. Henry was not put off by obvious reluctance on my part; in fact, it added to his momentum. He was now asking to come and meet my parents, and even starting to tell me how well he would be able to take care of me. That was alarming, but to see the cousin rise to his feet preparing to leave and hearing Henry ask him to close the door behind him, was terrifying. It was time to speak up.

I was very direct. The first word to come out of my mouth was *"No."* However, caution stopped me from continuing on to say: *"No,*

---

1   For a discussion of how, when and why I will answer questions, see Chapter 9, *"Attention Gives Opportunity."*

I don't want to go out with you, and no I don't want you to meet my parents." Instead I said: *"No, please don't shut the door, I need to see when clients come in."* It seemed important to offer an explanation for my behavior. I was almost certain the way Henry was coming on, that he would not accept rejection. I needed to give a reason other than the fact that I didn't want to be alone with Henry. I didn't want to antagonize him. I felt extremely vulnerable.

When the cousin moved out of the office to leave, I followed him into the reception area which was more open to the public. At least there was a slim chance someone might just walk in. Sadly, no one did. The cousin left and Henry and I were alone. Not even contemplating a refusal, Henry asked where and when he should pick me up for our date.

As gently as possible, so as not to offend, I told him I could not accept his offer. It was wasted effort, because he didn't accept my refusal and became even more persistent. He repeated his persuasion so often, that it rang in my ears for days: *"I like you, I want you for myself."* Now I knew I was really in trouble.

I didn't know how to avoid offending him. After all, he knew where I worked; if I upset him, he could return at any time. I wanted him to leave accepting his unrequited love. I asked him for time, but really was asking for distance, and suggested he telephone for my answer in the morning. I knew by then I would not be alone, nor could he exert physical force across a telephone wire.

When he was finally persuaded to leave and to telephone in the morning, I passed him the office card with our number on it. He was seated and looking me straight in the eye when he not only took the card, but also grabbed the hand holding it. His grip was strong and he pulled me toward him for a farewell kiss. When I resisted, he paused for a moment as though unable to understand. He explained that all the girls from his Island allowed the men to kiss them. I refused more emphatically. Undaunted, he grabbed me again, and pulled me to him. He was too strong for me to pull away, but at least I was able to turn my lips aside from his. When I continued to pull back from him, as if deflated by my resistance, he let me go. I immediately opened the office door, and stepped outside telling him it was time he left. The look on my face must have told him more than all the words spoken in the office, because he obeyed instantly.

When I did not hear from Henry the next day, I dismissed the incident as being all on the spur of the moment and gave it no further thought. At least, not until almost a week later when I was again alone in the office. In fact, it was the first time I had been alone since Henry had been there the week before. My heart sank when I saw Henry and a different companion walk in. I immediately regretted not having taken my mother's advice after last week's episode. I should have bought that rape whistle after all.

This time Henry was all dressed up. What's more, he said he was ready to take me out! He complained that he had come for me one night during the previous week, but the office was closed because we had gone home early. His tactics began all over again. He repeated the words used last week, *"I like you, I want you for myself."* I repeated my refusals, though this time I was more emphatic, to be sure he did not mistake them for reticence. After a twenty minute discussion, he finally agreed to leave, saying he would never forget me. He can be sure I will never forget him either.

Fortunately, such instances are rare. There is actually one thing that makes me even angrier than my experience with Henry and that is the suggestion that a non-lawyer friend of my mine made that I only succeed in the Court-room, because of the Judge's sympathy towards me. He even checked his theory out by discussing it with another lawyer who had seen me in action in the Court-room. I was furious; his suggestion belittled my ability as a lawyer.

It is true, I have described some allowances judges have made to accommodate my practice in the Court, but please note these are only related to matters of procedure and practice. In no way are allowances made in regard to the merits of the case, nor do they have influence on the decision of the court.

For my own satisfaction, I discussed the issue with a couple of legal colleagues. They assured me the suggestion was absurd. Incidentally, the lawyer my friend spoke to advised him I did as well as any other lawyer in the Court-room, if not better. I knew in my heart, that I never conducted my manner which would attract sympathy from the Court. What was there to be sorry about? My client was on the line, not me. I was arguing a brief in a professional capacity, and being paid for it.

I was also concerned as an Officer of the Court that the suggestion undermined the objectivity of those on the Bench. Cases are decided on the facts and the law which applies to that particular set of facts. There is no ground to persuade a judge to a point of view unless it can be supported by fact and law. Where a Judge is influenced by extraneous matter, such as the suggested dose of sympathy, the prosecution would be the first to rectify the decision by way of an appeal to a higher court. I had to agree with my colleagues and take issue with my friend, the suggestion was absurd. It still makes me mad that someone would think, let alone say, such a thing.

Success in practice becomes more enjoyable when a good relationship is developed with the judiciary. Judges look for competence, honesty, and reliability. Sympathy has no place. I have to get in there and battle as hard as any lawyer does. Sometimes I succeed and sometimes I fail. The successes do not always come easily, and the failures frequently bring heart-ache.

Just like other lawyers I have to bear the tongue lashing of many an impatient judge. I vividly remember the day a judge ripped into me when I requested that the guilty plea my client had entered before I took his case be withdrawn. The judge was furious with me and adamantly asserted that my client pleaded guilty after receiving counsel from the Duty Solicitor. Refusing to be intimidated by his anger, I had to explain to the judge that I had represented this client in non-criminal matters in the past and was aware that he was from Tonga and hardly understood a word of English. As a result, any advice from the Duty Solicitor would have gone right over my client's head and any guilty plea entered was without the assistance of counsel and without my client's full understanding of the charge brought against him.

Very reluctantly the judge called my client into the dock. Not willing to take my word for his English language ability, however, the judge determined after his own efforts to communicate with my client that indeed he could not understand English well enough to answer the charges. The Judge finally relented, allowed the guilty plea to be withdrawn and assigned an interpreter to the case. This was not a decision prompted by favoritism. The judge after a heated battle with me and an independent exercise of his own judgment was merely doing justice.

My share of lost cases also shows that judges do not favor me because of my size. The decisions do not always come with the judge's anger, but a decision against my client is just as hard to take. When my practice primarily related to family law, I represented many clients in their child custody claims. Hearing a judge determine that my client's request for custody must be refused was very hard to take, especially when the case was a close call and it was apparent that either parent could have provided what was in the best interests of the children. Despite the disappointment and knowledge that no one really wins a custody case, it was clear to me that judges weighed the merits of each case without being influenced by any sympathetic concern they might have had for me as counsel.

Being a Little Person and a member of the *"smallest minority"* [1] occasionally improves my effectiveness with clients. Many are themselves in minority groups being immigrants, alcoholics, solo parents and criminals. The fact that I belong to a different minority seems to be irrelevant. There is immediate empathy and recognition that we both have obstacles to face and overcome.

Often in my professional capacity, I advise people of the best approach to take in a situation. I believe many are inclined to accept my advice, because they realize I know what it means to have faced and overcome obstacles. I am living proof that you can make it even when the going is tough. After we have talked, people are encouraged to attempt to put the pieces of their lives back together.

My presence also seems to break down barriers, because I am not seen as a threat and there is no guard needed against what I might say. People will listen to my suggestions, not to say how often they follow them, simply because I manage to say what they must hear before they can erect barriers to block out my words.

People who operate their lives on a sympathy trip, because they are down and out, do not get far with me. Such a trip is phony to a person who has experienced battles equal to theirs. With my counsel, they have to face themselves and the facts, deal with each, learn from the experience, and go on with life accepting self responsibility. I try to instill hope and show that the future does not have to be a restatement of the past.

---

1   A phrased coined by Sonny Kleinfield in *"Our Smallest Minority --*
        Dwarfs," condensed from the Atlantic Monthly for Readers Digest
        (January, 1976).

I recall one client in particular. In two separate accidents, he had literally lost an arm, and a leg. The pain had driven him to drugs and the drug habit had driven him to crime. He had been before the Court many times; often enough that any other person would have been imprisoned for the same conduct. He came to me charged with yet another crime. This would give the court no choice but to imprison him if he were convicted. The client had been given many chances in the past, and there was nothing I could say in mitigation to change the fact that outside of prison there were no reasonable punitive options available to the court.

My client knew his time to face full responsibility had come. He decided to plead guilty to the criminal charges brought against him, and was fully prepared to serve a prison term. My plea on his behalf persuaded the court to reduce the term from six months to six weeks. My client was pleased with the result and served his time accepting it as fair and just. I often wonder if our meeting helped him to see there was a positive direction his life could take that was reliant on his own initiative and talent.

Humor is a tool which helps me make it through many days. It is highlighted when the relationship with the client allows that interchange. I reached this point with one client, for whom I handled three cases at the same time. They were all paternity proceedings and each was brought by a different woman! Consequently, this client was in the office regularly, and it was not long before I discovered his appreciation for a joke. He came up with some amazing ones, not all of which I would repeat, or even care to remember.

One particular day, he came into the office and was standing in the reception area waiting for my secretary. I came into the room and when I noticed he was standing, suggested he take a seat. He responded by saying, *"Don't worry, I'll stand and grow tall."* He was about five feet three inches. I grinned and said to him, *"I'm sorry to disappoint you, but it doesn't work."* Without any hesitation he replied, *"Oh I don't know, every time I see you, you're sitting down."*

In spite of the wisdom imparted, I returned to sit down at my desk. Maybe if I'd chosen to be a school teacher and been on my feet all day, I would have had a different story to tell.

Chapter Four

REFLECTED

The Genuineness of my Gaiety Questioned

Laughter peeled through the audience, but one laugh stood out above the rest. It had a distinctive ring, almost musical and definitely infectious. The laugh rang again, sparking off another rumble through the theater crowd. The cast standing back-stage had no need to peek through the curtain to see who it was. They all knew Angela was at the play tonight.

Many came to know me by that unique laugh, just as other Little People have become known for their jocularity. This characteristic even caused one physician to describe those with achondroplasia, the most common type of dwarfism, as having the happiness gene.[1] However, I know from my own experience that such appearances of happiness do not always reflect a genuine sentiment. This outward frivolity may at times mask deep sadness and much pain.

Most people assumed that I was a naturally cheerful person. But at seventeen, I met Dennis, the first person to even question the genuineness of my gaiety. Dennis met me and after hearing so much of my laughter, asked my girl-friend whether I was always so happy. He wanted to know how much of my apparent carefree attitude toward life was a cover for more deep-seated concerns. At the time, I laughed off Dennis' questions and did not dispute the answer my girl-friend gave him, *"No Angela is always laughing, she doesn't pretend to be happy."* It sounded like the right answer, but it caused me to reflect on the genuineness of my laughter.

---

1   Drash, *"Psychologic Counseling: Dwarfism, In Endocrine and Genetic Diseases of Childhood,"* 1014 (1969).

I had many reasons to be happy. I was loved by God, my family and my friends. I had long since come to terms with why God chose for me to be a dwarf. Contrary to what Dennis might have expected I did not cry out to God in anguish, *"Why did you let this happen to me?"* Instead I realized the more appropriate question to ask was *"Why not me?"*

I looked around at this physical world and realized that I had not been singled out to suffer. A birth like mine was no surprise in a world full of imperfections. I didn't believe God was expressing any malevolence toward me as punishment for misdeeds. That would hardly be fair. I was born a dwarf and didn't even get a chance to do anything wrong. I concluded there was just no escape from the imperfections of life on this planet. I just happened to acquire more symptoms of human fragility than other people. The dislocated bones of my body merely reflected the spinnings of a world out of joint.

Although I didn't hold God responsible for making me short, He did give me strength to live each day with confidence and peace. I would cling to many of His promises:

"I will never, never fail you nor forsake you ... I will never, never let go your hand ... I am with you always ... I will give you rest ... I will come again and receive you to myself; that where I am you may be also ... My peace I give to you. Let not your heart be troubled nor let it be fearful." [1]

I shared the views of the Old Testament writers who wrote:

"God is my refuge and strength ... my light and salvation ... a defense for the helpless, a shade from the heat." [2]

My disability was put into perspective for both my parents and me, when we accepted these words of Jesus:

"Two sparrows sell for a farthing, don't they? Yet not a single sparrow falls to the ground without your Father's knowledge. The very hairs of your head are all numbered. Never be afraid, then ... you are far more valuable than sparrows." [3]

I had come to realize that being little gave me a special opportunity

1   Hebrews 13:5; John 14:3, 14:27.
2   New American Standard Bible: Psalm 27:1, 46:1; Isaiah 25:4.
3   The New Testament in Modern English, paraphrased by J.B. Phillips, Matthew 10:29-31.

in spiritual matters. The saying, *"What a pity youth is wasted on the young,"* didn't have to be true for me. Instead of certain truths being thrust on me in old age, my body taught me in its infancy that lasting values and hope lie in the spiritual realm, not the physical. I learned as a young child that I was not indestructible and that the future of the human race depended on its relationship with God, rather than its supposed independent ability to succeed without Him.

My reflection revealed that the gaiety of my laugh does have a true ring. Life is satisfying and I am not angry at my lot in life. Likewise, other Little People are satisfied with what life has brought them, though not all explanations of our reason for existence have the same philosophical base. Ernest Ott has said:

"Society can emulate those who are achievers as 'heroes.' I'm not Superman in a cape who leaps buildings in a single bound, but I go out everyday and leap curbs in a single bound. Little People succeed by going a little bit further to get what they want. Maybe society will be a little bit better by our going out there and being role models." [1]

Walter Menning counted his odds. He had a one in 50,000 chance of being born a Little Person and in 1972 he wrote, *"I won --- we are especial people created to do a special job."* [2] He went on to say in a letter of encouragement to other Little People:

"Do you realize that your very appearance brings a smile on people's faces? That it brings amazement and joy to the most perceptive of all, the young children? We have a gift which we do not recognize, perhaps it makes some of us bitter. It should not do so ... if we insist on carrying a chip on our shoulders, we may rest assured it will be knocked off." [3]

David Hornstein, an attorney of four-feet-seven inches, has said:

"Short-stature will give you extra opportunities. It will lift you out

---

1   *"Just because you're short doesn't mean you're handicapped,"* the Baltimore Sun (June 28, 1981).

2   Excerpt from a letter to the Moore Clinic at the Johns Hopkins Hospital, Baltimore, Maryland (March 24, 1972).

3   Excerpt from a letter to the Moore Clinic at the Johns Hopkins Hospital, Baltimore, Maryland (February 28, 1972).

of the crowd. You will be noticed. You will get credit for more than you earn... It is a character builder... a friend maker .... It will give you a keen appreciation of the real values of life." [1]

My laughter was also an echo of the knowledge that my family loved and accepted me as I was. My parents taught me that my shortness of stature did not equate with *"short-comings,"* and did not diminish my stature as a person worthy of love and respect. I did not feel inadequate or less important because I was small. I knew that value had nothing to do with size. Even my sister had to learn this lesson as a young girl. She was happy to exchange her dime for the nickel that my brother and I would offer her.[2] She didn't know the nickel value was much less, even though it was greater in size.

Much of my happiness was also based in the knowledge that my friends accepted me as I was. I knew this for sure when at thirteen years of age, I wondered what it would be like to be the same size as my friends. I asked them if they would like me any better if I was taller. They said it didn't matter to them how tall I was.

My question had been prompted by newspaper reports of a hormone that was being used to make short people grow. I wondered what it would be like to be as tall as everyone else. However, my pondering came to an end with the next visit to my Orthopedic Specialist. He squelched any hope for adding inches to my height by explaining that I had all the growth hormone I needed and that this hormone only increased the height of those lacking in growth hormone.[3] Even if I had once been a candidate, it was too late for me; to be effective the hormone must be given before puberty and I had already reached that milestone. His words were easily accepted, as the idea of growing had not really germinated. Besides, I knew that staying short was okay, especially after learning that growing taller would not make me any more acceptable to my girl-friends. They liked me just the way I was. I

---

1   Excerpt from letter to a Little Person named Cathy (1967).

2   In fact my brother and I would offer my sister a penny, the United States equivalent to a one cent coin, in exchange for her sixpence, the equivalent of a United States nickel. (New Zealand changed from sterling to decimal currency in 1967.)

3   For more information about human growth hormone, contact the Human Growth Foundation, Executive Office, 4607 Davidson Drive, Chevy Chase, MD 20815, or write to the national P. O. Box 20253, Minneapolis, MN 55420.

could continue to laugh freely.

There certainly were many advantages to being short. After all, I could do lots of things my friends couldn't do. For one, I didn't have to line up waiting for the parade hours in advance. At the last minute, I could make way to the front row for a clear view and no one even noticed that I pushed in ahead of them. At other times, I could choose any row but the front if I had the misfortune to be attending a boring lecture. That way I could nod off to sleep without being noticed. Only a loud snort would disclose my secret slumber.

I actually did this once; nod off that is, I didn't snort. It was after a weekend camp and I was absolutely exhausted. While sitting in church Sunday night, it was impossible for me to keep my eyes open. I gave in to the struggle and decided to listen with my eyes closed. The next thing I knew, the service was over and someone was shaking me awake. Inspite of my bad manners, the Minister wasn't offended because he didn't see me sleeping. However, my slumber wasn't exactly a secret. All the kids around me were nudging each other and giggling. The choir-mistress couldn't figure out what set them off and was checking her appearance for any indiscretions. Not until afterwards did she discover the cause of all the commotion.

I could be more comfortable in a car as a peaceful passenger oblivious to traffic traumas because I was unable to see out the window. If I wanted to see out and didn't have a cushion, I could stand up. This was great on a long-distance trip, as when I had been sitting too long I could stand and stretch, perhaps even take a walk. Another traveling advantage was that more things can be fitted in the car by using the empty space beneath my feet.

According to one Little Person, being small even saves you housework, though it sounds like a bachelor story to me. This male says being little means you only have to make your bed twice a week. You sleep at one end for the first half and at the other end for the second half. He also uses this as an excuse to only change his sheets every other week!

So why did the answer my girl-friend gave Dennis cause me to question its accuracy? If I had the love and acceptance of God, my family and friends what was wrong with her saying *"Angela is always happy?"* Nothing really, except that it was only partly true. There were some things about being short which caused me great pain and unhappiness.

A woman I met one evening, who was well over six-feet, thought that my short-stature was so enviable that she wanted to trade places with me. Little did she know how similar our experiences really were.

I discovered this when I read a poem distributed by The Tip Toppers of Washington D.C.[1] I was amazed to find that almost half the experiences could be replicated under the title *"Being Short Is."* The parody of the Little Person's experience to that of the tall persons demonstrates that there was absolutely no point in the tall woman trading places with me.

> *The tall are asked if they play basketball;*
> *The short are asked if they're midget wrestlers or in the circus;*
> *The tall wonder what's it like to be short;*
> *The short wonder what's it like to be tall;*
> *The tall have friends that want protection from them;*
> *The short have friends that want to protect them;*
> *The tall are always being looked up to;*
> *The short are always being looked down on;*
> *The tall are always looking down;*
> *The short are always looking up;*
> *The tall have gas station attendants wonder how they*
> *fit in a Volkswagen;*
> *The short have gas station attendants wonder how they*
> *drive a Granville Pontiac;*
> *The tall have to sit in the rear of a classroom or a movie so that*
> *people can see over their head;*
> *The short have to sit at the front so they're not blocked by other*
> *people's heads;*
> *The tall are asked how the weather is up there;*
> *The short are asked how the weather is down there;*
> *The tall are asked if they're standing on something*
> *other than their feet;*
> *The short are asked if they're kneeling down;*
> *The tall don't need ID before they're 21;*
> *The short need ID after they're 21;*
> *The tall are able to touch bottom at the deep end of the pool*
> *and still have their head out of the water;*
> *The short are able to touch bottom at the shallow end of the pool*
> *and still have their head under water;*

---

1   A chapter of Tall Club International, a nationwide organization for men over 6 feet 2 inches and women over 5 feet 10 inches; for more information, write to 911 South Oakwood Drive, Tempe, AZ 85282.

> *The tall join a club for tall people;*
> *The short join a club for short people.*

Dennis question unsettled me, because I thought I was the only one who knew that my laughter not only expressed pleasure, but was also a mask to cover a persistent pain. A pain which grew stronger as I moved through my teen-age and into my adult years.

Dating Desires as Teen-ager

At the age of fourteen, the first nagging of emotional pain occurred when I realized that my acceptance by boys was more like a sister than a potential partner. It was then that I asked my mother when I would be allowed to go out with boys. Her concern was not so much when to let me start dating, but when to tell me I was not going to be swamped with invitations. She didn't say marriage was out, a line given to many Little People by their parents, but she did make it very clear that for someone to take an interest in me they would have to be very special.

Mom didn't have to worry about when to tell me, I already knew that boys were mainly interested in taking out the most attractive *"chick,"* [1] so they could impress the guys and boost their own egos. The trouble was, I wanted to attract boys as much as any girl does. My diary is full of entries about the boys I liked and dreamed about. It made my day if one of them so much as looked at me. It was painful to know that with me at their waist, they were not going to win compliments for their choice. I already knew it was more than likely the boys wouldn't pay much attention to me.

I had to treasure for years the few moments when I did catch a boy's attention. At a party to celebrate the end of ninth grade, we passed around a mystery parcel until we reached the final wrapping. The cousin of one of the boys in our class read the inscription aloud, *"To the sweetest girl in the room."* After looking around, he handed the parcel to me! I was thrilled and carefully removed the wrapping to find the gift. It wasn't exactly a romantic moment as there lay a hairy black spider! All the same, I treasured that spider and kept it for years. It was the thought that counted and that boy's were precious.

---

1   New Zealand slang for girl.

The emotional pain intensified throughout my years at high school. In all five years, I did not have one date! That hurt a lot; especially when my friends started dating regularly. At sixteen, I wasn't exactly *"sweet sixteen and never been kissed,"* but the kiss only came by way of chance in a game of spin the bottle at my sixteenth birthday party. When the bottle pointed at me, I got my first kiss.

It wasn't that I didn't have any female attributes that boys admire. In fact one day I was among the few girls in our maths class able to impress the boys. (Regrettably, it had nothing to do with my mathematical ability.) This day, the boys were telling the girls how you could determine whether your bosom had reached a size pleasing to men. If you could place and support a pencil underneath your breast, as far as the boys were concerned, you had made it.

Now we girls weren't so bold as to find out there and then, but in the privacy of our bedrooms that night, many of us used our pencils for something other than homework. The boys were asking the next day how we fared. I could boast.

Despite any attraction I may have had, it wasn't enough to persuade a boy to ask me out. As the years went by, it got harder and harder to accept. Almost everyone I knew had a boy-friend. Janet, my aunt who was six months younger than I was and lived with our family for three of her High School years, had lots of them; more than she could handle. When she tired of one, there was always another ready to take his place.

Inspite of feeling left out, I continued to circulate. I even went to a school dance alone. That was okay, because lots of people went without a date. I had been discussing it with Carol and told her I wanted to go, but probably wouldn't because no one would dance with me. She said that was nonsense and talked me into going. Actually, she did much more than that. She arranged for many of the boys in our class to dance with me. I was embarrassed, but did appreciate what she was trying to do. I enjoyed dancing with the boys, but somehow it wasn't the same. Popularity doesn't have a glow when you know it's pre-arranged.

By the time I was seventeen, I was well used to nursing my disappointments privately. I protected myself by using laughter as a defense. It had always been a part of my make-up and as a result nobody noticed when I began putting it to a different use. It wasn't that I lost interest in boys; rather my unwillingness to be hurt. I laughed at things that were not funny at all. That way people couldn't tell I was hurt and there was no way they could hurt me more. It helped me survive male friendships that never blossomed into romance. If a boy didn't know how I really felt, I was not vulnerable to his insensitivity or rejection.

I expected any male taking an interest in me to go a long way before I was willing to lower my wall of protection. I became so aloof that a guy paying attention to me had no idea that I was even interested. I would practically ignore him until he showed exceptional interest. Inevitably, I created a prison for myself; my true feelings were trapped inside. It wasn't until I met Andrew that I realized how locked in I was.

Andrew, a new pupil in my twelfth grade high school class, sat next to me in history on his first day and I got to show him the ropes. All the girls were drooling over his good looks, but I was also impressed with his manners. At the end of the day, he saw me struggling to place my chair on the top of the desk.[1] Without any hesitation, he took my chair and put it up for me. It was the beginning of a lovely friendship.

Andrew paid me a lot of attention. In class, we either sat together or near each other. We talked about lots of things and sometimes worked together on homework assignments. In the mornings, I would walk into the school grounds and when Andrew saw me, he would break away from the group of boys he was standing with, offer to carry my bag and accompany me to the locker room. In the afternoons, he would occasionally go home the long way, so that he could walk half way home with me.

Athletics was Andrew's special interest and every afternoon after school he would go for a run. Invariably, he would run past our house. I would just happen to be sitting out on the terrace and he would just happen to see me and stop for a chat.

I liked him very much and knew he liked me. Girls have their way of finding out these things. Gaylene was my source. She would tell me that Andrew liked me and she knew because her boy-friend Alec told

---

1   This was a daily ritual to clear the floors for the cleaners.

her; Alec knew because Andrew told him. Foolishly, Andrew and I never told our feelings to each other. I was sitting back waiting for Andrew to make the first move. I was reluctant to take the first step fearing his rejection or maybe even acceptance because he felt sorry for me. I had to be sure of his motives. How did I know if he really liked me? Hadn't my mother said that if I was to have a relationship with someone they would have to be really special? If he was such a special person then he would be willing to go the extra mile.

My mother had also cast an aspersion on Andrew's motives for our friendship by suggesting that Andrew might just be using me. She said this after I had helped him with his English homework a couple of times. I didn't think that her estimate was fair, but all the same I wanted Andrew to prove her wrong. To test him, I waited for him to take three steps towards me before I would take one towards him.

Even though I had set up all these barriers for Andrew to over-come, I couldn't understand why he never asked me for a date. Our en-counters were limited to seeing each other at school and a brief chat at the gate after school on his daily run. My friend Gaylene gave me an explanation that I clung to. According to her, Andrew was shy. I waited for his courage to build.

In retrospect, I realize that Andrew made many moves in my direc-tion. The most obvious occurred when all the senior high school clas-ses attended a film about a book we were studying in English. The room was crowded and I was easily lost in the crush. However, Andrew was looking out for me and saved me a seat next to him. That was especially pleasing, since I knew other girls were hoping to get his attention.

We settled down to watch the movie, but I couldn't see very well even though I was sitting on the end of the row. Andrew noticed right away and without any warning stood up, asked the other two on our four-seater form to stand also, and edged the form out into the aisle to give me an uninterrupted view. Now I was impressed with his looks, manners, and thoughtfulness.

When the film began, I placed my car-keys on the seat in front of us.[1] Andrew picked them up and grinned at me while tossing them in his hand. Was he asking me to take him home? I was almost certain

---

1   In my last four months of high school I had a car.

that's what he meant, but neither of us said anything. He just sat there tossing the keys and grinning. I knew it was the perfect opportunity, yet I couldn't bring myself to ask him. I wanted to desperately, but something stopped me. If I was the one to make the first move, how would I know if he was special; how could I be sure of his motives. I wanted him to ask me. But that was so silly, how could he ask me? I was the one with the car.

When the film ended, instead of offering Andrew a ride home, I said good-night. He rode home with the boys in another car and I took Gaylene home in my car. There was no doubt, I had missed a golden opportunity. I hoped it was not my last chance. The senior prom was coming up and I counted on Andrew asking me. However, I hadn't really learned anything from the film experience. I was still expecting Andrew to take the initiative.

The excitement buzzed as the days passed and girls shared who they were going to the prom with. I waited in anticipation for my invitation. As a prefect,[1] I was responsible to help with the decorations and I participated happily, optimistic that I'd get to enjoy them on the big night.

Eventually, an invitation did come my way, but it wasn't the one I was waiting for. Daniel suggested I come to the prom as a mermaid in the fountain. Me come as a mermaid! Of course he was joking, and I laughed because by now my laughter was automatic. However, the laugh was phony; I didn't think there was anything funny about the suggestion.

Daniels' idea hurt even more, because I thought he believed the only way I would get to the prom was in disguise. The trouble was I didn't have a fairy godmother to make that possible. Yet I could see one advantage to his mermaid idea. Those mermaid qualities might be just what I needed to entice Andrew. Yet, in reality, I hoped my invitation from Andrew was not dependent on fantasy.

My hopes diminished each day the prom drew nearer. They finally crashed on the day Carol came rushing into the locker room and asked

---

1   Prefects are fourth and fifth year high school students appointed and/or elected to set an example for and to help monitor the activities of other students.

everyone to guess who had asked her to the prom? We were all interested as she was both popular and attractive. Can you guess? I was crushed. Andrew had asked Carol! Why? He hardly paid her any attention. He and I were supposed to be friends, why didn't he ask me?

I was able to hide my tears, but there wasn't even the hint of a smile, let alone a laugh. I just stared out the window in silence. It wasn't fair!

Through Gaylene, I later learned that Andrew had wanted to ask me, but the guys got him to ask Carol. The peer pressure was stronger than our friendship. Besides, Andrew never knew from me just how strong my feelings for him were. I never told him I was interested in him. It should have been no surprise that he asked someone else.

If the clock could be turned back, I would be more assertive, more willing to take chances in expressing myself. I would know to trust my own judgment about Andrew and not be suspicious of his motives. I would know it was unreasonable to expect him to make so many moves before I was willing to make one. If Andrew had known my feelings for him, he might have resisted the peer pressure. Maybe if the guys knew we liked each other, they wouldn't have asked him to take Carol. If only.

My so-called defense shield had caused me more grief than anything it was designed to protect me from. However, the pain I experienced as a result seemed to make my need for the shield that much greater. Therefore, I continued to use the shield to mask the disappointment and hurt I experienced with Andrew and other men.

It got worse. My sister Deborah was four years younger than me, but she was dating regularly before I even got started. She often had several boys competing for her attention. Once I remember her talking to one boy on the telephone, while another waited in the lounge, and a third rode up the drive on his motor-bike. She could take them or leave them. If anything, her casual treatment seemed to attract them all the more. But Deborah's style didn't work for me. The nearest I got to having a boy-friend was to separate the two into boy and friend. I had lots of male friends, but none were willing to romance me. Or at least, I conducted myself in such a way that I never found out if anyone was interested.

It was about this time that I met Dennis, the one who asked my girl-friend whether I was always so happy. He was the only one to ask whether I was as happy as I appeared. Although I had laughed off his question it continued to haunt me. Deep down I knew the answer my girl-friend should have given, *"No, Angela is not always happy. She pretends that everything is okay to cover up the pain and heartache she really feels."* But, where was I supposed to turn? I was trapped by my own defense barriers. Inside waited a young woman who wanted to be loved and needed, and needed to be loved and wanted. On the outside was a young woman full of laughter and to all appearances coping very well with life.

Learning to like being a dwarf

At this time, I could well have understood the great lengths one man of four-feet was willing to go to reach his goal of average height. For him, being short was also very painful. Each morning, he would step into specially molded fiberglass feet that acted as stilts. They went beneath his trousers and gave him an additional fourteen inches. He explained his decision to wear stilts this way:

"When I have the extensions on, people treat me with more respect ... without the extensions I react differently ... I'm looking up to them. I'm not looking straight on. I feel more intimidated being with people. In a stress situation, I am not going to be as aggressive and demand my rights as I am, if I'm dressed up with the extensions." [1]

Such an extreme response is not common among Little People. Robert Van Etten,[2] responded with a letter to the editor, saying:

"Most of the 'little people' of America look the world in the eye the way God intended us to see it. In fact, it looks much better from down here. Most accept their small stature and learn to develop the talents necessary to live in average-size surrounding. Having a constructive self-image helps the individual ... deal with his fellow man." [3]

Although not faced with the choice of wearing stilts, at age twenty,

---

1   Mary Knudson, *"New Studies help dwarfs look world in the eye,"* the Baltimore Sun (December 24, 1978).

2   An active member of Little People of America, Inc. who went on to become the organization's national president from 1980-1982 and 1984-1986.

3   *"Little People,"* letter to the editor, the Baltimore Sun (January 23, 1979).

I faced the question whether I would like to grow taller. It wasn't something I had searched out; rather the question came up when I attended a week-long Christian Life Convention in Tauranga. I joined a camp of twenty people on the beach front of Papamoa with my close friends Lynn and Judy.

Each day, we traveled into Tauranga to hear the teaching of Derek Prince and Harry Greenwood. I had only heard of Harry and if I'd known in advance that he was one of the main speakers, it might have put me off coming to the conference. You see Harry Greenwood was a faith- healer and, in the circles where I mixed, had the reputation of a *"show-man."* I didn't object to his ministry of healing, but was very suspicious of his motives. However, after watching and listening to both these men, my suspicions relaxed and I accepted their ministry as genuine. The flamboyant nature of Harry was counter-balanced by the more serious style of Derek. Harry even confronted some of the criticisms people had of him by saying. *"People can say whatever they like about me, but one thing they can't dispute is that I love Jesus."* That I had no trouble accepting, the love of Jesus shone from his face.

Well, it turned out that both Derek and Harry had a ministry of healing. At every meeting, people went forward for the laying on of hands. I wasn't bothered by any of this until I was confronted with the question of how their ministry fit into my life. I began to wonder if I should be going forward for healing. I started joking with my friends and said. *"I wonder what Derek would do if I went up there to be healed?"* I imagined he would be quite perturbed. Most people were coming forward with simple aches and pains, but my demand would be to grow two feet and for a total transformation of the joints. How much faith that would require!

I knew God could heal and in spite of my joke, began to think -- if it was okay for all these other people, why not for me too? Before I could answer this question, two other questions had to be answered: did God want to heal me, and did I want to be healed?

As I wrestled with these questions, I was in total turmoil. Much of my attention was focused on the loneliness I was feeling at the time. Although I was concerned that not going forward for healing might mean missing the opportunity God wanted me to take, I also considered that it would mean continuing to live with the pain and disappointment of never getting married. And yet going forward meant uprooting my whole life and identity.

I couldn't imagine what life would be like if I wasn't short. Even so, I wasn't naive enough to think that growing two feet would remove all my troubles. Deep down, I knew that one of the reasons I had no close male friend was because of the barriers I created to hinder such a friendship. Would changing my size make any difference to my ability to enter meaningful relationships? I didn't really think so. That was something I would have to deal with no matter how tall I was.

I shared my quandary with Lynn and Judy and we decided to talk to Derek Prince's wife, but she was no help at all. She had zero perception of how traumatic such a change would be for me. Her advice was very simplistic and implied that the only reason I was not already healed was my lack of faith. I was asking for help, and she lacked the understanding necessary to give it. So we left her none the wiser and even more frustrated. The three of us walked back to the car quite overwhelmed. I was so distraught that I just burst into tears. What was I supposed to do? I had no idea.

As I pondered the dilemma, I came to see that the big question was: what did God want for me? Once I knew the answer to that question, I would know what I wanted. I certainly didn't have the wisdom or prophetic ability to know the answer. My friends and I turned to God for that. Our days were filled with meetings and people and so the only way to get some quiet time for meditation and prayer was to rise with the sun. For me, that was almost impossible. A seven o'clock start had been hard enough after a midnight retirement. So this night, I prayed for God to wake my early so we could have time together. At 5:30 a.m. I was wide awake. That in itself was a miracle, considering that I'd slept through earth tremors the night before. (The Bay of Plenty, like San Francisco, is on a fault-line and is frequently shaken by earth tremors).

Our camp was right on the beach so I took my Bible into the sand-hills that overlook the ocean and searched for the answer in God's word. I turned to Hebrews 12:12-13 and the words jumped right out at me:

"Therefore, strengthen the hands that are weak and the knees that are feeble, and make straight paths for your feet, so that the limb which is lame may not be put out of joint, but rather be healed." [1]

No words could have been any closer to my situation. My knees are stiff, my feet are crooked and extend outward, and all my joints are dislocated. The words *"be healed"* appeared to leap right off the page. Here was my answer!

I first shared the passage with Judy and Lynn and later with the whole camp. Everyone was excited. I didn't know whether to laugh or cry, and frequently did both. It was both wonderful and frightening.

Otis, the camp leader, called the fellowship to a day of prayer and fasting. In the day-time meeting, we were strengthened by the teaching of Derek Prince on the power of collective prayer and fasting. Otis learned from Harry that his gift of healing was limited to the faith we had. We saw our responsibility and prayed earnestly for the gift of faith. We met as a group and spent time alone. In my further meditation, I was encouraged by the scripture in Isaiah 5:10-12:

"For as the rain and the snow come down from heaven:
And do not return there without watering the earth
And making it bear and sprout,
And furnishing seed to the sower and bread to the eater;
So shall my word be which goes forth from My mouth;
It shall not return to Me empty,
Without accomplishing what I desire
And without succeeding in the matter for which I sent it.
For you will go out with joy,
And be led forth with peace; the
mountains and the hills will break forth into shouts of joy before you.
And all the trees of the field will clap their hands." [2]

Following that day time meeting, the camp was filled with an atmosphere of confidence and expectation. We all went off to the evening meeting and discovered it was the last to be led by Harry. We were just in time. After the meeting we waited more than an hour for Harry to pray for the many others who came to him for healing. It was almost midnight before he finally turned to our group.

I was introduced and he said, *"Hi, or should I say low?"* Very corny, but it worked as an ice-breaker. After ministering for four hours,

---

1   New American Standard Bible.
2   ibid.

Harry was relieved to sit down while he talked to me. He asked me to close my eyes and said, *"Acknowledge in your heart the way Jesus originally intended for you to be, thank and praise Him for His healing, and hold on in faith to what you cannot yet see."* I did this and so did the other twenty who had waited and fasted with me. Harry laid his hands on me and prayed for my healing.

I'm not sure what we all expected to happen next, but whatever it was it didn't happen. It wasn't disappointing as I didn't anticipate an instant result and accepted that God would work in His own time and way. My faith was to be truly tested.

For months I waited and prayed, even fasting once a week. I was not to be discouraged and found strength in the knowledge that Abraham not only inherited the promises by his faith, but also by his patience.[1] My friends prayed with me. After more than a year there was still no visible physical change. We were all very puzzled as we had thought the experience and guidance was so real. God had made everything so clear. Where did we go wrong?

A year after going forward for healing there were still no answers or signs of physical change. Because I thought the prospect of growing was God's idea rather than my own, I didn't know whether to be pleased or disappointed when nothing happened. I was certainly puzzled.

I questioned why I had this experience. There were many possible explanations. Maybe it was all in the words of Harry, *"Acknowledge the way Jesus originally intended for you to be."* Perhaps I was always meant to be a Little Person. But if that was the case, why was I prompted to seek healing? Maybe the healing promised was the one I would experience and could look forward to in eternity. Yet that didn't make any sense either. I was already waiting to 'leap as an hart' in heaven[2] and expecting the first bow of my knee to be at the feet of Jesus in heaven or on earth at His second coming. Was it a lack of faith? Did I get my wires crossed and God didn't tell me to seek physical healing? But how could twenty of my christian friends also get the

---

1   New American Standard Bible, Hebrews 6:12-15.

2   Isaiah 35:5-6.

wrong message? There was also the possibility that Harry was a phony after all, and didn't really have a gift of healing. The explanations and possibilities seemed endless, but a satisfying answer was not to be found.

The time came for me to stop wondering why and to get on with my life. I knew I had to respond like Job. Although he did not get answers to all his questions, after seeing the awe and majesty of God revealed to him his questions no longer seemed important. Job went on with his life trusting that God knew what He was doing. I had to do the same thing.

It was apparent that no change to my physical body was going to take place. Any healing and escape from the pain and frustration I had felt with men would not be found in adding extra inches to my height. This would have to come from a healing of my wounded soul and spirit. I had to come to terms with myself as a dwarf.

Working towards a satisfying male\female relationship

I came to realize that the happiness I enjoyed in my relationship with God, my family and friends was possible because of the mutual exchange we shared. I had not put up any barriers to prevent our inter-action. If there was to be any hope for my finding a satisfying relation-ship with a man, I had to learn how to break through the protective bar-riers I had built around myself.

It was a continual emotional struggle. I continued to be cheerful. Sometimes it was a charade and other times it truly was genuine. In-deed it actually made sense to put on a happy face, as a friendly, happy person is attractive to others. If I projected the image of a negative sad person people would naturally keep their distance. I wanted to control and channel my feelings so that people would not start avoiding me. It worked.

In my early twenties, I found a number of male adult friends who I could call on and who would call on me to accompany me to dinner, movies, concerts, theater, parties and other activities of mutual interest. We had good times together. Yet, despite the warmth of these friendships the one thing I was hoping for was still missing. A romance with me was not on any of their minds. If the subject ever came up it was usually to talk about their progress in a relationship with another woman.

This became harder to accept as one by one my friends became engaged and married. It hit me really hard when I was a brides- maid for the third time. The wind was knocked right out of me when some 'kind soul' told me that, *"If you're a bridesmaid three times, you'll never be married yourself!"* That was the last thing I needed to hear.

Although often teetering on an emotional tight-rope, I managed to stay on my feet. The saving grace came in my relationship with one very special person, Jesus Christ. I knew He shared my tears and anguish and understood rejection and loneliness better than I ever would.

I poured out my longings to Jesus. At times to help clarify my thoughts, I would write Him *"letters."* Here is an excerpt from one of those *"letters"* written when I was twenty three:

"Dear Lord,

There are so many songs about life and love that I often wish that someone would sing them to me. I listen soulfully and wish --- I can't hear anyone singing them to me, but my imagination is great and I see someone all starry eyed singing of their love for me and I dream of how it could be after the song was over when everyone else had gone and, and, and, and then I feel like screaming. It's not happening and hasn't ever happened and might never happen. I pride myself on being a realist, I still hear myself telling people that I am a realist. Well then why do I spend so much time dreaming, pretending that one day there will be someone who wants to love me, as a woman? I can't stand the thought that there may never be such a day. --- Lord I know you're my best friend, but I need another one, I'm lonely."

Actually, when I wrote this letter I had a particular person in mind. It was Gerald, one of the men I would go places with. The same letter went on to talk specifically about him:

"I'm at peace when in his company and I would defend him against any critic --- yet I don't know whether to tell him my feelings or not --- whenever we've been together there has never been quite the right moment. Or is it that I don't want to be the one to say anything for fear of rejection? I don't want to be rejected that is for sure, --- my heart aches for the return of his love to me --- does he know that I offer him my love? I haven't said it in so many words."

Gerald was about five feet five and I'd been in love with him for years. Yet to all appearances we were just good friends. I hated to admit it, but there was never even the hint of romance between us. I wanted there to be so much more. One time, I got all excited, because he actually asked me out for dinner as his date! My secret hope for a lovely evening together was kindled. The day before the dinner he threw cold water on any sparks of hope when he invited another woman to join us.

That was only one of many disappointments. Although none extinguished my feelings for him, they were enough to keep me from expressing them. I had every reason to fear being held at a greater distance if I told Gerald of my love. When he left town to travel overseas, I let him go without ever telling him how much I cared for him. I regretted this and continued to express my longing on paper:

> *"My heart is crying*
> *and hurting for the love of one,*
> *who does not love me?*
> *I feel a sadness as he is gone,*
> *without knowing my love for him,*
> *how it hurts*
> *to want to touch someone*
> *and speak of the love you feel."*

Years before when Gerald was away at school, I did try to tell him how I felt. We had been writing occasionally and in one letter I told him I loved him and asked if he had any feelings for me. It was a moment of total abandon. The moment passed and I whited out every word retreating into my safe shelter. I dared not expose myself. What if he should reply by saying he felt nothing for me? I wasn't ready to hear that and decided against the risk. However, I did send the letter, which mysteriously had one third of its face blotted out. The only thing I managed to arouse in Gerald was a curiosity as to what on earth was written beneath the white out. I never told him.

When Gerald returned, our friendship continued much as it had before. I loved him but didn't say anything and had no idea how he felt about me. Actually nothing had changed because I was still expressing myself in poetry. In *"the Pain of Love"* I wrote:

> *"I long to be near him and share my most private thoughts,*
> *Even though when we are together I dare not.*
> *I long to touch and love him,*
> *even though he offers no lead for such contact,*
> *I long to be identified as his companion,*
> *Inspite of his bachelor sufficiency.*

Reason says:
he does not need or love me,
he will be my friend,
but he will never come with his hand in love.
I cannot sing of the beauty and the happiness.
My love is my sorrow."

I desperately wanted to learn from my mistake with Andrew. I was now twenty-six years of age and it would be foolish for me to continue sitting back, waiting for Gerald to make all the moves. This was not the time to let history repeat itself. There was no reason why, after ten years of friendship, I could not tell Gerald how much he meant to me. It might be the only way I was going to find out if he cared about me. Maybe he also had built a wall of protection around him and was unwilling to take any chances by expressing himself to me. Whatever the reason for his silence, I was ready to start dismantling my wall of protection.

It had taken me a long time to get to this point, but the time was right. True, it meant taking a risk as Gerald might not feel the same way about me, but at least I would know. I was ready for the relationship to go forward or to finish.

Gerald's decision to move to another neighborhood gave me the opportunity to say something of my feelings. At first, I couldn't bring myself to tell him how much I cared, but I did muster the courage to tell him that I cared for him a lot and couldn't stand the idea of his just walking out of my life. It was a good start, because he responded by saying I meant a lot to him too.

Our friendship grew stronger. We continued to see each other regularly for meals, movies and shows, and to talk. Yet, as before, the talk was never about us. Despite the obvious pleasure we found in each others company, there was a tremendous gulf which kept us far apart. Although we often went places together, I never felt like we were a couple. I was never comfortable referring to Gerald as my boyfriend. I could never count on him to be there for me. There was much about him that I didn't know or understand and I suspected it was that unknown part of his life which was keeping us apart.

What made it harder was that Gerald never showed any signs of affection. He never even touched me; not even a gentle touch on the hand; no arm around the shoulder; no good night kisses. It was amazing that a man and woman could share as much as we did and yet be separated by so great a chasm.

If it hadn't been for my friend, Gary, I might have started to believe I was not attractive to men. Gary helped me to see that was not the case. We had met years before at one of the meetings of the Little People of New Zealand. For all those years, we had been good friends when suddenly a new spark in our relationship fired. A certain chemistry added a new dimension to our friendship. We became much more than just friends.

We lived hundreds of miles apart and only saw each other for a few days at a time; each visit being months apart. We made the gaps bearable by writing. Yet, neither of us were ready to promise commitment to the other as we each held a deeper love for another, me for Gerald and he for Andrea. However, because of the special problems we each had with our other love, we reached out to each other for caring and companionship. We enjoyed the luxury of being able to communicate eye-to-eye and the unspoken communication of knowing what it was to be short-statured. We found a new love. It was wonderful to have Gary relate to me as a woman, not just as a friend. His closeness and affection helped me understand my ability to love, and the reality of having someone love me in return.

Yet, inspite of our shared laughter and happiness, my relationship with Gary was destined to be temporary. Neither of us were ready to give up our separate dream to share our total love and life with Andrea and Gerald, respectively. We were not willing to make a complete commitment to each other. I knew for certain where Gary's loyalties lay when I called him in the hope that he would sense my low spirits and offer to come and visit me. He did not respond because he was with Andrea. When forced to choose between us, he chose Andrea.

I too had made my choice and that was to be with Gerald. The question remained as to whether this was something Gerald wanted. After many months of pondering the reason for not being able to get any closer to Gerald, I decided it was time to know where we stood with each other. I found out the night we celebrated my twenty-seventh birthday.

To my total amazement, Gerald was the one to start talking. It was ironic. I had longed for him to make the first move and here he was doing just that. But what he had to say was far from what I wanted to hear. It wasn't a discussion about us, so much as an explanation of where Gerald was at. I'll never forget the way he began. *"People aren't always what they appear to be."*

Gerald explained that for years he had struggled with the question of his sexuality and finally he had come to terms with the fact that he was bi-sexual. He not only spoke of his bi- sexuality, but explained that he had adjusted his lifestyle accordingly. The man he shared his apartment with was not just his room-mate, but his lover.

I was the first *"straight"* person that Gerald confided in. He realized that his telling me might mean the end of our friendship, but was willing to take the chance because it was time for him to give up the lie he had been living. It was also time for me to give up the hope of sharing my life with Gerald.

In a strange way, Gerald's decision to choose me as the first person to confide in demonstrated how close to me he really felt. Although it was the beginning of a bridge to span the gap between us, it wasn't the kind of bridge I had hoped to build.

Certainly after Gerald had demonstrated such courage in telling me about his lifestyle and despite the certainty of rejection, I still went ahead and told Gerald I loved him. He said he understood in his head, but didn't feel anything in his heart. I couldn't feel anything either, but mine was the numbness associated with shock.

Gerald went on to say that he had long been aware of my feelings, but felt it would have been unfair for him to take advantage of them knowing that he wasn't prepared to make a commitment. He had deliberately kept his distance and cared enough about me not to exploit my feelings for what could only be short-term pleasure. He did care about me, but again, it was not in the way I had hoped.

For hours, I tried not to let the meaning of Gerald's words sink in. However, as my feeling started to return, the reality of their meaning began to take hold of me. The next day, when I drove myself to a peaceful place in the hills, I finally let myself feel the full force of Gerald's words. There I could let the tears drop to soothe the pain in my heart. Unfortunately, the beauty of my look-out could do nothing to ease my sorrow.

So, after all this time, I finally had my answer. I didn't want to believe it. Gerald didn't love me. Oh, he tried to break it gently by saying there was caring and a close friendship, but how could he soften the news that he did not love me. There was just no way.

For a short time, I held onto Gerald's words that he was bi-sexual. Surely that meant he could choose whether to love a man or a woman. Why couldn't he choose to love me? However, the more I talked to Gerald, the more I realized he had already made a choice to continue in his relationship with Tom. I had to accept that there was no hope for a love relationship between Gerald and myself.

For a few months, I couldn't even express myself in poetry. All my hopes for a shared love with Gerald were destroyed. It took me a long time to deal with those feelings. Eventually I was able to write again:

> *"It's late*
> *and my head spins with exhaustion,*
> *flopped on the bed,*
> *sleep is near*
> *closer is the distance of my loved one.*
> *I need him,*
> *now*
> *beside me, and he is not here!"*

I finally had to accept that he never would be there. He was not the one who would love me *"until death do us part."*

Although I did not cherish the prospect of a future without Gerald, I had the satisfaction of knowing love. True, Gerald didn't return it, but that could do nothing to wipe out the love I had for him. It was real and very powerful. My love for Gerald even stood the test of rejection; I continued to love him even though he didn't love me.

The loss of my hope for sharing my life with Gerald left me despondent but certainly not in despair. I knew there was still hope for both of us even though we would not find it together. My final poem about Gerald went like this:

> *"Laughter or tears?*
> *I can't choose.*
> *The gift of love is reason to laugh,*
> *but the sound is trapped,*
> *The love is not shared.*
> *Yet the tears cannot flow,*
> *There is still hope,*
> *and the dream of love to come."*

After my breakup with Gerald, I felt it was important to straighten things out with Gary. He had broken up with Andrea and the knowledge that we were now each free to make a commitment to the other, made me think it was the right time to find out if there was any future in our relationship. I was no longer prepared to hang on to a relationship that was going nowhere.

I visited with Gary and his family for a week to help me decide what I wanted from our friendship. Although the trauma of our two separate relationships breaking apart drew us closer together, the pain of Gary's break up with Andrea was very recent and he wasn't ready to talk seriously about our future. However, I was ready.

During the week, therefore, I quietly began to assess our compatibility. I concluded that our love was not one we could share in marriage. We had different values and goals in life. Our common size was not a sufficient base on which to build a life together. Although there was no formal decision not to continue a romance, at the time of parting, we vowed always to remain friends. It was as though Gary also knew that we would not be committed to each other in the future. We would each pursue our own goals.

So finally, at age twenty-seven, I had come through years of struggling with a desire for male companionship. My pain caused me to put up barriers to protect myself from the hurt of disinterest. Eventually, the pain caused by the protective shield caused me to look for a way out. I thought I had found the answer to my problems when I responded to a call for physical healing, but in reality the answer was to dismantle my protective barriers and to accept the challenges of each relationship. My size had nothing to do with the loneliness I was feeling. The unhappiness I experienced was caused by my unwillingness to accept the realities of pain and love which exist in any relationship.

Ten years after Dennis questioned whether my laugh truly reflected genuine happiness and pleasure, I could say my laugh did ring true. I no longer used my laughter as a protective cover for my true emotions. Sure, it meant that at times I had to cry many tears, but finally I understood it was better to feel the water on my cheeks than carry the lonely ache inside. I could laugh and cry and experience both happiness and sorrow.

Through all these heartaches and soul-searchings, I had acquired a sense of confidence, I knew the depth of love I was capable of giving and was strong enough to offer it even knowing it wouldn't be returned. I also knew I was worthy of love and should not be surprised if someone paid attention to me. There was no reason why someone shouldn't love me. Somehow, once I started believing that, I was no longer all consumed with the desire to find a husband. I had found my own value and knew I was able to live happily ever after as a single person. I could only marry if I found a man who was worthy of my love; one who would love me in return.

Chapter Five

AT YOUR
PHYSICAL PLEASURE

"I wouldn't be in your shoes for anything!" That's the view shared by many when observing the life of a Little Person. Although in general, I reject this sentiment as lacking in any understanding of how fulfilling the life of a Little Person can be, I agree that with regard to gaining access to public facilities trading places with me would be no fun for an average-sized person. The design and construction of public facilities is truly at the physical pleasure of average-sized people.

A Little Person will relate to what I'm saying right away, but an average-sized person will need to step into my shoes for just a few hours to know what I'm talking about. If you're average-sized, I'm willing to share my shoes with you for an afternoon; if you're a Little Person feel free to tag along. Are you game? Please don't be shy. Besides, you'll be invisible so no one will know you're even with me. Come for a trip into fantasy land that you'll never forget; a fantasy trip that will be a true reflection of reality; a real experience that I dream will become a fantasy.

Let's go into the city by bus. It's a great day; at the bus-stop, I appreciate the warm sun and blue skies. The bus approaches and I hail the driver. No one else is waiting. The driver sees me and pulls into the shelter. For some unknown reason, he halts a good three paces out from the curb. The blue sky does little to improve my irritation.

I step off the curb onto the roadway, which makes the step-up from the road to the bus almost impossible to mount, especially as there is no rail for me to grab and pull myself up. The driver looks down to see why I'm still standing on the road. I no longer appreciate the warmth of the sun, as a roaring heat flares from within. To make things worse, the driver doesn't budge to offer a helping hand. I am mad enough to refuse it even if he offers. I would rather crawl. But first, I try to make it on my feet.

I hoist my right leg onto the step, grasp onto the folds of the collapsible door with my right hand and lean my left side hard against the doorway. This gives me some support and I pull with a quick jerk hoping that my hold on the door is firm enough to bring me up onto the first step. Today I'm lucky, I make the bottom step. The remaining stairs are easier to manage, because now I can reach other fixtures to grab and pull.

The driver may have been frustrated with his passenger who delayed his schedule by a couple of minutes, but the delay could have been avoided. It would have been a different story if he had pulled to the curb and if grab rails had been there for me to use. Finally, I get to buy my ticket and flop into a seat. I have an hour to get over the look of being hot and bothered and for my heart to return to its normal pace.

Today, we can be thankful for an easy boarding experience. On other days, I haven't been so lucky. There is plenty of time during our ride for me to tell you about the day I stood in line waiting for a bus at rush hour.

On that day, there seemed to be as many buses as people pulling in and out of the stop. However, when my bus came the stop was crowded out by other buses and the driver had to board passengers in the mainstream of traffic. Everyone poured onto the street. The driver waited impatiently and became more anxious by the second in his wish to unjam the traffic flow he was causing. But not so fast, I stood last in line; right in the path of another bus!

As my bus threatened to depart without me and the bus behind prepared to drive over me, I could easily imagine some passenger sitting passively on the bus later reciting the incident as evidence at a coroner's hearing. Fortunately, for me I lived to tell the story myself. However, my escape did not come until the last moment. It occurred when the woman ahead of me in the line reached down with the arm of rescue and plucked me away from the wheels of the approaching bus.

A violent jerk of the bus reminds me that today's good fortune might be short-lived. I almost lose my seat. Every time the bus goes around a corner or stops suddenly, I lose control over my position in the seat. I slide around, because my feet don't touch the floor and my hand doesn't reach the over-head grip. I gain some stability by holding onto the seat and pressing my feet against the seat-back in front of me. I suggest you do the same if you don't want to be sent flying every time the bus stops suddenly.

The hour passes and about a mile before the stop I prepare to exit. How best to tell the bus driver where I want to get off? He's the grumpy sort, so there's no point in disregarding the warning sign above his head, *"Passengers are not permitted to speak to the driver while the bus is in motion."* I do know about the cord which would give the appropriate signal, but I can't reach it. (Now don't forget you've lost your height for the afternoon and can't reach the cord either). The best thing to do, is approach the elderly woman seated across the aisle. But, I'll have to be quick, because I can hear the bus driver racing through the gears accelerating towards our stop. In fact, ours is now the next one.

Trying not to show any signs of panic, I ask the lady to pull the cord for me. She misunderstands and moves across to the window, making room for me to sit down. In desperation and to ensure that she hears me, I shout at her. *"Please pull the cord."* She understands, but age delays her response. We might as well give up on getting out at our stop; the bus is about to sail right past.

Curses, but not from me as you might expect. It's the driver. The traffic light turned red against him and he has to stop. While the engine idles at the intersection, the woman successfully pulls the cord. Now we can make our move to exit. We must use the front door, as the driver will not see us if we use the back door.

The driver pulls into the stop and you may share my relief that he gets close to the curb. Although it helps to be close, it's not enough to make the exit anything less than a major undertaking. You see, my only way out is to jump, because my knees don't bend and this makes it impossible for one leg to lower the other to the step below.

When I jump, the drop from the bottom step of the bus to the sidewalk is big enough for the jar to reverberate throughout my whole body. Pulling in close to the curb removes a couple of those inches, so today the shock absorption will not be quite so traumatic. I make careful preparation for the jump, to avoid the all too recent memory of catching my heel and falling flat on my hands and face. A bruised pride and the task of picking pieces of pavement out of my hands make the memory of that experience far from funny.

Yet children often find the sight very amusing and make a great game out of mimicing my descent of stairs.[1] Unfortunately, it's no game for me and I adopt a strategy as seriously as though I was about to make a target jump from an airplane. Today I land successfully on the side-walk. I hope your landing was as safe.

Now we can set off toward my place of business. It will pay to be mentally prepared, in view of the obstacles yet to be overcome. The first looms up very fast --- a flight of stairs leading to the foyer of the building to be entered. It is the only way in!

I stand at the bottom and scan the climb to be made; once again without the assistance of a railing. Don't be discouraged, we can do it and we won't even have to crawl! Most definitely crawling is an inferior way of ascending stairs for two very good reasons. First, nobody sees you at their feet and in all probability you arrive at the top with flattened fingers, or worse; and second, to put head down and tail up is to advertise your brand of underwear without getting paid a cent for the effort!

Now I'm not so proud that I won't accept or ask for help, but I'll only ask when it is necessary. I think it's necessary when I can't make it alone with dignity, or to refuse means I will be left behind. In these cases, I accept help graciously.

When traveling in Malaysia in 1978, I found to my exhaustion that almost every place of scenic interest was on a hill at the top of a long flight of stairs, with no support rails of any description. After traveling thousands of miles to get there, I was not going to be left at the bottom. For example, unless I accepted the helping hand of our tour guide to mount the granite laid steps leading to the Buddhist temple of *"Kek Lok Si"* on the island of Penang, I would have missed out on seeing a grand and lavishly laid out temple topped with a structurally unique seven storey pagoda which combined features of Burmese and Thai design.

Sometimes a pull by the hand will not be enough to set me on the step above, especially if the step is very steep. I remember being asked by the photographer during the first year I was enrolled at University,

---

1   For a discussion of the child's mimic, see Chapter 9, *"Attention Gives Opportunity."*

to step up onto a stool so I would be in the range of his camera. I was perturbed. It was not possible for me to make the step alone and no way did I want him to lift me.

In my first year, I was too timid to resist his persuasion and inspite of my distress I allowed him to lift me onto the stool. My only pleasure was that the black and white photo could not record the color of my red flushed cheeks. At the time, it seemed like my only option as I was the one who fell short of the camera.

However, by my second year of University, I was no longer too short for the camera! No, I hadn't grown in the interim, rather I had made a discovery. I had learned that the environment is built by people for people --- it is not our dictator. In practice, this meant it was not for me to follow the camera, but for the camera to follow me. The second year when the photographer saw that I was below the camera sights and wanted to lift me onto a stool, I refused to be lifted. Instead, I asked him to take the camera off the tripod and to take the photo at my level. The quality of the photos unfortunately did not improve.

As a last resort, I will agree to be lifted, but there must be no other way. It was an easy decision to accept the lift into the cock-pit of the airplane in which I had been promised a ride. To refuse would have left me standing on the ground miserable as I watched the plane taxi away and soar into the air.

Enough reminiscing, I'm sure you want to know how we are going to make these steps today? My agenda includes neither sight-seeing in Malaysia, nor air travel. No, today's task is quite ordinary; a simple matter of climbing a flight of stairs. The stairs are not so steep that I need a helping hand, but steep enough that it will take every ounce of energy concentrated on each single step to reach the top without losing my balance.

I will make it, but the heat combined with the exertion of the ascent adds to my discomfort. Take it from me, we need to walk slowly to recover strength and regain composure. I wipe the beads of perspiration rolling off my upper lip into my mouth. The salty taste makes me thirsty, but there's no time for a drink. The appointment time approaches and I must push on to my destination on the fourth floor of the building. You heard me right, the fourth floor. However, there's no need to panic. There is an elevator.

No one else is waiting, so I press the button and stand watching the

light to record the elevator's descent from the sixth floor. The bell
rings, the automatic doors open and I step in. For a moment, we can be
grateful for the day's technology. However, this sense of gratitude will
not last long.

The doors close quickly behind me. I turn to press the fourth floor
button and notice I can't reach one single button; not even the one to
open the door! My heart sinks, and I sense yours falling even further
than mine. The urge to scream is overwhelming, isn't it? Well, you
have my permission to scream. But before I'll be taken over by such an
outcry, my thoughts are diverted to the narrow-minded short-sighted
idiot who designed the elevator in the first place. My urge to scream
turns to anger, but even that is no release. Actually, it is a waste of the
energy needed to get out of this trap. Yet suddenly, my anger and
frustration give way to reason. I see you have the same idea. Being
stuck in an elevator is an emergency, so why not use the emergency
telephone. How could I be so stupid as to forget this means of escape?
I reach for the phone and discover in desperation that it too is out of
reach!

Now it seems that I only have one option left. I'll have to wait for
someone to find me. Someone is bound to come along soon, surely!
How long could it possibly be? --- five, ten minutes at the most. In this
age of rush and bustle, maybe I should be pleased to get a few quiet
moments. Yet somehow, I don't feel the least bit grateful. I like to
choose when and where those moments will be. How about you?

Minutes pass and no one comes, but by now I'm too tired for an
emotional outburst. My foot taps in irritation as I wait impatiently.
With nothing better to do, I look at my foot as it taps and another idea
comes. I can take my shoe off. Yes, it will increase my comfort in the
time of waiting, but there is a more important reason. I can use it to
reach the fourth floor button. Brilliant! (Thank goodness, it's summer
and I'm wearing scuffs which are easily removed. In the winter I
would have a terrible time getting my boots off and on).

I remove my scuff and stand with it in hand, when I hear a very
familiar noise --- the whir of the electric doors opening. A young man
stands looking at me very surprised. I greet him with a broad smile. He
looks puzzled, no doubt by the warmth of the welcome from this
woman who is not only a stranger, but behaving very strangely holding
a shoe in her hand. He's too polite to say anything and responds to my

request to press the fourth floor button. As soon as the doors open I step out quickly, leaving him to ponder over my apparent aggressive tendencies.

I notice you rushed out ahead of me. No need to explain, I understand completely. Yet as angry as we might feel and as useful as it might be for us to vent our frustrations, this is not the time. Now there are only ten minutes left before my appointment time.

I hurry toward the door leading to my place of business. The door is solid wood from the floor to a level above my head. (The window begins at the level of the average person's shoulders and is designed to warn people on the other side of your approach). Even if my hair was wind-blown and standing on end, there would be no whisper of my presence at the door. I'll have to enter by taking a chance that no one is approaching from the other side. If someone is leaving as I enter, there will be an interesting variation of Indian wrestling,[1] with odds on I'll be flattened against the wall.

Hopefully, the receptionist isn't watching the door. Any cynicism she might have as to the existence of the supernatural will dissipate as the door appears to open by itself. I want service when I reach the counter, without having to deal with any shattered nerves or piercing screams.

I enter safely and unnoticed. The well oiled door, the soft carpet to muffle my footsteps and the four feet high counter all mean the receptionist has no idea that I have come in. I am completely over-looked. Take a seat and watch what happens.

It doesn't seem right to shout out for service, but all other options smell of bad manners or eccentricity. I could throw my papers up onto the desk to announce my arrival and cause the receptionist to look around and see where they came from. I could open the door of the office and enter forbidden territory. I could even succumb to the temptation of wearing and extending an aerial with a flashing red antenna.

---

1   Indian wrestling is a game where two people place their elbows on the table, clasp their hands together, and push forward to see who can flatten the other's arm onto the table first. Two people pushing, one on each side of a door, would provide an interesting variation in that the winner would flatten the other into the wall behind the door.

That would get me noticed!

At least when there are other people waiting, I have some chance of getting the attendant's attention without going to such lengths but that doesn't always work out. Often I am lost among the legs of other customers and they will push in ahead of me. In Malaysia, the only ones served are those able to physically push the others out of the way and themselves to the front. I'd still be there waiting my turn, if I didn't have a friend bigger and stronger to transact my business.

Today I wait alone. To attract attention, I take the chance of being considered bad mannered and shout while waving my hand above my head. My voice is loud enough to break into the world of the person on the typewriter. I learn the person I've been waiting for is female when she comes to the counter.

The receptionist offers her help. An offer no doubt given hundreds of times in the working day. Although I realize the offer is not open-ended, I can't help wonder how she might improve relations between busdrivers and passengers and access into and around this building. With a great deal of restraint, I confine myself to her area of expertise, applications.

I pass her the form completed the evening before. She reaches to take it and after a cursory perusal hands it back for me to sign in her presence. She scouts the counter for something hard for me to rest the form on and passes a book down to me. Now I search for a surface to lean the book and form against. The wall is no use; ball-point pens give out when they are held up-side down. The support of a leg, usually mine, has been used many times, though this is not the best way to develop a good writing style. Finally, the receptionist, seeing my predicament and no doubt concerned about a future challenge to the authenticity of my signature invites me into the office to use her desk. I accept, and the form is duly signed.

Have you had enough of a break? Good we're on the move again. I will now be interviewed by the person appointed to process the applications. The receptionist directs me towards the office and I follow the long corridor leading to the room. I pause at each door and consider the type-written labels way above my head. I have to presume they describe the people occupying the rooms but I can't be sure. At least I know my interview is in the room behind the sixth door on the left. I count very carefully. At number six, I stop and peer up at the label to be double sure I have found the right room. I still can't read it with any precision, so I must rely on my arithmetical ability.

I knock hoping the person doesn't call out *"come in."* A strange thought I know, from someone who wants to be made welcome. An invitation to enter does sound like a positive way to begin, but I know it will create a problem. You can see that the door handle is set too high and I won't be able to follow the direction. Even to stand on tip-toes will not make me tall enough to reach it. To try, would mean being so stretched out that once attached to the handle I wouldn't be able to let go without falling. When my curious interviewer opened the door to see what was going on, I would literally swing into the room. A spectacular entrance to be sure and certain to assist in the recollection of which applicant I was. Nonetheless, I prefer not to risk such an entrance having no need to find ways to stand out in a crowd. I do that without even trying. I learned long ago *"once seen, never forgotten."*

As feared, my interviewer does call out *"Come in,"* and I have to speak to him through the closed door. When I tell him that I cannot reach the handle, he comes to the door not too sure if someone is playing a joke or not. He opens it and finds me standing there. Then he's sorry for his impatience, but not half as much as I am.

The interview is soon over and I stand back and allow the door to be opened for me. This time there is no hesitation about whether as a feminist I should expect a man to open the door. There is simply no other way. Besides, I would have allowed a woman to do the same thing. He opens the door and I pass under his arm happy to accept the social graces of the middle-aged gentleman.

After the interview, I'm well ready to use a rest-room. You must be ready too. I locate it on the same floor and enter with no greater demand than the effort required to push hard against a swing door. You might as well forget taking any time for grooming, as the room offers no opportunity to consider your reflection. It should be no surprise by now to find that the mirrors are set too high.

A cubicle is vacant and I enter, close the door and turn to lock it. No such luck. The lock is too high. I can turn it if I stretch, but then wouldn't be sure of reserving sufficient energy to get it open again.

I remember too well the time I locked the toilet door in the airplane taking me to Malaysia. That time I took the risk and locked the door anyway. There seemed to be more at stake. Unless the door was locked, the light would not come on, and I would have to leave the door wide open. I did not fancy exposing myself to the strangers waiting in line outside the door.

When ready to leave, all my energy failed to release the lock. I was trapped. After several attempts I sat back on the toilet, lid down, exhausted. The thought of spending the rest of the flight in there did not thrill me at all. A person can only spend so much time sampling the lotions and potions. I should have been grateful that they were in reach.

My eyes settled on the emergency button. It was so attractive that I pressed it, twice. Nobody came. I felt relief and panic simultaneously. Relief, because I didn't really want to be rescued from the toilet and be associated with the usual child victim; and panic, because I had pressed the emergency button twice and nobody responded! There was truly no escape.

The panic subsided as my strength returned. It didn't take as long as Samson's hair to grow, but I suspect that in the single moment when I needed extra energy to stretch up to the lock, I was given divine help. I reached up again and the door sprung open. I was relieved to get out of there in more ways than one.[1]

This time, I decide not to tempt fate. I'm sure you'll agree with that decision. We don't want to be in here any longer than necessary. I use the toilet without locking the door, even though it means the door swings wide open. I could of course prop my shoe against the door and hold it closed, but I don't bother as no one else is using the bathroom. (Manufacturers would be amazed to know the thousand and one alternative uses their products are put to).

When ready to wash my hands, I discover the taps are out of reach. They're not too high, just set too far back in the hand basin. My mother's well worn advice to always wash my hands after using the bathroom must be put to rest this time. The words don't die easily. Of course, reaching the tap was only the first of three steps necessary to accomplish the joy of clean hands. After the tap comes the soap and then the hand-towels. In this bathroom, I can't reach any of them.

It's even more frustrating to come across a bathroom where you

---

1   I have since discovered that the airline steward or hostess can protect
     your privacy by locking the door from the outside and unlocking it again
     upon a prearranged signal.

can reach some of the amenities but not the others. To be offered the sensation of water running over your hands and be denied the cleansing effect of soap is infuriating. To have the water pour from the tap and extend to a flow from the wrist to the armpit as you reach in vain for the hand-towel is drenching. To have the air dryer not only diminish the quantity of water on your hands, but also destroy the style of your hair is enough to make you blow your cool.

However, today the rumbling noises in my stomach turn my mind to other things. They remind me it's been a long time since breakfast. Going to a coffee shop for a bite to eat seems like a good idea. Agreed? Well, despite a consensus, our stomachs must be over-ruled. There is a place in the next building, but our already dirty hands will be blackened after use of the dust-coated banister leading to the food bar. Then there are the four flights of stairs to contend with.

Besides, I'm not really partial to lucky dips. That's how I view my selection of food in most coffee shops. The food is displayed on high shelves, no doubt to protect each item from the sticky roving fingers of children who can't make a choice without touching everything they see. This means, I have to rely on the ability of my companion or the assistant to describe the food. Often the description differs profoundly from the item which turns up on my plate.

I suggest we ignore the stomach rumblings and hold out until we get home. I hope you can last that long. First, I must make a telephone call. There is a booth nearby and I have the right change. I enter the booth, have no problem removing the handset from the hook and on tip-toes can reach the number dial. The hitch comes when I attempt to insert the coins. The slot is out of reach and there's nothing to stand on to gain additional height.

Phone books can no longer be used as they are usually chained in place or missing altogether. I have two options: hope that someone walks by, or ask the operator to put the call through for me, either collect or by transferring the charges.

One operator was quite taken aback when I asked to make a collect call for the cost of a local call, which at the time was only six cents. She couldn't believe someone could be that close to the bread-line. When I explained that I couldn't reach the coin slot, she put the call through for nothing, for what she described as 'my honesty.' Calling the operator is only possible, however, if I can reach the handset and the dial to call the operator. If not, I must turn to my first option and wait for a passer-by to help. Most are very willing. The trouble is people are not always there when you need them.

Today I'm lucky and someone puts my coins in for me. On this phone I can reach the number buttons, and button "A," so I can take the call from there. It would be a bit more complicated if the phone had a dial face instead of push buttons. In that case, I would have to dial numbers without being able to see them. I know it's possible, because I've done it before. I found the correct number by quickly counting back from either end of the dial, but it had to be fast or else the phone would return to dial tone and I'd have to start all over again.

The call is concluded and we are ready to make our way home. I return to the elevator and see the button for descent is already pressed. The building is now buzzing with life and people from all over the place are also waiting. Where were all these people when we were trapped in the elevator?

The elevator's arrival prevents any response to the question and the open doors beckon our entry. I make this load and find myself jammed in the middle. To be sure I don't get sandwiched or stabbed by a stray umbrella, I make sure people are aware of me by prodding the knees of everyone close by. To interact with their shoulders is not only impossible, but wouldn't get their attention. In a crowd, people expect to get jostled, but no one gets prodded in the knee by accident. That has to be deliberate. They immediately look around for the culprit and will discover me when it occurs to them to look down. The likelihood of my being stepped on is now diminished. You can relax; we will get out of here in one piece.

The elevator begins its descent and as I can't see which buttons are pressed, I bargain that most will be getting out on the ground floor and someone will already have pressed that button. My gamble pays off and I find we are at ground level in the fresh air, released from the stale odor of people's bottoms.

My business is accomplished and I sing quietly to myself, *"I'm tired and I want to go home."* I'm pleased to be on my way and try not to be daunted by all the bridges yet to be crossed. I can't wait to get home and put my feet up. When you see what's coming up, you might be more inclined to sing, *"One more mountain to climb,"* even if it is down all those stairs.

I'm sure you can clearly recall the stairs we mounted on the way into the building and have already realized that they now have to be descended. The three stairs off the bus were bad enough, now there is a whole flight. There is no banister to reduce the impact of each jump, nor as an insurance should I catch my heel.

Even though critical of accumulated dust on banisters, I still prefer dirty hands to a broken neck. A banister saved me from a terrible fall when I was in school. That day, I tripped and was falling head first. By dropping my school bag and grabbing the banister, I saved myself from disaster.

Today, each step is approached with great care. In all probability, this day will be like ninety-nine times in a hundred and will bring a descent without catastrophe. However, passers-by will still become alarmed at the sight, and may even offer to carry me down. Though their concern is appreciated I can manage well enough and usually refuse their help. Besides, I often doubt their ability to transport me safely to the bottom.

The same criterion for allowing someone to lift me up steps, applies to letting someone carry me down. There has to be no other practical mode of descent and I must have exhausted all reasonable efforts to do it alone. This was the case when I accepted the offer of a Malaysian gentleman to carry me from the railway carriage to the station platform.

When I reached the door expecting to step out, I found the train had pulled into the center track a good distance from the platform. I looked to see how far down the jump was going to be and to my horror saw a man's head level with my feet. He was looking up beckoning me to jump onto his shoulders. He must have been fooled into believing that my size indicated a matching weight. That was a big mistake. He was not in the best position to appreciate that my body carries a number of components not found in the body of the child he was comparing me with and weighs considerably more.

I seriously doubted his ability to carry me to the platform. Yet inspite of his puny frame, I realized he was my only hope of getting there. I knew for sure that he would never stand the onslaught of my jumping onto his shoulders, so I managed to lower myself onto the step below as he swept me off my feet.

Many girls dream of this happening one day, but my experience was not the usual romantic picture. From where I stood, I didn't know if he was tall, dark, or handsome. I only knew he was a stranger. What's more, my assessment of his strength was fairly accurate and it was only his total exertion that landed me safely on the platform.

Today, no one offers help, neither do I need it. The descent is without incident. I do not fall, and no one is disturbed by the clatter of my shoes jumping down each step. Not like the morning I broke into the meditative silence of my praying friends.

That day, I was the last one to arrive and had hoped to slip into the meeting quietly. I failed miserably. The room was at the bottom of a stairwell and every jump I made echoed into the room below. At first, the closed door at the bottom encouraged the thought that my approach was undetected. The delusion was apparent as soon as I opened the door --- every eye was on it. My feeble apology for lateness fizzled, as one by one each person lost control by convulsing into laughter. I had to join them.

Today, I find no reason to laugh, and there is no one to laugh with me, that is, apart from you and you had better not be laughing. However, if you have any inclination to laugh, I suggest you suppress it. Remember, we still have the journey home to face and that's no joke.

Chapter Six

ATTITUDES
DISABLE

The air line hostess began to plump my pillows to make me more comfortable. I was impressed with the personal service until I noticed this special treatment was not being given to other passengers. The offer of a glass of milk betrayed the attitude of the hostess -- I was to be treated like a child. Her attitude toward me was paternal even though she knew I was traveling on an adult ticket.

I seldom have to guess what a person's attitude is, as their behavior makes it perfectly obvious. When their action is negative it is a clear indication of what's going on in their head. When confronted by negative behavior, I know the person does not regard me as an equal, and will be compelled to treat me differently. Although the person with the negative attitude doesn't realize it, their behavior disables both of us.

I am rendered incapable of doing something which is within my ability, and excluded from an activity that I would like to participate in. The situation with the air line hostess demonstrates this. She did not perceive that as an adult I would like to drink tea, and automatically excluded me from that simple adult ritual. I gave up milk years ago, especially since it does nothing but give me bad breath.

The person carrying the negative attitude is also saddled with a disability. This attitude may lead to any number of impairments: blindness; loss of hearing; reduced mobility; retarded socialization skills; and/or mental delusions. The behavior of the hostess demonstrated her lack of vision. She was blind to my adult characteristics and could only see to treat me as a child.

I hate to say it, but she is not the only one with impaired vision. Many adults with all the faculties which contribute to the notion of intelligence cannot see me as their peer. It's hard to accept the adult's reaction when even children can discern I am not one of them. True, the child may not fully understand and will ask why they aren't allowed to drive a car if I'm allowed to. Yet their expressions show their perception of my adult years. I often over-hear children saying such things as: *"There goes a baby lady,"* or *"Look at the little lady."* If children can see it, why can't adults?

I have no problem accepting that at times it is reasonable for a person to mistake me for a child, especially if the person's view of me is from a distance. It's easy to accept that from a distance all a person catches is the image of someone standing at a height equal to that of a three year old. The features of a full grown woman are blurred.

For instance, one evening I was looking for my parents in a lounge bar of the hotel adjacent to the room where we were planning to eat dinner. Other women of nineteen were easily mistaken for the legal age of twenty, but not me. From a distance I was mistaken for the age of three. I no sooner walked in the door when the bouncer began to gesticulate from the other side of the room and moved toward me. When he was making his approach, my father intervened to explain I was not a young child. The bouncer saw that for himself when he got closer and was sorry for the fuss he made.

Such errors are in fact not that unusual. A restaurateur made the same mistake. A group of us were standing close together, when the host observed my head at the level of their rear ends. He took the opportunity to advise my father that child portions were served. There were no children in our party, so he had to be talking about me. I turned around to see how my father was going to handle this one. Dad didn't have to say a word as the host immediately recognized his mistake when he took a second look at me. He apologized profusely.

A couple of months later, when at the same restaurant with the same people, the same host made the same mistake! This time he only made it part of the way through his offer of the half portion for children, when he wanted to bite his tongue off. Instead, he tendered his apology with a bottle of wine on the house. Those sort of errors are easy to forgive.

However, most have no excuse. The behavior of the people clearly demonstrates their beliefs. They make no mistake about my appearance. Many will stand in full view of me and respond in the same way they would to a child. Some fumble in their pockets to give me small change to spend on an ice-cream. Their sentiment is twenty years too late and the change is hardly enough to give me a lick of the ice-cream promised. I know it would be childish to ask for more, but I have been tempted.

Others have a very curious problem. I will be walking on the street, when I notice someone who is approaching suddenly twist their neck around to face the opposite direction. They cannot look at me, not even out of the corner of their eye, or to sneak a look when my back is turned. Instead they will continue walking in this fashion until I am actually out of sight. In the meantime, they are blind to and have denied my presence altogether.

"An honest reaction beats being ignored." [1] I strongly believe this and was pleased to see my comment used as a headline in a newspaper report about me. When a person blocks me from their view, there is no opportunity for us to communicate. There is no way I can break through, because as far as the other person is concerned people like me don't exist.

Not everyone is blind to my presence, but in overlooking my ability to think and speak for myself, they demonstrate tunnel vision. Many with this limited sight will speak to the person in my company instead of directly to me. It's as though I am outside their line of vision.

On one such occasion, I was standing at an airline counter arranging a seat assignment when the hostess asked my friend whether I would like to sit next to the window. My friend didn't presume to answer for me and just looked at me wondering why the hostess didn't ask me directly. Good question. Not willing to accept this procedure, I asked the hostess to repeat the question. This forced her to speak to me, and to get the seat request from the person who would be using the seat. Maybe the hostess also got the more important message -- Little People can speak for themselves.

What's more amazing to me was the traffic officer who signaled for me to pull off the road. When he came to the window, he said I was

---

1   Mainly Women, the New Zealand Herald, Auckland (February 10, 1981).

driving too fast in wet conditions. Lucky for me and my passengers, he only issued a warning. However, he asked a few questions before letting us go. Would you believe he addressed his questions to my passengers, with me the car owner and driver sitting at the wheel?

An attempt can be made to broaden the view of those with tunnel vision by getting their attention and refusing to be overlooked. I believe Jack Purvis, one of the cast in the 1981 film, *"Time Bandits,"* did just that. He was in a bar with a friend when someone asked his friend if *"he"* would like a drink. Jack, who was not to be kept off this person's visual screen responded, *"Yes, I'll have a double brandy, thank you."* The person not only had his eyes opened, but also his wallet.

Others have a totally short-sighted view of my ability. They totally under-estimate it, and persist in wanting to help and do things for me when the help is neither requested nor needed. I have even had a toilet-attendant in a public rest-room use the master key to burst into my cubicle to see if I needed any help! How did she think I managed before she came along? Believe me, when I need help I will ask. She should have known it is polite to ask before literally bursting in.

I'm not just being stubborn when I say this. A lot of harm can be done by these over-zealous helpers. I struggle to gain independence, only to have it whisked away by these so-called 'acts of mercy.' It's very hard to make a person understand this, especially when you're the vulnerable one sitting on the toilet and find the graffiti on the walls become a living face.

Extreme consequences result when someone does for you what you could do for yourself. The helper is not only short-sighted, but both society and the one being helped become disabled. In time, the Little Person becomes dependent on the helper for the service being provided; and society is dismembered because of its loss of access to the ability and contribution of the Little Person.

The end result is that a relationship of provider and receiver is established. The provider gains control, becomes superior, and decides what will be given and when. The recipient is subservient, and accepts the help given gratefully. However, the people being provided for become removed from day-to-day activities of society. Their dependence on the provider will eventually render them incapable of functioning independently. They will no longer be able to participate fully in education, the work force, family or public life.

The recipient's dismemberment from society causes the individual to be at the mercy of charity, which fluctuates with the changes of the economy and the mood of the day. No doubt recipients will be cared for as they always have been --- with minimum benefits. However, they cannot ask for more, as they are lucky to get what they do, and any complaints may threaten the supply for which there is no other source. As much as it is, it will never be enough.

When Little People are forced into this type of subservient relationship by the well-wishers who take away their independence, they typically respond to the low expectations of self, by producing and achieving according to their size --- very little. Their equality is sacrificed for the supposed fringe benefits of being disabled, such as: not having to work; riding half-fare on buses; and getting into movie theaters at half-price. Without their independence, these Little People now need all the help they can get.

In time, the provider appears justified for continuing to provide, as the service given has created people who actually do need help. However, after years of providing, some providers begin to resent their paternal relationship. It could even dawn on them that the recipients may in fact be capable of providing for themselves. Unfortunately, those recipients who have never been allowed to exercise independence cannot be left to fend for themselves. They have been placed in a cycle of dependency from which they are incapable of breaking free without a lot more help.

Both the provider and society will suffer if they cut themselves off from the contribution Little People can make. Yet the only way for this functional loss to be avoided is for Little People to exercise their right to independence, and for well-wishers to allow Little People to be independent, no matter how reluctant they might be to do this.

One airport sky-cap, who brought me from the gate to the baggage claim area in a wheelchair, was very hesitant to let me go off with the people who were meeting me. When I first pointed in the direction of my friends, the sky-cap couldn't see who I meant until I described them: *"That Little Person over there and the man carrying a white cane."* He was obviously reluctant to pass me over to these two; one a dwarf and the other blind. In his mind, we were all helpless. Fortunately, he was helpless to do anything about my chosen companions and to his dismay I left the airport with them.

Besides, it's in the interest of the helper to recognize my ability and independence, otherwise they may end up penalizing themselves. This happened to a sales-woman trying to sell me a painting I liked. The painting was at a good sale price and I was about to make the purchase, when she surprised me by offering to reduce the price even further to fit my size and purse. She foolishly presumed that my size was a reflection of my income. It wasn't. I had been both willing and able to pay the greater price.

The vision of some people may not be impaired, but the sight of me totally immobilizes them. In their amazement, they become fixed to one spot and stop to stare. It was total disbelief which gathered a very large crowd outside of an Indonesian fabric store where I was shopping. The crowd gathered in the shop entrance and were so many in number that the natural light was dimmed to the point that I could not distinguish any of the colors on the fabric. I already knew that a white person was a curiosity in Indonesia, but a white Little Person brought everything to a stand-still.

Not everyone is immobilized, but for some my presence does impair their mobility. They may experience awkward stumbling movements. I saw this phenomena one afternoon when a girl walked out of the school grounds with her bike. She was so amazed at my appearance that she lost total regard for what she was doing. She continued to look backwards while walking forwards; not surprisingly therefore, she ran straight into a wall and fell in a crumpled heap on top of her bike.

The impaired physical mobility which occurs as a result of the person's reaction to the sight of me doesn't bother me any more. I am well used to being stared at, and almost had to say to the girl falling on her bike, *"It serves you right."* The behavior of such people causes them more grief than it does me.

However, I become quite distressed when the immobility of the person is figurative. In such cases, the immobility may be translated into a refusal to respond to my requests. At these times, I may become disabled by such a person's attitude. For example, I am disabled when a person, fixed to one spot, refuses my requests for improved access.

"Cities are the mirror of our attitudes. They are built in response

to the way people think." [1] The thinking has been disabling because of its immobilizing effect on the community, the Little Person, and the average-sized. Yet we can all have mobility, if people take positive steps to restructure the environment.[2] We can all experience equal access without the loss of freedom, independence, convenience, dignity and safety. I am waiting for and working towards that day.

People are not only blind and immobilized when they encounter a Little Person, they also experience a hearing loss. It is especially noticeable when they are asked to do something. The request often falls on deaf ears.

Many employers are unable to give a hearing to prospective job applicants. This failure to listen causes a problem to Little People of all ages. The loss has serious consequences as the attitude of the employer results in discrimination. It is a denial of any qualified individual's right to enter the occupation or profession of choice.

Many employers are deaf when they fail to hear the qualifications of an applicant. A medical technologist and Little Person tells how one laboratory supervisor all but accused her college professors of lying about her abilities in their letters of recommendation. The employer did not even want to hear about her credentials. Her story can be echoed by many others.

A male Little Person in his twenties tells how, ironically enough, he was applying for a job as a 'short-order' cook. The employer took one look at him and straight out said, *"You're too short."* He never bothered to ask what his job qualifications were.

A Little Person nearing sixty years of age, tells how it was her size which made it difficult for her to gain employment. A male in his forties says: *"Just by sight, I have been turned down for jobs."* A male in his thirties agrees and says: *"You can pick the employer unable to listen by the tone of voice and the look in the eye. The discernment comes with years of experience of being rejected because you are a dwarf."*

Little People not yet in the job market have listened to the tales of

---

1   Charles Eskridge, *"Access for All is a Goal of Barrier Free Design."*
2   For a discussion of the effect of environmental barriers, see Chapter 5, *"At Your Physical Pleasure."*

older Little People and so anticipate this unwillingness of employers to hear them out. One young man studying for his Masters degree and not far from actively seeking employment said this: *"You're aware that you'll lose ninety percent of jobs you apply for, but the job you get will be great, because you'll know they are people oriented."* He could also have said: *"You'll know they are people prepared to listen."*

The unwillingness of an employer to listen to the skills and qualifications of Little People to perform the job indicates the presence of two handicaps. The employer is both deaf and blind. This person is unable to see the accomplishments and achievements of the many Little People who have entered all manner of occupations and professions. To attempt a list would be limiting, as inevitably someone's trade, profession, or skill would be omitted. It is safe to let your mind run wild as to the possibilities, because there are few occupations where Little People are not represented.

The employer's double handicap often carries through to discussions about making accommodations on the job-site. They are simply unable to handle them, even though most of the changes, which make it possible for the Little Person to be employed, cost next to nothing. The change may be as simple as placing a box under the feet of a person working at a desk, a cushion on the seat and in the back of the chair to increase height and comfort, and perhaps removing the legs to lower a desk. For those working at high counters, a stool gives the height needed to reach things. It is no excuse to say the person might fall off the stool. I doubt there is any group more experienced in the use and value of stools!

Employers may be willing to hire a Little Person, but they have not listened to the whole story if the job offered is one which greatly underutilizes the talents of the individual. The person gets the job, but there is no recognition of potential. When it is time to talk of a promotion or pay increase, there may be no one listening.

One Little Person tells how his employer would always have his discussions about promotion when standing in the hall. That way the employer could literally tower over him and physically impose his superiority. The tactic worked every time, because peering up made the employee feel helpless to argue and the chance of getting a raise was doomed to failure.

Some employers have not heard of the right of equal pay for equal work. To make it worse, the employer cannot even hear the contributions the employee is making to the company and so refuses to offer a full salary. Yet some Little People are so desperate to obtain employment they are willing to accept a lesser income. It is their only way of getting work.

Well, actually there are some other ways of getting jobs. However, not all of them are worth pursuing. I was appalled to learn of one government scheme which assisted people with disabilities to get work. A Little Person friend of mine was one of their victims.

In this scheme, to persuade the employer to hire, the government sold out my friend and many other individuals they were supposed to be helping. Oh, my friend got a job all right, but for eighty percent of the usual salary! This, combined with the fact that the salary was only minimum wage, made it very difficult for my friend to live independently. In effect, this work-scheme extorted twenty- percent of my friends wages as payment for the *"so-called"* privilege of employment.

The consequences of an employer's disabling attitude is very serious. Otherwise capable people are kept unemployed and dependent, and the so-called able-bodied population impairs its progress by carrying a social welfare burden far greater than is necessary. If *"people like us"* were given the same opportunity to work, the government could put its tax dollars to better use. Ears and eyes should be opened to this unnecessary waste.

Not everyone experiences immobility, deafness, or blindness. Some people disable themselves through their insensitivity. Socially they are retarded because of their inability to recognize I am a person with feelings. Through their social bumbling, they hurt me with their ridicule, overt curiosity and patronization.

Ridicule is often the past-time of children, who delight in making fun of you. Children are experts at mimic and love to find all manner of names to describe you to their friends. The names used are expressive of their imagination. *"Pint-size,"* and *"elf"* are some of the more original, and *"king vitamin"* and *"mighty mouse,"* which is how a Court Orderly used to describe me, I can even enjoy. However, most names are down-right derogatory and hurtful, such as hunch-back, midget, runt, stumpy and dolly. They are demeaning and not in the least bit appreciated.

Children can be handled successfully if they are alone; however, it is almost impossible to control their behavior when they are in a group. They are encouraged by each other and their antics proceed from bad to worse. When confronted by a group, I have found it is best to avoid them altogether. If I need to go into an area and it is around the time children are let out of school, I seriously consider delaying my business to avoid the hassles.

Adults are more sophisticated, but still delight in making fun when they see Little People. One evening I was coming out of a shop and was greeted by a group of women. They saw me and began nudging each other to make sure no one missed the sight. One of them said loud enough for everyone to hear including me, *"Make way for the little lady."* They all snickered. Another one spurred on by the hilarity continued, *"Watch out, don't get too close, you might shrink too!"* They didn't realize that to my mind they already had.

The curiosity of some is so extreme that their behavior is obnoxious. They are ignorant of the feelings of the person involved. One Little Person in reflection of her childhood recalled the reaction of the children when she first started school. Crowds followed her in the playground and even into the bathroom. When she used the toilet, the children even crawled on the floor to look underneath the door.

My heart still begins to gallop when I think about the curiosity of one man I met. It was vacation time and I was out with my brother Greg, sister Deborah, their respective fiancees and some other friends. There were seven of us.

We were at a place so crowded, I feared to move too far from our group in case I couldn't find them again. Deborah went off to look for people she had arranged to meet hoping to find enough seats for us among them. She finally returned and beckoned us to follow. It was hard to believe that she could have found either friends or seats in this crowd, but we followed her anyway.

I was very careful when weaving around people's legs to anticipate whether they were about to move forwards, backwards or sideways. They had no chance of seeing me and I had to look out for their movements. I was particularly wary of fire-lit hands. One wrong move and my hair would be singed or a pit burned in my face. I followed very close in Deborah's wake, taking advantage of the pathway she was clearing.

We reached Deborah's friends in one piece and they squeezed together so I could sit down. I was introduced, but didn't enter the conversation too much, as Deborah and her friends were busy catching up on old times. I sat quietly, watching the crowd, and listening to the music.

Before long, I noticed one chap in particular talking with Deborah. I assumed he was one of their group as he was being very familiar. In fact he was making her a fast play, so fast that he was not in the least deterred by the engagement ring on her finger, or the presence of her fiancee somewhere in the crowd. In the middle of his flirtation with Deb he leaned over to me and said, *"Smile."* His concern was an interesting diversion and I had no difficulty responding to the request.

The only way Deborah could communicate her lack of interest was to walk off and leave him and it wasn't long before she did just that. When she left, it was not leaving him to his own devices, but rather leaving him to me. He moved into the place where Deborah had sat and again asked me to smile. This time he offered practical assistance and placed two of his fingers at each corner of my mouth to make sure I did smile.

I did not need his help and he was pleased when I smiled again. He moved closer saying, *"Little People are supposed to smile."* That's where our conversation began and if I had known what was to follow, would also have been where it ended. But I had no idea of what was to come and allowed the man to introduce himself. The name he used should have been a clue. He called himself Demon. Even so, he seemed harmless enough and I played along saying my name was Angel.

He frankly admitted his curiosity about me and began to ask what it was like to be a Little Person. I knew he had been making a pass at Deb and probably should have told him to get lost when he turned his attention to me. But I didn't want to. It was unusual for such a good-looking man to take an interest in me and I was flattered by his attention. For once I wasn't the wall-flower watching the ups and downs of other people's encounters. Tonight I could experience one of my own.

I talked and he listened. Now he was smiling. He looked at me the whole time very intently. I had a captive audience. (Little did I know that he planned to make me his captive). He moved closer.

I attempted further conversation, but his interest in conversation had lapsed. Now there were other things on his mind. My encounter was turning into much more than I had bargained for. I could only guess what he might be thinking, but didn't have to wonder for long. He wasn't one for keeping his thoughts to himself. In fact he didn't want to keep much to himself at all. He came right out with it -- his thoughts that is. He said, *"I could slip one right up you."* I couldn't believe my ears. He couldn't be serious, could he?

My look expressed shock and embarrassment at the suggestion. I tried to play it cool by replying with a question, *"Is that right?"* The tone in my voice told him *"That's what you think buster!"*

Even though I was shocked at his declaration, I didn't really think it was more than an idle remark. I had no idea that it was an indication of his real intention. My experience with men had never gone beyond conversation. The men I knew were friendly, but they had never made any sexual advances. That was only something I dreamed about. I had no experience fending off a man who was coming on strong. I couldn't even tell if he was serious or joking!

When his eyes began to wander from my face and around my body, as though in preparation for the experience, things began to clarify very quickly. It was his next words which made me absolutely certain of his intentions. He looked into my eyes and said softly, *"I really would like to."* Now I knew he meant every word.

I didn't know what to do. I had encouraged him to stick around and made it obvious that I enjoyed his company and the attention he was giving me. But he had interpreted everything wrong! I had to make it absolutely clear that I was not interested in a sexual encounter. I said NO in every way I knew, with my voice, eyes and body -- all the areas he was taking an interest in.

He was not in the least rebuffed by my refusal and said, *"Well you don't really have any choice in the matter."* Again I was shocked. He couldn't mean it? I reminded him that I was not alone and would call for help if he persisted. He laughed saying, *"That doesn't worry me, call your brother and friends, anyone you please, I'm a black belt in karate."* His tone of voice was not threatening, but my concern increased as I realized the power of Demon's physical presence. He appeared to be deadly serious and from his appearance I could easily accept his claim to a black belt.

He moved closer again and continued exploring with his eyes, while scanning my body with his hands hovering above the surface, as though measuring me for size. He did not touch me, but I objected to his anticipation and grabbed his hand to stop him. He tried to convince me that to allow him to screw me would be a very interesting experience for him because he had never been with a Little Person. I was expected to show him what it was like!

I was not willing to move from social to sexual intercourse. When he realized I was not about to satisfy his curiosity, he attempted another line of persuasion. He spoke softly and gently into my ear, about how beneficial the experience would be for me! I still said no. By now, I was almost overcome by his physical presence as he had me covered in all directions. His arm was around my back and left side, his butt and torso at my right, and he was leaning across me at the front. Yet in spite of his efforts to overcome me physically, there was nothing he could do to overpower my will. My answer was still no.

His face drew closer and closer to mine. I couldn't move away. He was finished with persuasive words and closed the distance between us, by placing his open mouth on my lips. When he pushed his tongue into my mouth, I realized that talking was not going to get me out of this one. The word no had no significance in his vocabulary! I turned my head away and insisted that he stop. His earlier threats were becoming a definite reality. He intended to follow through with his objective, regardless of my wish. I had no doubt about this when he lifted me from the seat and began walking off with me into the bushes. HELP!

I didn't have to call for it, as Deborah looked up from her conversation at just the right moment. She came running after us calling out, *"Hey, where do you think you're taking my sister?"* It was perfect timing and sufficient challenge for Demon to put me down immediately. He laughed and said, *"I've been trying to freak her right out."* He had been very successful.

It was a relief to be rescued and to see him go away. I told everyone what he had threatened and attempted and asked them to stay close by in case he should come back. I was not left alone again, not even by Demon. He returned very soon afterwards and sat down next to me again. This time two of the girls sat at the table with me.

Before long, Demon was beginning his advances again, even in the presence of the girls. Three of us attempted to discourage him this time. However, he was not to be told what to do by anyone. Every time one of the others spoke up, he would get very nasty. Helen, told him if he carried on the way he was going she would have to call my brother over to stop him. Greg had been close by since my earlier request and almost as though he heard Helen, moved in to stand next to us. Demon took his presence as a direct challenge to a fight. However, before beginning, he took time to warn Greg that he was a black belt in karate. Greg indicated he wasn't perturbed in the least, saying he was pretty good with brown bottles.[1] A fight was imminent. Demon's arm which had been behind my back and hidden to me, I now noticed. His hand was clenched into a fist directed at Greg. Demon rose to his feet ready to act. Everyone took their positions, including Bryan, Greg's best mate who moved quietly behind Demon with a beer bottle in his hand. Demon's eyes were blazing with anger. There was no one to call on for help now --- they were all here and about to get their heads knocked off.

Violence was not my idea of the best solution, so I attempted to dissipate the anger and tension in Demon. After all, it was me he was interested in getting, and there was some hope that he would listen to me. Surprisingly, he responded to my suggestion that he sit down. He calmed quickly, but like a dog with a bone, returned to pursue his objective.

It didn't take long to realize that there might not be a peaceful solution. His next move confirmed that. I found myself lying flat on my back. It wasn't exactly skillful preparation for the experience Demon was looking for. He had picked me up as suddenly as before, but in swinging me off the seat, lost his balance and dropped me. I shrieked as we both went down. He had no opportunity to take advantage of my position as everyone rushed to the rescue.

I reacted by shouting angrily at Demon, *"You can just pick me up and put me right back where you found me."* There was no worry he would take off with me again; everyone was present to stop him. It was instinctive to direct my anger at him and to expect he should be the one to put things back together again.

To my amazement he did pick me up and put me back on the seat, without even a murmur. His instant obedience I took to be an apology.

---

1   In New Zealand, this is a colloquial way of referring to beer bottles.

Finally, I followed Deborah's earlier example, when he made solicitations to her. I left him to it. Bryan (who I don't hesitate in comparing with Sir Gallahad) made that possible by asking me to dance. I accepted immediately and we walked off, this time leaving Demon to his own devices.

Maybe all this would have been avoided, if I had followed my grandmother's advice. She always advised against speaking to strangers. But how was I to know that Demon was a stranger? I thought he was among the group of my sister's friends. With the wisdom of hindsight, I may have been able to change the course of events, if I had done this or hadn't done that, but such wisdom is not available in the heat of the moment. By the time I realized his intentions were not honorable, it was too late to change anything --- he could not be stopped. Demon was determined to carry his curiosity to the most objectionable extreme. Sadly I must say that other Little People have been sexually abused --- all in the name of curiosity.

Patronization is another form of abuse. It is an insensitivity to my wish to be treated as any other person. It shows itself when people pat you on the head or take you by the hand when they walk alongside you. I find it especially frustrating, because often the person cannot be told their behavior is offensive. Many times they are people in authority over you.

Many things happen at annual Christmas parties and some people's behavior leaves a lot to be desired. Yet people are often excused for what they do or say because it is something they only do once a year. It is generously called *"letting your hair down."* One year, I indulged myself.

It was the Christmas party at the Court where I often appeared as a lawyer and I was talking with a group of three or four other lawyers. A Justice of the Peace before whom I regularly appeared during the year joined our group. He greeted me by patting me on the head and asked how I was doing. At this point, I let him have it trusting that my behavior would later be excused as one of those things people do when they let their hair down at a party.

I spoke to the Justice of the Peace very directly and said, *"I was fine until you patted me on the head."* One of my friends, standing behind him, reeled back in shock. He didn't have to say what he was thinking, it was written all over his face. *"How could you be so rude to one of the hierarchy?"* My answer is simple, *"It's easy, I'm tired of being patronized."*

It's no surprise that my remark made no impact on the Justice of the Peace. He was as oblivious to the comment, as to my feelings as a person. At least I had the satisfaction of saying what I felt, even if it didn't make any difference. I tried.

The reaction some people have to a Little Person causes me to wonder about their mental stability. The imbalance manifests itself in the form of delusions in which I am envisioned as someone who is better than other people. In extreme cases, people even fantasize that I am a super-woman.

People suffering from such delusions regard any accomplishment I make as something of great moment. Their applause is thunderous, far more than for others receiving the same award. They set me apart as someone outstanding, and in so doing place me on a pedestal.

I can still remember my embarrassment at hearing the increased volume of applause at my law school graduation. Why did they applaud louder for me? It was not and should not be a marvel that I as a Little Person should graduate. I have both the ability to study and succeed. There was no reason for people to be astounded at the fact. My graduation was no more credit-worthy than that of the other students. They worked just as hard as I did. My graduation did not make me any better than they were.

What may be worse than the fact that many people have such delusions, is the attempt to delude Little People into thinking that they are better than others. One instance of this happening is when a Little Person applies for a job. The individual is told to advise prospective employers that they will be a more conscientious, cooperative, punctual and efficient employee. This is supposed to offset the negative reaction the employer may have to the Little Person's appearance.

This approach, however, is not only disabling to the one experiencing these delusions, but also to the Little Person. The immediate effect is that the individual who is promoted as someone better is elevated above others and separated from the day-to-day routines in society. In the long term, the delusion of superiority is revealed for what it is -- a delusion. As a result, unless the Little Person is actually above average, he or she will be toppled from the pedestal. Consequently, those who are average will be seen as falling below the mark, and there will be no hope for those with less than average skills.

In reality, Little People have the same range of differences in ability and talent as other people --- some are better, others are worse, most are average. In order to be accepted for who we are, Little People should not have to prove they are better. As Dr. Leonard Sawisch so aptly put it: *"Little People are not better than most, but are potentially as good as the best."* [1] If it's true that Little People have achieved more than other groups in society, I don't think it's because as a group we are more talented or have more ability. Rather, our achievements come because we are more determined and have to try harder to get anywhere. Many have gone a long way because of the development of skills which others have, but waste. The attitude of having to prove it can be done, takes a Little Person that much further. For someone to tell us we can't do it, only spurs us on to show how wrong they are. *"Just you wait and see!"*

I feel it would be helpful if people understood the concept put forward by Cass Irvin, an activist in disability rights and an editor and publisher of Disability Rag, a leading magazine on disability issues, who says:

" ... if people would quit saying they're equal and meaning by it that they're the same, and start saying instead that we have a right to our own way of life and my way of life is just different from yours. It isn't more or less, just different." [2]

I don't believe I'm better or worse just because I'm a Little Person. Nor does my size make me more or less equal. I think of myself as ordinary, and want others to see me that way too. I only achieve equality when people do not raise me up or put me down with their favors, praise, or rejection.

The negative reaction some people have to disability is something researchers have spent years trying to understand. What is the cause? How can it be prevented? I ask the same questions about the disabling influence of people's attitudes toward Little People. Where does all

---

1   Leonard Sawisch, PH.D., is President of the Little People of America
     Foundation, and President of the Mid-Michigan Chapter of the Little People
     of America, Inc.

2   Mary Breit, *"Free the People."*

this negativism toward us stem from? If we could find the cause, we could work toward prevention of the effects.

The disabilities created by the attitudinal barriers are not terminal, nor do they need to be permanent. There is a cure! It can be implemented when the particular cause of the negative attitude is located. At that point, an education program can be planned to at least remove the negative attitude and where possible implant a positive one. I know it won't happen overnight. The process of rehabilitation requires extensive long-term therapy of individuals and support from a community which recognizes the rights of all and is willing to protect them through legislation.[1]

To effect a cure is in everyone's interest. We will all be released. I will be free of the disabilities imposed on me and will be free to be myself. In the exercise of my independence and equality, I will contribute to rather than be a burden on society.

The average sized people will be free to participate with the Little People that they previously excluded from their circles. When they regain their mobility, sight, hearing, sensitivity, and mental stability, all people will join the age of enlightenment and discover that the world of disability is not flat. Little People have a worthy role to play in the twentieth century. Our globe will be rounded again when we are free to help ourselves and others.

---

1   For further discussion of the dual role of education and legislation, see
     Chapter 10, "The Rise and Fall of Dwarf Throwing."

Chapter Seven

DOING THINGS
DIFFERENTLY

Short-stature is no excuse

I listened with interest for the answer to the television interviewer's question, *"Is there anything you can't do?"* The Little Person paused before answering thoughtfully. *"No, I can do everything I want. My size has not stopped me doing anything."* The response settled well with me. Without even being told that the young man was a third year medical student, I knew immediately that he was not allowing his short-stature to be an excuse for achieving less. Sadly, not all Little People have reached this plateau. Only a year before hearing the interview, I had tried to discourage an eight year old little person from using his size as an excuse.

Kevin, the eldest of three children, and the only Little Person in his family, was having trouble accepting his short-stature. His parents were doing their best to raise him as an ordinary kid, but Kevin was not cooperating. He was obviously put out by the fact that his brother, three years younger, was already taller than he was.

In talking to Kevin, I heard complaints of how small he was, and the things he couldn't do. He frequently complained that his father made him wash the car. He didn't think that was fair because he was too small.

Kevin soon realized that mine was not a sympathetic ear. I told him that as the oldest, he should be pleased to take some responsibility. His size was no reason to shirk work. I knew if he didn't learn this soon, he would find himself missing out on a lot more.

He was free to reject my advice, but would only hear it echoed by many other Little People. Bammer of Florida says, *"There isn't anything I can't do. I don't let things stop me."* [1] Mary also of Florida says, *"Why would I just sit around and do nothing --- I like to see how far I can go."* [2] If not persuaded by the feminine view, maybe Kevin would be challenged by the male Little Person I heard interviewed on television.

The interview time did not allow a discussion of the skills developed to allow the man to do everything he wanted. Yet I know many of his activities must have been achieved by *"doing things differently."* It was these hints that Kevin needed to hear.

Bammer explains, *"As long as I can get a chair, I'm okay --- if you just sit down and figure it out, you can do it some old way --- being determined is probably one advantage to being small."* [3]

John Strudwick said, *"If there's something you have to do, there's always a way. You have to adapt, or you can't survive."* [4] Robert Van Etten believes little people can do anything. His resource is to work with other people. He says, *"I've learned to cope with people. People are willing to work with you."* [5]

Adaptation as a way of life

Eight year old Kevin could achieve whatever he wanted. However, he first needs to know that his way will sometimes differ from his younger brother's. He will be just as successful, but his accomplishments may not come until he learns adaptation as a way of life.

Kevin will learn adaptation by developing skills such as: initiative, ingenuity, determination, patience, perseverance, and a sense of humor. Often a task will look too difficult, yet when faced with the responsibility of getting it done, you will figure out a way of doing the task. I was faced with such a challenge one day as I was about to leave the of-

1   Bob Arndorfer, *"These Little People Meet Full-Sized Problems Head On,"* the Gainesville Sun (July 25, 1976).

2   Dee Whittington, *"She Won't Say Can't,"* the Palm Beach Post (1978).

3   supra 1.

4   Reenie McAllister, *"Little Person Here Has No Trouble Dealing With Life,"* the Sunday Times, Salisbury Maryland (June 2, 1974).

5   supra 1.

fice.

Closing the windows was not my usual job, however, this day I was the last to leave the office, and the bathroom window had been left open. It was up to me to close it even though it was way out of my reach. No one could help me, as everyone had left the building. (That was the first thing I checked). I was completely dependent on my own resources.

I started out by dragging a chair into the bathroom to help me climb onto the toilet. (The window was behind the toilet; the room was too narrow for the chair to be placed alongside the window wall). It was a precarious climb onto the chair, but even more uncertain was the decision to stand on the plastic toilet seat and cover. They literally buckled under my weight. Fortunately, I didn't fall through.

However, when I delicately balanced myself on the edge of the seat, my reach was still short of the window. Total frustration! The temptation was to just leave the window open, but I knew that was out of the question. It wasn't just a matter of overnight, the office was closing for the Christmas vacation week.

The other option was to call my boss when I got home, and tell him to go back and close it. I knew that wasn't fair, especially since he had gone off to enjoy himself at a string of seasonal parties. Anyway, I didn't know where to find him.

Not wanting to risk a catastrophe, I carefully descended from my toilet perch. Once on the ground, I could plan another strategy. I roamed the office to find something to hook onto the latch. I found a piece of wood and returned to the bathroom. My second climb was also successful, and my footing on the seat balanced just as carefully. I extended the wood-piece out the window and slipped it between the latch and frame. The pressure applied in a thrust forward and down was not enough to pull it in, as the window had been extended to its limit.

I had almost reached my own limit, but was not going to give up that easily. Several stronger thrusts, in short bursts, edged the window closer. Finally, it was in far enough that I could reach out and pull it in with my hand. I closed it! It was a feeling of triumph, well preparing me for my own Christmas celebrations.

Determination and perseverance can get the job done. But there are times, when a sense of humor is also necessary. Rowan discovered this one day when fixing his car. Even a stool couldn't give him enough height to tinker with the engine. His solution was to climb right in. Somewhat unconventional, but it was the best way to get the job done.

One day, this practice became quite alarming for a passer-by. Rowan was working on the car when a man walking past heard muffled sounds coming from the engine. They were most unusual noises for a Datsun to make. The man came closer to investigate the human noises coming from within. He heard a plea that sounded like *"Help, help."* His curiosity got the better of him and he lifted the hood. He was so taken aback he almost dropped the hood. Was he seeing things? He couldn't believe his eyes when a little man stepped out and thanked him for the rescue? There was Rowan shaking the man's hand, dusting himself down, and laughing about his predicament.

What else could Rowan do? He certainly wasn't going to pay a mechanic, when he could fix the car himself. Only then would the joke have been against him. This one he could enjoy, and share as an occupational hazard.

Physical limitations

Yet, even with all the required skills, frustration can only be avoided if an initial adaptation is made: to accept that there are some things in life which are impossible. Even though John Strudwick said *"There's always a way,"* his mother Priscilla wrote, *"A little person must early in his life be taught to strive to accomplish those things that he can do, and to accept those things that are -- in fact -- impossible for him to achieve."* [1] Inspite of John's optimism, he had not ignored his mother's teaching.

No, the key to John's understanding is expressed in his own words, *"There's always a way, if there's something you have to do."* And one of the things that has to be done is to recognize your limitations. They are different for every Little Person, and depend on the type of dwarfism.

Most of the limitations are determined by characteristics other than size. It is my dislocated joints and fused knees that stop my participation in sky-diving, ballet-dancing, gymnastics, pole-vaulting, and

---

1   *"The Story of John Phillips Strudwick, As Seen by his Parents."*

skiing. However, these activities are rarely found in the average person's repertoire and I have no trouble joining the masses as a spectator. I easily accept the elimination of some options and appreciate how many remain. There is no reason to be frustrated. The crisis is not coping with lost functions, but trying to fit everything I want to do into an already over-crowded schedule.

I can join Bammer, Mary, John, and Robert to say, *"I can do anything I want."* But like them only choose to do what is possible for me. I forgot this, the day I went horseback riding.

I had seen young children riding. They were fully supervised while riding the horse as Murray guided them around the paddock. The horse seemed so docile, any question of danger or risk was remote. I was game to try too. After all, none of the children had been harmed. I started riding double with Anne, but we had trouble both fitting into the hollow in the ancient horse's back. We could appreciate the shape of his back because we were riding without a saddle. Anne dismounted so I could ride alone.

Murray still held the reins, and I continued to sit astride the horse's back side saddle minus the saddle. (I had to sit sideways because the dislocation of my hips makes it impossible for me to straddle a horse). I soon found riding side saddle was impossible without a saddle. I also got a very fast lesson in the anatomy of horses as each step caused the top of the horse's legs to move up and down. (I now understand the relationship between horse-power and cars. The tops of horse's legs are like engine pistons and go up and down, up and down, over and over). My discovery was more than academic, the motion had a drastic effect on my ride.

I was not on the horse long enough to feel queasy, instead I started sliding off. Without a saddle, there was nothing for me to hold and every step of the horse inched me closer to the ground. In a controlled shrill voice, I let Murray know I was falling. The horse apparently understood my half-way position and decided to put me in my proper place. He changed his gentle amble around the paddock into a canter. My friends standing on the other side of the horse could do nothing to stop me sliding straight down the horse's side into the ditch.

It was an easy fall, but my left ankle took the brunt. No more bareback riding for me. Horse-riding did not have to be on my no list, but riding without a saddle was just asking for trouble. I now know that only experienced riders can leave the saddle behind, and only fools ride sideways without one. But when you choose to wear your brains in your pants, you learn the hard way.

Knowing the difference between what can and can't be done, comes from sound parental guidance, plain common sense, and sadly enough, sometimes from limping around for a whole week on a sprained ankle. It does not come from Kevin's attitude of assuming it can't be done because you're too short.

It is best to assume the activity can be done, even if at first glance it looks out of the question. That doesn't mean you rush in and try everything, rather you stop to give the project serious thought before giving it up. How a project can be accomplished may not always be obvious. The uninformed may say, *"No you can't possibly do that."* Yet by doing things differently the Little Person will often show a relationship between a will and the way.

Driving and accessing a motor vehicle

One summer, I totally shocked a supposedly educated man who was a staff lawyer where I was working as a law clerk. Someone told him I drove a car but he didn't believe it. *"How could she drive a car?"* He only accepted it after one of the other office clerks told him, *"Yes she does, I know because she drove me home at lunch-time."* I find it just as hard to believe that anyone could be so amazed. Yet he is not the only person I have surprised.

One afternoon, I was pulling into the curb to park. I left plenty of room between the car in front and behind, and got out to lock my door. The man watching, whose image I caught earlier in my rear view mirror, was very impressed. He came up and extended his hand in congratulations. It wasn't in sarcastic relief that I hadn't bumped his car parked behind me. That wasn't his car. No, he just hadn't realized Little People were able to drive, and thought the feat was marvelous. I have long since taken it for granted.

All I need are pedal extensions, cushions behind and beneath, the seat moved forward, a smaller steering wheel, and an automatic drive. The smaller wheel is necessary, otherwise the increased height offered by the cushions makes it difficult for me to fit between the wheel and the seat. The sports car racing wheel is the perfect size, and leaves me plenty of room. I also appreciate the better grip and control that a smaller wheel provides.

Some Little People prefer to use hand-controls. When I was assessed for driving, I tried hand-controls, but it was recommended that since my legs had adequate strength it was better for me to use pedal extensions. An automatic was also recommended to allow full concentration on road management, without the distraction and effort required for changing gears. Why not make things easier if you can?

When learning to drive the automatic, I was encouraged to only drive with one foot, to avoid the temptation of resting one foot on the brake at the same time as the other foot is accelerating. My left foot is the natural choice as it is the stronger. However, the drawback in doing this is the discomfort of lifting my leg across the brake to the accelerator on the right.

In my hurry to get on the road, I was willing to sacrifice comfort. Many Little People do the same. I later learned that this sacrifice was not needed. It is possible for me to both drive with my left foot and be comfortable. Instead of lifting my leg across the brake, I now use a left foot accelerator. The accelerator extension is positioned at the location where my foot naturally sits, on the left. Now I can drive greater distances without feeling tired.

Further fatigue and discomfort is avoided by building a platform on which to rest the feet. This removes the risk of the driving foot falling asleep, or any delay in reaction time. The platform also saves the strain of suspending your feet in mid-air, and stops the temptation of resting your non-driving foot on the brake.

Many Little People do not wear their seat-belts, because the fit is uncomfortable. The shoulder harness tucked under the arm removes the risk of strangulation, but cuts into the skin when short summer sleeves are worn. Rather than suffer, many don't bother belting-up. Others don't even have the choice. The shifting forward and raising of the seat make it impossible to fasten because the seat-belt is then too short to reach around them.

I am one of the lucky ones. My seat-belt will pull out far enough to fit around me, but that's only because I don't have to pull my seat too far forward. Even so, I cannot sit comfortably until I know that all Little People have the same opportunity as other people to ride safely in motor-vehicles. That is, vehicles equipped with seat-belts that save injury and death, not cause it. I'm looking forward to a redesigned seatbelt which does not hang loose unused, or cause the user's neck to be hung up in it.

It doesn't matter how many precautions a person takes, there is no way to eliminate the risk of break-down. When it happens, no one likes it, least of all a Little Person. Chances are even the slightest trouble cannot be handled without help. I discovered this only a few months after getting my first car.

Even though conscious that I should know how to change a tire, when the time came my knowledge was no help. I could not loosen the nuts to remove the wheel, or get the spare tire out of the trunk. My girlfriend was with me, and though able to remove the tire from the trunk, she was unable to loosen the nuts. We almost went nuts in the sweltering heat, waiting more than an hour for help to come along that lonely country road. The second time I got a flat I was alone on the freeway in rush-hour traffic. The only effort I made toward repair, was to walk in the direction of the emergency telephone to call the Automobile Association. I never found out whether I could reach the phone, as a Good Samaritan pulled over and called me back. He was happy to change the tire for me. I was most grateful.

It can be a risky business accepting help from strangers, especially when you're stranded at night. I've not been too happy about the chances I've had to take. However, these can be reduced by carrying a Citizen Band Radio, or an emergency pennant. When you break down, instead of taking a walk, you can call or signal for help and wait for a person in authority to come along.

There is one very important thing to remember when driving a car. It can easily be forgotten or stretched to the limit. You have to fill the car with gas! I have learned that lesson the hard way, twice. The first time was a kindly warning. I ran out opposite a gas station! It wasn't enough to stop me doing it again, however. Even so, the second time I only missed the station by a half mile. Now I try not to push my luck.

When I was learning to drive, the instructor anticipated one difficulty I would have. He predicted that when reversing, I just might miss seeing a trash can sitting behind the car. He was absolutely right. Not long after getting my license I knocked one over when backing out of a friends driveway. However, because of the instructor's cautionary words, I was moving slowly and the can was left intact.

To limit such accidents, I check the vicinity of the car before getting in, and have installed good rear-view mirrors. I prefer to have one on both doors, and a rectangular convex one in the center. The curved center mirror gives panoramic vision through the back, and out the side windows. Working with all three mirrors, I can eliminate blind spots. Of course, the mirrors only work if you keep your eyes open.

Driving your car is one thing, using it is another. It's great when you can do both. Such is not always the case for Little People. At least, not without adaptation. Many cars restrict their access to Little People, the most offensive area being the trunk.

Often the lid opens half way up the back of the car. This means you have to drop things into the trunk, and hope there will be someone around when it is time to get them out. Or else get them out yourself by using a stool kept for that purpose in the trunk. (That is, if you can reach in far enough to get the stool). If you're looking for something in the trunk, it is impossible to see without climbing in, or using the stool.

I have found a way to both drive and use my car. I buy a model where the trunk opens and lifts from the bumper level. I can slide things in and out without any help, and have no excuse for not being able to find what I'm looking for.

The frustration of the automatic glide sailing the trunk door into the wind, and out of reach, is easily solved. I attach a piece of rope to the latch and pull on that. Once closed, I just wrap the rope around the bumper so that it doesn't drag on the ground.

I have seen a more sophisticated arrangement, where a vinyl strap is inserted inside the car. It looks nicer, but has one bug left to iron out. When you're closing the trunk, you have to watch that the strap doesn't get caught in the lock.

The trunk which opens at bumper level is great when you're doing your grocery shopping. You can just slide the bags in, and pull them out without injuring yourself. That is of course, if you know how to make shopping easy.

Grocery shopping

Making shopping easy is only possible by developing some adaptive techniques. It all begins by choosing the right store. Not only must the prices be manageable, so must the facilities. I will choose the store with the lowest profile fruit and vegetable display stand, the plastic and paper bag dispensers set within my reach, freezers I can see into, helpful and polite staff, and grocery carts where I can reach the bottom and see over the top.

It all sounds rather ideal, but many stores today are bending over back-wards to please all their customers. When I moved to a new area recently a staff person said, *"If there's anything we can do to help you, just let us know."* I decided to test just how far the offer went.

I told the staff person how great it would be to have a low-profile cart, one where I could reach into the bottom. It would be just wonderful to stand at the check-out counter, and unload my own groceries. Would you believe, when I returned to the store a couple of weeks later, the store proudly presented me with a cart just my size? You can be sure they won my regular patronage.

Even though I have a check-list when choosing a grocery store, there will always be features that I cannot deal with alone. This is when a helpful and considerate staff is a necessity. It is a relief to know they will be happy to do self-serve chores for me, such as weighing fruit and vegetables, reaching items from high shelves, and only half-filling the grocery bags at the check-out. Some will even go that final step, and load the bags into the car. That is icing on the cake which guarantees I will come back for more.

Where the staff are too busy, or not within calling distance, the public are an invaluable resource. When I spot what I want on a high shelf, and another shopper is close by, I don't hesitate to ask the person to assist me. Most people are only too pleased to help out, and after the first request are on the look out to help again.

There is only one drawback. Unless you want your shopping to take all day (by having to go and search for help every time you want something) it means you have to shop when there are plenty of people around. It really is a catch twenty-two, because if you do shop when there is a crowd, you're shopping does take all day.

However long it takes, eventually the job is done, and the half-filled bags make it easier to carry them into the house. It also helps to have your own cart at home to save many trips from the car to the house. The bags can be lifted from the cart without too much effort, and the job of putting things away begins.

Why adjust when you can modify

But where will I put everything? I can't reach half the shelves in the kitchen cupboards even when I'm standing on a stool, and the last thing I expect to do is stand on the counter. The answer to the question will depend on two things: my philosophical perspective, and who else lives in the house with me.

Some Little People refuse to make any concessions to their size. They will not scale utilities down, or build anything up. To them, modification is seen as giving in or opting out. Their real world is at the height of average-sized people, and they perceive themselves as managing very well leaving things just as they are. They choose to adjust to the average-sized person's environment.

A newspaper report revealed that the five stars of the movie 'Time Bandits', felt this way.[1] Dave Rappaport[2] was reported as saying, *"The great pit into which you mustn't fall is to reduce things to your Lilliputian size."* Tiny Ross added, *"Never lower even a shelf, if you build yourself a doll's house you opt out of real life. If you can't draw the curtains or reach a light switch, use a walking stick."* Dave Rappaport continued, *"There's not a kitchen unit I can't scale, once I've worked out the north face."*

My reaction is to say that lowering a shelf is an acceptance of reality. It is an appreciation that constant climbing and jumping onto kitchen units is a hazard, unhygienic, and excessive wear and tear on the joints. To never lower a shelf is to opt out of reality. It is an unreal attempt to live life as though in the shoes of an average-sized person. The mirror reflects my true image, why shouldn't my environment? Why adjust to something that doesn't have to be?

Many Little People don't see the alterations as a sell out, but they don't make them because the changes will hinder the chances of being able to sell the property. With so few Little People represented in the population, the market for homes with lower facilities is limited. To sell the property means reconverting the facilities to average height.

---

1   Jean Rooks, *"Facing Up to Life from Waist Level,"* the 8 O'Clock, Auckland, New Zealand (August 29, 1981).

2   The lead actor in the United States 1987 T.V. series, *"the Wizard."*

The expense is prohibitive to many.

There is a partial answer to this dilemma. That is to have two sets of units built. At the time of reconstruction, instead of throwing out the regular sized units, they can be stored, and removable modular units can be installed at more convenient levels. When it is time to sell the property, the modular units can be removed, the original regular sized ones reinstalled, and the mobile modulars made ready to install in the next home. True, there is the initial sunk cost of building the second set of units, but thereafter its just a matter of removal and installation.

Many people *"make do"* because they have to, not because they choose to. They can't afford the changes, or don't have the option. Landlords have been known to frown on lesser changes. Alterations to the level of kitchen cabinets and counters would not be likely to earn their approval.

Even though some Little People have both the opportunity and the finances, they still choose not to make major changes. They don't see the modifications as a sell out, rather the decision is out of consideration to the average-sized persons living in the same household. More often than not, there is only one Little Person in a family, and if changes are made the average-sized members will be inconvenienced.

A member of the Little People of America told how his five feet seven inch tall son would bump his head on the kitchen cabinet when bending over to use the sink. He was the only person of average height in a family of three Little People. The parent's did not intend to make life difficult for their son. No, at the time of his adoption, they were told that he too would be a Little Person. However, he just kept growing.

Well, I still haven't answered the question, *"Where will I put my groceries?"* They will defrost if I don't hurry up and decide.

My philosophy allows me to modify my kitchen. I don't see such changes as opting out of real life. Unlike David Rappaport, I will not scale the units on the north face, rather I will scale them down with my pencil. I prefer to put my groceries away without any need for a mountain climbing expedition.

If I want to please Tiny Ross, instead of lowering my shelves, I could have the floors raised. Yet my preference would be to scale the units down, (no one would be inconvenienced as the only other person in my household at the time of planning is a Little Person). I do have a problem though, my landlord would not consent to such changes. In actuality, I step up onto platforms which raise me to the sink, freezer and stove.

I stop dreaming, and get on with the job of putting the groceries away. On high cupboard shelves, I place items infrequently used. However, I still need an aid to reach all but the bottom shelf. I gain an additional eighteen inches by using a reacher. It has a grip claw at the end, which I squeeze tight around an object. (It works best with light weight articles). I raise the object to the shelf, and place it toward the front, so that I can see what is in there. A space is left between each item so that the reacher can easily slide in between when its time to remove items.

Well that takes care of the light-weight goods. Where will I put everything else? Canned foods are too heavy for successful reacher transport. Most of the lower cupboards in the kitchen are covered by the platforms, and those still available are full of kitchen utensils and dishes. Besides, even without the platforms, I would only use the front of the cupboards, as I have difficulty reaching the back.

After a few weeks of living in the apartment with a cluttered counter, a cupboard was converted into a pantry. The shelves were built at my height, and finally there was a place to store groceries. The excuse for an untidy kitchen was removed. I can unload the rest of the groceries into the shelves, freezer and refrigerator. The job is finally complete. At last, I can put my feet up and relax. I certainly need it. Shopping wears me out.

Designing my dream house

I lay back on the couch and muse about my dream house. If I were at the drawing board, how would I lay everything out? It's not totally fanciful -- one day my dream will come true. I will own a house and be able to walk in, and have access to everything without climbing and reaching. It will be just wonderful.

My mind wanders back to the kitchen. I will remove the platforms for the last time, glad to end the routine of shifting them every time the floor needs cleaning. A large walk-in pantry with lots and lots of shelves is built. The floor space will be greater, so that I can have more shelves at a lower level. The only way I would consider floor to ceiling shelving is if I could install the shelving I once saw demonstrated.[1] There were a row of shelves at the front, and another at the back. At the push of a button, the shelves would rotate in a complete circle. Instead of riding the ferris wheel, I could stand in one location and view the contents of the whole cupboard as each shelf passed by. When releasing the button, the shelf needed would stop at my height. It would be a great asset to my kitchen, but a sorry sight for my bank account. But, maybe one day.

I turn to the wall cabinets. The bottoms must be lowered to my eye level, so that I can reach the shelves.[2] To make full use of the back shelf space, otherwise out of reach, I include either Lazy Susan trays, or shelving that slides right out like open-sided drawers.[3]

The counter work area is set at less than or equal to my elbow height.[4] Maybe chopping and preparing meals will eventually become a pleasure. For a moment, I come to my senses and realize I must be getting carried away. Well, if not enjoyed at least I wouldn't hate cooking chores. Pleasure may be possible, if I plan a sit-down work area. I need an open space beneath the counter to store a stool, and to slide my legs under when I'm sitting down. This way my endurance level in the kitchen would be at least doubled. The stool could have coaster wheels, so that when I'm really tired I could just glide around the kitchen to get what I need.

The sink will have long arm spigots, so that I don't have to dip myself into the soapy water when reaching across to turn the taps. The oven and stove controls will be at the front and end the precarious moments of stretching over hot elements and steaming pots. Of course, it goes without saying that both the elements, and the oven will be set at convenient levels. The door of the oven will open vertical to the ground, so that I don't have to lean across it, when reaching to remove the contents. Goodbye to the days of leaning across the side of the

---

1   A patented product known as the *"Kitchen Jeani"* and distributed in the United States by Rich-maid Kitchens Inc., John C. Lehman, Inc., of P.O. Box 1167 Lancaster, PA 17604 can provide further information.

2   Mary O'Donnell, *"The Idea Machine: a booklet of handy hints for more convenient living by everyone"* (about 1978). This hint at I(C)(2)(e), p 5.

3   ibid, I(A)(1)(d), p 3.

4   ibid, I(C)(2)(a) page 5.

door, angling dishes in and out. One casserole lost to the oven floor is one too many.

The controls for the hood vent and lights will be mounted on the counter.[1] The switch for the waste disposal unit and outlets for electric appliances will not be on the wall behind the counter. That is out of reach, and instead they will be mounted on the front, or at least placed on a wall that doesn't require reaching across something else.

The dream continues as I leave the kitchen, looking for other design challenges. There is no temptation to draw split-level housing. One level ranch style sprawl is the most appealing. Stairs have no attraction and the mere thought of them starts the pencil in my hand quivering.

A calm returns as I gaze through the window. Yes, the windows must be low in profile. There is much more to see than the sky. Movement along the street, and the relaxing effect of surrounding nature must not be blocked by solid walls. The breath of life must be free to flow in windows that I can see through. I shall be sure to have the latches within reach, so I can breathe in fresh air without the struggle of climbing on a chair to open the windows.

I turn back to the room and consider how nicely the picture frames are hung. Through art and photography, I can fill my world with what the window view lacks. I will set them for my comfort. No more straining of the neck to appreciate a painting or photograph. They will be hung at my eye level.

My friends will enjoy the wall hangings just as much, but they will have to sit down for the best view. After all, visitors are expected to relax and it would be good to see them put their feet up. It doesn't worry me that the kitchen facilities won't suit them, they're not supposed to work in there anyway. If they insist on helping with the dishes, I'm sure they won't break bending over for those few minutes.

The furniture will be convenient for everyone. At the most, I might indulge in a rocking chair designed primarily for my comfort. Other chairs and couches will be of regular size.

---

1   Mary O'Donnell, *"The Idea Machine: a booklet of handy hints for more convenient living by everyone" (about 1978)*. This hint at I(C)(2)(c), p 5.

I have no intention of building a doll house. The first image that pops into my head when someone mentions doll house is everything in miniature. Even the ceilings of a doll house are lowered. That is ridiculous. Apart from making the house unsaleable, I would be isolating myself from all but Little People. Perish the thought. What about my family and other friends?

I am not inconvenienced by regular sized ceilings, so would not even think of lowering them. My dream design must include, not exclude. The changes made consider the needs of everyone, not just a few. I want all my friends, and family to have access to my home. For this reason, I will also make sure that the doorways are wide enough for friends who use wheelchairs. The access into the house will be barrier free. A level entry -- no steps!

I may be tempted to lower the dining table and chairs a few inches, but not so much as to make sharing it with average-sized people impossible or uncomfortable. I value my friends, and would not consider putting them through the mill. I would prefer using a cushion to gain the extra height rather than be so inconsiderate.

Of course, no one would be inconvenienced by what I plan in my bedroom, low profile dressers and mirrors, and a bed that doesn't require a step-ladder to get in or out. Nothing spectacular, but everything usable.

Other Little People have succeeded in scaling down certain utilities without building themselves the doll's house so much despised by the Time Bandit stars. (I have yet to meet a Little Person who has done such a thing). They have catered to the needs of both short and tall. Instead of furnishing their home with miniature furniture some have chosen low profile contemporary designs comfortable for a person of any size.[1] A married couple of Little People from New York, *"furnish their bedroom and kitchen to account for their size, with vanities that are thirty inches tall and shallow oval sinks to accommodate their short reach. The bathroom shower head is lowered. However, everything else in the house is average-size, because they entertain average-size friends."* [2]

1   *"In a world made for big people, little people are learning to cope,"* the (Dallas) Sun (February 24, 1981).

2   William Neugebauer, *"Their stature can't be measured,"* the Daily News (March 23, 1980).

As far as the office goes, forget the chair which raises me to the height of an average-sized desk. Instead, I plan a low profile desk with a chair to match. Then, I can sit and have my feet touch the ground. You can't get closer to reality than that!

The telephone rings. I hear it, but don't hear it. It rings again. Not until the third time do I realize it is my phone. Reluctantly, I abandon my dream, though I know it's high time I stirred. I sigh and put my feet back on the ground.

At the fifth ring, I answer it. My sister is on the other end, she knows to wait a while before hanging up. At the best of times, I take a while to get there. (Another thought occurs, I will have a telephone in every room, so that I don't miss the calls of people who don't know to wait. Yes, I'll even put one in the bathroom).

Preparing for an outing

Deborah speaks to me, *"Angela, are you there."* I reply, *"Oh Deborah, excuse me I was just coming out of a dream. What's up?"* She continues and brings me right back to earth. *"I was wondering if you were doing anything tonight, maybe we could go to the movies together."* I don't have anything planned, and agree to meet her at the theater at seven-fifteen.

First, I must keep my appointment with the hairdresser. A glance at my watch tells me to get moving. I have to shower and get my clothes ready. Now that I'm going to the movies after the hairdresser, I will make an extra effort to look nice.

What will I wear? The clothes are still in the dryer, so I walk over to pull out something appropriate. (The dryer is loaded from the front and convenient to use). I find a blouse and decide to wear it with a jumper.[1]

Ironing is not my favorite occupation, and I consider wearing it unironed. A closer look shows the wrinkles will spoil the whole effect. There is no way to avoid it; if I want to look presentable, it has to be ironed. It's no trouble really, the ironing board does collapse to my

---

1   A jumper in New Zealand is called a tunic.

height. I let the iron heat, while I go and lay my other clothes out on the bed.

I flick through the hangers in the wardrobe until I find the jumper. There is no high reaching. The rod is only about three inches above my head.[1] It was easily lowered with a spring loaded adjustable closet rod[2] and secured by wiring between the upper and lower rods.

I lay the jumper on the bed with my underwear, and return to iron the blouse. The wrinkles removed I switch the iron off, bring the blouse to the bedroom, and head for the bathroom. It is not enough to just have clean clothes.

The landlord's design did not consider a stature as short as mine, and I must turn the light on by pulling down on the piece of wooden dowel hanging from the switch. (After my lease expires, I don't think the landlord will notice the small hole I had drilled in the plastic part of the switch). The dowel has a hole drilled in it too, and is joined to the switch by a safety pin threaded through both holes.[3] Simple, but effective. (In my dream home, of course, the lights will be within reach).

A piece of dowel is also attached to the end hooks of the shower curtain. This means I can pull the curtain backwards and forwards without ripping it, and separating it from the hooks. I can no longer be falsely accused of being in a tearing hurry. With the dowel, I can lift and slide the shower curtain. By chance, the taps are within reach and no tall Jo has sent the spray shooting across my head to cascade down the walls of the shower. In my dream house, none of this would be left to chance. Never again would I need to climb out of the shower to find a broom to angle the shower head at the floor and away from the walls. The head would be detachable. To save always holding it, I would install a grip for it at two levels: a lower one for me, and a higher one for my guests. As a final touch, after a hard day at the office, I would be sure to install a seat where I could blissfully sit under the soothing spray.

I'm dreaming again, and time is running away with me. I turn the

---

1   Mary O'Donnell, *"The Idea Machine: a booklet of handy hints for more convenient living by everyone,"* I(C)(4)(a), p 6 (about 1978).

2   ibid, II(C)(3), p 10.

3   ibid, I(C)(6)(b), p 6 (about 1978). An alternative is to fit a light switch extender over the existing wall switch. Such a device is available from the Central Florida chapter, Little People of America, Inc.

water off and climb out to dry myself down. The towel is within easy reach and I mop up all the drips. Even daily calisthenics wouldn't help me reach my toes and I must dry between them with a cotton bud.

The vanity unit is only accessible with a stool and I climb up to clean my teeth. (I could have saved this step by cleaning my teeth in the shower, but I was so engrossed in planning my dream home that I forgot to get my toothbrush). Now there is no more time for dreaming, but it takes no imagination to know that there would be no need for that stool in my design home.

I presume all looks clean and sparkling (I can't see into the bathroom mirror to check even when standing on the stool) and return to the bedroom to dress. As usual, I'm racing the clock and must rush out of the house without putting on any make-up. Anyway, it would be wasted effort as it would only be removed at the hairdresser's.

At the hairdressers

I walk in the shop relieved to be only a minute after the appointment time. My aunt works there and is pleased to see me. She invites me to follow her to the back of the salon.

Unlike the average customer, when I sit in the chair at the basin to have my hair washed, my head does not lie back in the cradle. Efforts have been made to increase my height with cushions and boxes. Although they make me taller, everything slips from under me when I lean back to place my head in the cradle. I quickly lose my lofty position.

I finally put an end to the discomfort and paraphernalia. Instead of sitting in the chair and leaning back, I now stand on the floor on two telephone books, and bend my head forward into the sink. My face gets wet (which is how I lose my make-up), but it's no different than washing my hair at home in the shower. The job is done without any great fuss; that's how I like it. (Another way is to wash your hair before you go to the salon and let them dampen it again with a water spray).

I chit-chat with my aunt while the hairdresser does her work. Finally, the hair is cut and combed into place. My aunt conducts me into the drying room where I am boosted under the drying cylinder with a bulky cushion. She leaves me to put on my make-up and returns to her work, but not before bringing me a cup of tea. The noise of the dryer cuts me off from the rest of the world, and I concentrate on drawing straight lines with my eye-liner brush. The hair is soon dry and I climb down from the dryer. I pay the fee, farewell my aunt and walk out to the car.

Parking

The parking lot is busy and I take care not to walk behind a parked car without checking if there is a driver preparing to pull out. My presence would not alert them that the way was not clear. They have no chance of seeing me, so I must be on the lookout for them.

I make it to the car safely, and begin my drive into the city to meet Deborah. I park the car in a nearby parking building, and walk the short distance to the theater. Since I can't walk very far without getting tired, I always park as close as possible to where I'm going. I applaud the day that brought in parking permits, and facilities for drivers with disabilities to overstay parking meters without extra cost.

At the movies

I approach the theater and see Deborah is waiting for me. That's not surprising since I'm running late, but there is no time to fret about it. We need to hurry in and get our tickets. Deborah buys them, while I get us some nibbles. The theater lights are out when we enter. The usher shines his flash-light[1] into the center of the row. We thought it better to follow instructions than disturb everyone with whisperings about better seating. Instead, we disturb only those people whose feet we stumble over on the way to the center. Finally, we are seated. There's only one small problem. I can't see, not even by sitting on the upturned edge of the seat. (Today, I forgot to bring a cushion, but the few inches it gives wouldn't have helped any).

We were in such a hurry we never thought to arrange an aisle seat at the ticket office. We conferred for a moment, and Deborah decided to track out past everyone again. She would look for the usher, and see if he couldn't find us better seating. It was embarrassing, but I wasn't going to waste my money staring blankly at the outline of a person's

---

1   Referred to in New Zealand as a torch.

head. I have yet to find one that is transparent.

The usher was especially helpful and practically fell over himself with apologies for not having thought. Deb beckoned for me to follow her, and I tripped over everyone's feet again on the way out. We were shown to a seat where we both had a clear view, and finally settled back to enjoy the movie. The trailers were just finishing.

To my surprise, the usher was soon back at my side. He was offering us prize seats at no extra cost. We appreciated his concern, but declined to make a third move, especially as the seats offered were upstairs. At the end of the movie, I needed to use the conveniences. (I have long since learned that public bathrooms are more an inconvenience than a convenience). However, I do not let that stop me from using them. Tonight, I am fully prepared.

In this bathroom, there is a partial concession. I can reach the lock on the toilet door. It must have been an accident, because I still can't reach the tap or towels to wash and dry my hands. The solution is to carry moist towlettes in my handbag. When I can reach the tap but not the towels, I use the water and dry my hands on toilet paper. Since the bathroom mirror is mostly out of sight, I carry a hand-mirror in my handbag. Poor design does not have to prevent me from keeping up appearances.[1]

At a night-club

It's just as well I tidy up because as I leave, Deborah suggests we go to Oscar's night-club where we can have a dance or two, and get something to eat. Not having been there and always game to try something new, I agreed. Besides, I hadn't eaten dinner, and the idea of food was appealing.

We were approved for entry by the doorman, and walked in. What a crowd! There were people everywhere. I walked very close behind Deborah so as not to get trampled. On the way across the room, she met a waiter friend. She wanted to introduce me. He came up to us car-

---

1   For further discussion of barriers in bathrooms refer to Chapter 5, *"At Your Physical Pleasure."*

rying his tray, and was obviously pleased to see Deborah. They chatted for a minute or so, but the two feet difference in our height meant I couldn't hear a word they were saying. The club lent itself to intimate conversations, as you had to be very close to hear anything above the noise of the band.

In these circumstances, when I want to have conversation with someone, I invite them to sit down so we can talk eye to eye, ear to mouth. The only problem is that you have to be very forward to suggest this to strangers. I usually don't.

Deborah did try to include me in her conversation. She turned to me and said to her friend, *"Oh, I'd like you to meet my sister."* He looked around for me and said, *"Where? I don't see anyone."* She pointed down and said, *"Here, this is my sister Angela."* He looked down, but still couldn't see me. I was hidden beneath his cocktail tray! He was so embarrassed to find me standing beneath it, that he only managed to say hello, before using the same tray as an excuse to return to his work.

We ordered a drink, but changed our mind about the food when we saw the prices on the menu. One guy at our table got into a conversation and shared a dance with us, but Deb was disappointed not to find any of her friends. She said it was a dull night and we left in less than an hour.

We said good night to each other and drove home to our separate houses. On the way home my mind returned to young Kevin and the many Little People like him struggling with their identity. I hoped that he would have the courage and determination to learn the skills of *"doing things differently,"* so that he could join in the chorus, *"I can do everything I want. My size does not stop me from doing anything."*

Chapter Eight

SHARED

First Encounters with Little People

I was enjoying the show like any other eight year old kid in the crowd. It was the school holidays and this was our family treat. We didn't get to many live shows and this was one of the classics. The story was very familiar, as it was read to us as kids over and over again: *"Snow White and the Seven Dwarfs."* The play was great, but somehow I don't think it was the performance which makes the drama stand out in my mind. No, I'm sure it was because this was my first time to see other Little People. My mother took the opportunity to explain, that when I grew up I would be short just like the Little People in the play. It registered that although the dwarfs had not grown up in the regular sense of the words, they were in fact 'grown ups.'

At the time, it was no *"big deal;"* I already knew I was different from the other kids. Now, I also knew that I would still be different when I grew up. (I can't ever recall thinking, 'one day I will be like everyone else'). My only interest in the dwarfs, was to try and work out how old they were.

I didn't see another Little Person until I was thirteen. The experience was far from the delight of the childhood fairy tale. This time there was only one dwarf and I couldn't have cared less how old he was. The further away he was from me, the happier I felt.

We met in my first year of high school. Our encounters usually happened when my girl friends and I were walking around the school grounds in a morning or lunch break. Whenever I saw Tim my reactions were extreme. I would try to hide behind the skirts of my girlfriends, or sometimes even duck away down the side of the closest building.

I didn't have to wonder how old he was. He was a year ahead of me in school and I didn't need anyone to tell me he was a dwarf. That was very obvious! My reluctance to meet was nothing against him personally. No, it was the way his boyfriends reacted when Tim and I were anywhere near each other. Every time they saw me, they would chant at him riotously, *"Here she comes, here comes your girlfriend."*

Neither of us appreciated their antics and Tim was just as diligent in his efforts to avoid me. We exercised a self-imposed quarantine from each other, but we were not always successful. On the days we failed to avoid meeting, Tim would have to resist his friends' efforts as they pushed him toward me saying, *"Go on, go on, kiss her, kiss her, she's just right for you."* That was all I ever heard, as I would disappear long before there was any chance of a successful thrust.

At no time in our two years at the same school, did we ever speak to each other. Our only communication was mutual recognition of the other's embarrassment. I sincerely regret this now, as we had so much to share. It hurts to know that we never shared any of it with each other.

A common heritage

As Little People, Tim and I shared a common heritage recorded in both history and folklore. Our concerns in life had to be so similar: contending with the disabling influence of others' attitudes;[1] learning how to deal with all the attention we get;[2] living in a world at the physical pleasure of others;[3] and finding self-esteem.

If things had been different, Tim and I could have shared many aspects of our history. We could only regret that people like us were regarded as freaks and living exhibits in fairs, dime museums, traveling shows, carnivals and circuses. The General Tom Thumb exhibit was billed as, *"the most interesting and extraordinary natural curiosity of which the world has ever known."* Many Little People were a fascination to the mocking public who paid a fee to come and gawk and make fun.

---

1   See Chapter 6, *"Attitudes Disable."*
2   See Chapter 9, *"Attention Gives Opportunity."*
3   See Chapter 5, *"At Your Physical Pleasure."*

At the same time, Tim and I could boast about other Little People who were smart enough to take advantage of their appeal. They became valuable members in the courts of monarchs and households of the upper classes. They cashed in on their attraction and made themselves very comfortable.

Tim and I could have occupied ourselves for hours discussing the achievements of many Little People: Henri de Toulouse-Lautrec; Charles Steinmetz; Michael Dunn; Charles Stratton (more popularly known as Tom Thumb); -- - the list is endless. Hy Roth and Robert Cromie in their book *"The Little People,"* [1] well document some of our achievements in history as spies, scholars, military and religious leaders, politicians, artists and photographers, writers and people in advertising. Tim and I had much to be proud of. In days of extreme prejudice, Little People established themselves well enough to make the history books and share with us their example.

A comment credited to General Tom Thumb, at the time he met the young Prince of Wales in the English court of Queen Victoria could have helped both Tim and me. Tom Thumb is said to have measured himself against the Prince, and when noticing the Prince was taller went on to say, *"The Prince is taller than I am, but I feel as big as anybody."* [2] Indeed this was a double challenge, as Tom had ranked himself equal, not just in size, but also in the importance which belongs only to royalty.

Of course, Tim and I would have to puzzle about where our place in history began, though depictions in cave-drawings indicate it must have been thousands of years ago. Yet, we knew enough to recognize that the day's events soon slip into yesterday and the day before and last week and in time actually become part of our history. We could have been challenged to take responsibility for our heritage, to live each day so that it would slip into yesterday with dignity and make our history something to be proud of.

Tim knew as well as I did that Little People are no longer servants

1   Everest House Publishers, 1133 Avenue of the Americas, New York, N.Y. 10036.
2   ibid.

and 'side-show' exhibits, but we could both ask whether we are still 'on show.' We may not be billed as *"Great Curiosities,"* but we still attract great curiosity and interest; we may not be exhibited as the tallest and the shortest, but we know people are still delighted to see the two height extremes.

I could tell Tim about the day I entered a store to buy something. A man followed me in and asked how tall I was. When hearing I was three feet four inches he was ecstatic. I thought his reaction was very strange, until he told me of his experience in England many years before.

He had been passing a building when he came across a great crowd waiting for someone to exit. He joined them not wanting to miss anything. Before long, a woman came out. He considered his wait worth every minute when he saw the woman was over seven feet tall. Seeing me put him into ecstasy, because now he had seen one of the tallest and one of the shortest. There's no doubt in my mind that he would have paid to see us exhibited together.

History gave Little People like Tim and myself two choices: to be an exhibit; or to hide away from the public view. Who knows what choice we would have made. Many Little People chose to hide. Yet even the 'hidden people' became known. What society could not see, they depicted through their imaginations in folklore. Even today, Tim and I could marvel at how people mistake us for elves and sprites, *"the children of nature."*

At Christmas, we are expected to be Santa's helpers. I don't really mind that, since people of all sizes are assigned fictitious roles at Christmas, but I do object to the invitation to be a leprechaun on Saint Patrick's day. I have no resemblance nor desire to dress like an old man wrinkled and knobby.

If it's a person's profession to represent such creatures, it is understood they play a role in fantasy. However, we're not on stage and in reality do not expect an invitation to be leprechauns. For me it's not enough that I have green eyes and green is my favorite color. Anybody trying to entice me, soon learns I'm too much a handful!

You might think all this sounds ridiculous; who really thinks of today's Little People as leprechauns? If you're having trouble, here's an experience I shared with another Little Person.

We were having a meal in a restaurant on Saint Patrick's Day when an Irishman targeted our table. He asked for permission to tell us a joke and proceeded to do so before we could say no. As expected, he did not settle for one joke and was just finishing his third, when my friend interrupted him saying, *"Well, thank you very much, we enjoyed your jokes, but really there are some things I want to discuss privately with Angela."* Surprisingly, the man got the message straight away and prepared to leave. His parting words however, were the biggest joke of all. He invited us to be his leprechauns at the local Saint Patrick's Day Parade. For him it wasn't make believe, we were the real thing!

Folklore has given people many misconceptions about Little People. One tale instructs that we are always happy. The folklore, talks of dwarfs (the generic name for dark elves) who live in forests and mountains and are known to be 'good natured creatures.' Tim and I could both dispute that one. We have just as many ups and downs as other people. Besides, a thorough student of folklore would know this species of dwarf is almost extinct.[1]

Others believe that we, like gnomes, live for hundreds of years without aging. If only that were true. It must have been this confusion which continually led people to mistake a middle-aged couple of the 1980's, for the aged couple who lived in the same area in the 1940's. For the 1980 couple to be the Little People of the 1940's, they would now be in their one hundred and thirtieth year!

Tim would know how some regard it as good luck to meet a Little Person. We are mistaken for pixies who are known to guide travelers at night and for fairies who protect and are special friends to children. Although this often means people's response to us is warm and friendly, it also means we're not to be taken seriously!

Yet some folklore reflects a reality that we can live with today. For example brownies, the good natured Little People of Scotland, are known for helping farmers with their chores and as very hard workers. If people want to mistake us for one of the 'hidden people,' why not mistake us for brownies? Then maybe Tim and I would have a better

---

1   Nancy Arrowsmith and George Moore, *"A Field Guide to the Little People"* (1979).

chance getting our employment applications favorably received.

Knowing the wisdom of *"the Little Elf Man"* would have been very helpful to us. When he was asked why he didn't grow, he replied, *"I'm just as big for me, as you are for you!"* [1]

The thriving folklore market was something for Tim and I to ponder. A quick drive in suburbia would lead to an easy conclusion that the garden gnome is alive and well. But, would we notice the gnomes shaking their heads, or even know their reason for doing it? Folklore says, *"it is in wonder at the narrowness and stupidity of men."* [2] We could certainly relate to that part of the gnomes' identity. We could even join the garden gnome and shake our heads in wonder at the inability of people to understand the distinction between reality and fiction. Why don't they understand that we are real people with feelings and not animated creatures of fantasy?

Coming to terms with identity as Little Person

Yet in spite of our shared heritage and experience, Tim and I shared nothing with each other. Actually we would never be free to share with each other until we came to terms with our identity as Little People; could accept other Little People as equals; were willing to give up the pedestal given us by society; and could comfortably live in the world of both average-sized and Little People.

The first task for Tim and myself was to come to terms with our identity as Little People. Maybe that was part of our problem in high school and the behavior of his aggressive boyfriends was only a convenient excuse for our avoidance of each other. If that's the case, we wouldn't be alone. Many Little People have difficulty coming to terms with their identity.

You can see it clearly when two Little People meet on the street, well, almost meet. The one not able to accept his or her size, will immediately look for a means of escape. To make sure there is no contact they will disappear down the nearest side-alley, or dart as quick as

---

1   Gyo Fujukawa, *"Come Follow Me --- to the Secret World of Elves and Fairies and Gnomes and Trolls."*

2   Wil Huygen (text) and Rien Povitvliet (illustrations), *"Gnomes"* (1979).

lightening into the closest store. (Sounds awfully like my escape from Tim doesn't it?).

When you haven't accepted that you're a dwarf, meeting another Little Person is very traumatic. Until you're confronted by another dwarf, you can successfully deny or forget you are different. The meeting destroys the fantasy and the reality of your true size is reflected in the other person. For many, the image is too painful and they refuse to see themselves as they really look.

Many Little People confess to having felt this way at one time. One person reported to Joan Ablon, a medical anthropologist from the University of California in San Francisco:

"if I saw another Little Person, I'd go around the block because I saw myself. I just didn't want to look at that. I couldn't stand to look at myself. Because I wasn't a dwarf, (sarcastically), I just had rickets." [1]

Ironically, one way for Tim and me to learn self-acceptance is to mix with other Little People. The interaction forces us to look at ourselves and other people. We would see ourselves as we really are, as other people see us, as dwarfs. Some have even gone so far as to say, *"You can't ever see yourself, until you see other Little People. You have to relate to yourself as a Little Person, by relating to others as Little People."* [2]

Yet the solution is not easily accepted and even when Little People know each other it is common for them to avoid and be antagonistic toward each other. Roberta, a friend of mine who is a Little Person, told me how Tommy, a boy in her class, reacted toward her the day of their graduation.

Tommy was about four feet six inches. By total coincidence, Roberta and Tommy were paired together in the procession. He was so disturbed by this, that he forgot all rehearsal drills and took off, leaving Roberta trailing behind. She says, *"He literally ran up the aisle and left me. I had no way of keeping up with him."* Roberta's analysis is simple. *"He didn't want to be seen with me; he saw himself as short,*

---

1   Joan Ablon, *"Little People in America: the Social Dimensions of Dwarfism"* (1984), Praeger Press.
2   ibid.

but no way did he want to be seen as being a dwarf." She believes that
Tommy perceived any association with her as being likely to invite his
being labeled as a dwarf and that was the last thing he wanted to happen.

This denial and pretense is fueled by the view the public has of Little People. To be a Little Person or have a child who is a Little Person
is seen by some as tragic and an unbearable burden. Many people react
negatively to the sight of a Little Person. There is ridicule, shock, con-
descension, pity, over-protection, and misconception, to name only a
few reactions. These alone make it necessary for some Little People to
avoid seeing themselves as they are. That is where the real tragedy lies.
Little People are not only denying their size, but are also denied the opportunity to share with others of short-stature.

Fortunately, not all Little People practice self-denial and for those
who do it is possible to change. With time and encouragement, it is
possible to come to terms with yourself. However, self-acceptance is
only the first step Tim and I must take. Our sharing will only be meaningful, if we can accept each other as equals.

Dwarfs have no edge on sensitivity

Dwarfs are not immune to the temptations average-sized people
have when meeting someone shorter. Little People like anybody else
can be quite overwhelmed. We may even be guilty of asking that infuriating question, *"How tall are you?"*

One person of three feet four inches says he had never met anyone
shorter than himself. He couldn't believe it when he met someone
several inches shorter. He introduced himself saying, *"I am so pleased
to meet you."* The shorter woman was impressed at the warmth of his
greeting and replied, *"Well thank you, I'm very pleased to meet you
also."* Her bubble was soon burst when he continued, *"You know, you
are the first person I have met who is shorter than me. Tell me, how
tall are you?"* He didn't know how close he was to getting hit on the
head. Of all people, he should have known better.

Another Little Person when finding that he was one of the taller
members present wanted to go around helping everyone. When he
called one woman, *"Honey,"* he was quickly censured. She reminded
him of his own dislike for people endearing themselves with such

patronizing descriptions. He couldn't believe it. He had behaved in exactly the way average-sized people do when they first meet him.

I read a newspaper report about some of the Little People in the cast of *"Under the Rainbow."* [1] They spoke about the shortest member of the cast, who was two feet nine inches. Who do you think were the ones saying how cute he was, and how much they would like to pick him up and cuddle him? It was the Little People!

Actually Little People share a lot of the stereotypes demonstrated by average-sized people. This is especially apparent when male and female Little People are paired up. The male looks for someone shorter and the female looks for someone taller. People too tall or too short are rejected. I actually heard a dwarf woman tell a dwarf guy several inches shorter than she was, *"I can't go out with you because you're too short."*

The plain truth is that we Little People do to each other, just what others do to us. We are a part of the society, which makes life difficult for others, yes, even for other Little People. We do not have an edge on sensitivity. That is something we must all learn.

Rejecting the position of prominence

Society has had another inhibiting effect on the ability of Little People to share with each other. All our lives wherever we have gone people have looked at us and taken a special interest. After years of people reacting this way, it's so easy to accept this extra attention and very hard to reject it. Yet until we are willing to give it up, Tim and I will have extreme difficulty sharing with each other.

This struggle is most apparent at Little People meetings. The majority of people present are short-statured and size is no longer something which makes you stand out. You are just one of the crowd. The sudden loss of automatic distinction and popularity can be a great shock and may account for why so many Little People cannot share with others of similar stature.

While society may place Little People on a pedestal, it has not

---

1   A film released in the United States in 1981.

removed our right to accept or reject the position. If Tim and I are to have any chance of sharing with each other, we must reject the elevation. We must step down from the pedestal. I first discovered this in 1968.

It was the inaugural meeting of the Little People of New Zealand and I was sixteen. I considered myself to be a well-adjusted adolescent and was oblivious to the existence of any pedestal. I arrived at the meeting totally unprepared.

I expected to stand out in the group as someone extraordinary. I thought I had it all together and would be able to contribute so much. After all, I had a good mind; was moderately good looking and had always been very popular. It was total deflation to discover I had no position of prominence or popularity. If anything, I was very ordinary. For the first time in my life, I was truly just one of the crowd.

I realized that all the special attention over the years had led me to see myself as being more important than other people and certainly more important than I really was. My ability to share with other Little People was very limited. In the presence of so many other short-statured people my perception of superiority was shattered. I learned that I was no more or less, just equal.

My ability to find a place in the group was totally dependent on the real me. Height no longer shielded me from meaningful interaction and the eye to eye communication left little room for pretense. I learned to appreciate the opportunity to base relationships on factors unrelated to size. I knew that when other Little People chose me as a friend, it had nothing to do with misguided sympathy or admiration.

The best of both worlds

Yet even after giving up that special place, there was another barrier which could prevent Tim and me from sharing. It was my hang up for a very long time.

I feared that if I mixed with Little People, the public would limit me to socializing with Little People and separate me from the mainstream community. For years, I struggled to find an equal place in the world of average-sized people and I was concerned that if I joined an organization for short-statured individuals, a social boundary would be drawn around me limiting me to the group where they thought I belonged. I didn't want to take the risk of losing my position among the average-sized.

Admittedly, this fear didn't stop me from attending my first meeting (my curiosity was too great), but I was very careful not to be seen in public with Little People. I didn't overcome this fear until I recognized that I was responsible for drawing my own social boundaries and that other people's attitudes should not govern my activity, especially when their attitudes dictated who I should spend my time with.

I finally decided to exercise my right to associate with whomever I pleased. Until I reached that point, my sharing with Tim or any other Little Person would only have been superficial. I'd always be worried about someone seeing us together.

I realized that 'making it' in the average-sized world is not synonymous with rejecting my place in the world of short-statured persons. Many boast of their success among the average-sized and have used as their index, lack of the need to associate with Little People. They see the need to be with Little People as a stage you grow out of. It is certainly a stage, but now I know it is a stage you grow into.

Little People have a place in both worlds, all we have to do is find it. In fact, we have the best of both worlds, that is among both short and average-sized people. I appreciate the wisdom of Dallas Ziska, a member of the Little People of America, Inc., who put it this way:

> *"a person who finds happiness in both worlds,*
> *(small and big)*
> *has nothing to lose to society or himself,*
> *but a person who hides in one of the two worlds,*
> *must always live with the fear of evasion or*
> *contact with the other world.*
> *For this person there is no real truth,*
> *not even to himself."*

Only after Tim and I had knocked down all the barriers would it be possible for us to share a meaningful relationship with each other. At that point, we could add a whole new dimension to our lives. However, the danger is that once Tim and I are able to share with each other, we will decide not to. We may become too engrossed in our own lives and we won't make time to help people who have problems and need counsel from those who have succeeded in similar battles.

Yet even if we reach the point where self-interest is our only motivation, it will still be in our own interest to step in and help. That's because the public sees us as one and the same. I'm sure that as self-sufficient Little People, we wouldn't want to be mistaken for the maladjusted! We will be remembered by our least common denominator!

Finding other Little People

Tim and I may both be ready, willing and able to meet and share with other Little People, but if we leave it up to chance the opportunity will rarely present itself. A chance meeting of two Little People is uncommon. That is because the incidence of dwarfism in the population is rare. Just how rare is a subject of medical debate. For example, the incidence of achondroplasia, the most common type of dwarfism,[1] has been reported over the years by different studies at widely variant rates, ranging from one in 10,000 to one in 40,000 births.[2] It has recently been said that a reasonable estimate for the United States is that achondroplasia occurs once in approximately 30,000 births.[3] This estimate compares well with actual Italian Birth Registry statistics which report the incidence of achondroplasia as one in 27,000 births.[4]

---

1   David L. Rimoin, *"The Chondrodystrophies,"* Advances in Human
     Genetics, Volume V (about 1974).

2   Willard R. Centerwall and Seigried A. Centerwall, *"An Introduction to
     Your Child who has Achondroplasia,"* Light for the Way Series,
     Booklet No. 30 (1986).

3   ibid.

4   Judith G. Hall, *"Summary of the First International Conference on
     Human Achondroplasia,"* Newsletter of the Little People of Canada
     (1986).

Inevitably, the varying reports of the incidence of achondroplasia, combined with estimates of the numbers of dwarfs in the other one hundred or more different conditions of short-stature,[1] has resulted in varying estimates of the dwarf population in the United States. The estimates have been as low as 20,000 and as high as 100,000.[2] However, until dwarfism becomes a subject of census analysis in the United States, the debate will continue. Without the benefit of reliable statistics[3] it is necessary to continue estimating the number of Little People in the United States. In the United States, just to give an idea of how unlikely a chance meeting of two Little People with achondroplasia is, there may be as few as 5,750[4] or as many as 23,000 spread throughout the country.[5]

However many more or less dwarfs in the population, it is true to say a person could live for years and never meet another Little Person. This is even more likely if the person lives in the smaller population of a rural community and seldom moves out of the area. This means when we see another Little Person, it pays to take advantage of the situation, because chance may not offer a meeting with another Little Person again. Consequently, it won't be of much use for Tim and I to sit around waiting for a chance meeting. Rather, we'd be better off actively seeking the company of other Little People.

Actually, we might begin our search for an entirely different reason. If we experience physical problems, we may come to a clinic or medical symposium in search of qualified advisors specialized in at-

---

1   John G. Rogers and Joan O. Weiss, *"My Child is a Dwarf,"* Little People of America, Inc., and Little People of America Foundation (1979).

2   Joseph A. Bailey, *"Disproportionate Short Stature: Diagnosis and Management"* (1973); Joan O. Weiss, *"Social Development of Dwarfs"* (1977); Charles I. Scott, Jr., letter to Robert Van Etten of the Architectural and Transportation Barriers Compliance Board (April 23, 1981).

3   David L. Rimoin has stated that there are no adequate studies available based on accurate diagnostic criteria to provide an accurate prevalence figure, see *"The Chondrodystrophies,"* Advances in Human Genetics, Volume V (about 1974).

4   This estimate is based on the incidence of one in 40,000 births and a population of 230 million.

5   This estimate is based on the incidence of one in 10,000 births and a population of 230 million.

tending to the medical needs of Little People. At the same time, we may discover a room full of Little People also waiting to see a physician. This presents the opportunity to attend to our medical needs and to begin relationships with the Little People we meet at the clinic or symposium.

Public reaction to groups of Little People

Yet Tim and I don't have to wait for a medical problem to find other Little People. We can locate the nearest organization of Little People and begin attending their meetings. That's not to say joining the group will be the end of all our troubles. If anything, the fact of our meeting will add another burden, the compounded public reaction.

To see one Little Person is more than some people can handle politely, but to see two or three together throws them into delirium. Their behavior can become quite obnoxious. My aunt told me how she felt when attending a film with two Little People. She said it like this, *"The stares of the public were something to be endured and ignored, but when there were two of like stature, the public became almost offensive."*

I vividly recall an occasion of such offensive behavior. I was waiting in the car for two Little People doing the weekend shopping. There were a group of young teen-age boys standing at the corner of the supermarket when the two girls came out and started walking toward the car. The boys couldn't believe the sight of two Little People together and had a wonderful time at the girls' expense, mimicing, jeering, gesticulating, you name it, they did it.

The girls walked on without the bat of an eyelid, quite used to hearing such nonsense. What's more the girls made no comment when they got in the car, as if they had blocked out the whole performance. However, I was not in the mood to do that. I was furious and wanted to go and tell the boys where to get off, but I knew my appearance on the scene would have been like a red rag to a bull. I did nothing but fume quietly. However, you can't hide the smoke forever.

People are not always so rude, though their behavior can be very tiresome. There are people who find it difficult to distinguish between us. Even when a Little Person has known someone for many years, when another Little Person comes into the room, the person sometimes can't tell us apart. The confusion can even be between two Little People who look nothing like each other. This happened to me when attending a wedding with my friend Cathy.

Her sister was being married and all the family and neighbors were present. Cathy is four feet four inches with blond straight hair and I'm three feet four inches with dark curly hair. We don't have the same type of dwarfism and so our body proportions are quite different. In fact, the only similarity between us is our feminine gender. Cathy and I were together most of the day and so the guests were well aware that there were two Little People at the wedding. We had been noticed. The confusion occurred at the party after the wedding.

One of the neighbors came up to me and said, *"Hello Cathy. How are you?"* An aunt, quite horrified, interceded saying, *"This is not Cathy; this is Angela,"* and looked at me apologetically. Somehow the neighbor still didn't comprehend. When Cathy came and sat down next to me, the neighbor was obviously confused. Ironically, Cathy's two average-sized identical twin sisters were also at the wedding. This created a double puzzle, for the people had to distinguish between the twins and the dwarfs.

Others mistake us for each other and refuse to be told they are in error. It doesn't matter what you tell them. Take for example the person installing a telephone in my office. He asked if I went to the local technical college. I told him no, but he insisted that I did because he had seen me there. Even though I said it must be another Little Person, he refused to accept it.

Occasionally it is excusable for a person to mistake one Little Person for another, as some of us do look alike. This is especially common when the two Little People are about the same age and have the same type of dwarfism. Among ourselves, Little People will even comment how much resemblance there is between two short-statured people.

The mistake is most likely when the two are not together. A group of us have joked about two Little People doing an exchange, just to see how many would notice. One company manager is sure that a male Little Person of the same type could walk into his place of business, which is closely controlled by security and where he has worked more than twenty years and not be challenged as an intruder.

However, the confusion is not always a laughing matter. A conse-

182

quence of continually winning the look alike contest and being taken as having the same interests as another Little Person frequently means people have difficulty accepting us as individuals. Not to be recognized or known for yourself, time after time, can result in suppression of your own personality. There is a danger of losing it altogether.

Maybe it would be all right to be known as someone else, if the other person was everything you ever wanted to be in terms of wealth, looks and ability. But how often would that happen? Tim and I have two choices: to accept the preconceived image of the other Little Person and become like that person; or break-free and be ourselves. I'm sure our choice would be no different than that of most people. We would choose to be ourselves.

People mistake us for each other when they know more than one Little Person. It is also common for them to attribute the interests and abilities of one Little Person to the other. The classic illustration of this belief is when you are approached and asked if you're in the circus or a midget wrestler. (People usually ask me if I'm in the circus; I must look more like a clown than a wrestler!)

One day such an approach was made while I was waiting to cross the street. I noticed a man looking at me, but didn't think anything of it as people look at me wherever I go. The road cleared and as I started crossing the street the man called me. By the time I had the car unlocked, he had crossed the road and came over to my car.

He said he had a job for me. I told him I didn't need a job, as I was already working. This didn't put him off at all. He said he had a better job (even though he didn't know what my job was) and offered me a position in the circus! Here was my opportunity for travel and excitement. He honestly thought that was all I could be looking for and couldn't understand why I turned away from my destiny.

Others believe that Little People all know each other. Sometimes I try to figure out where these crazy ideas come from, but it is mostly wasted energy. I've yet to find a satisfactory answer. However, it has occurred to me that the notion may be linked with the belief that Little People all travel the world together in the circus and of course that is how we get to meet and know all Little People!

This idea that Little People all know each other was presented to me by an Englishman at the time we were introduced. He was the friend of a friend, and visited our home just before taking his return flight to England. His opening remark was, *"I know your friend."* At first I took him at his word and began to think of friends of mine in England that he may have met. After a few questions to find who he could be referring to, I discovered that his reference was to another Little Person. At the time, I knew no Little People in England. I was most irritated. He was one of those who not only believed all Little People know each other, but also that we all have similar interests. Based on these two premises, he concluded that we also had to be friends.

How ridiculous this is. How could Little People possibly have the time to be friends with everyone? Apart from that, we do not all share the same interests. Our height may be all that is common; after that, we represent the same range of differences and likenesses as any group in society.

In a large meeting of Little People, we are very likely to find people who will become our friends, but the process is the same as for other people. All Little People will not be my friends, neither will I only have friends of short-stature. To limit my field for choosing friends, to a group less than four feet ten inches disturbs me. Tim and I should refuse to limit our circle to people within inches of our height.

Sizing up a suitable marriage partner

Members of the public frequently see some Little People as much more than just friends. Automatically a male and female Little Person are paired as a ready-made couple. You may have dismissed my earlier description of the boys at school pushing Tim and me together as teenage antics which are only left on record in a school girl's journal. I wish that were true, but my experience as an adult demonstrates that although the boyish style of prank is left in the youthful years, the belief and expressions are not.

I remember being at a weekend conference of Little People. We were at the railway station to greet some of the arriving members. Gary and Helen were walking ahead chatting cozily. They were pleased to see each other after a long break and showed their pleasure by holding hands, not such an extraordinary thing to do really. Men and women do it all the time; in fact, other men and women were holding hands on the same railway platform. Their behavior did not cause anyone to react.

Yet a man on the platform came up to Gary and Helen and extended his hand to Gary offering his congratulations. They were not in order. We could only guess at the reason for the man's delight. No doubt he interpreted their holding hands to mean they were hitched. He had no idea if this was the beginning of a friendship, if they were engaged, or even married. However he assumed (as do many others) they were well-matched because they were both Little People.

The same thing happened to Gary another day when he was walking with me and we were not even holding hands. The security person of the building where Gary worked came to him saying how pleased he was that he had found himself a wife. It was the first we knew about it! Gary knew from experience, that courting and compatibility are not so easily found.

Many beliefs that people have about Little People sound so absurd (at least I hope they do) I can hardly believe them as I write. I would even like to think these ideas belong to an eccentric few, but there is no evidence to support such a view. There are just too many instances of this sort of thing happening.

Little People mostly dismiss the behavior as foolishness. Some of the incidents even make amusing anecdotes and can bring great hilarity to a group of us, each trying to top the others story of *"what about the time --- ?"* Some of the behavior and attitudes expressed however, are cause for great concern and have grave consequences.

The most serious effect is on two Little People beginning a relationship. They are not given time or breathing space to find out if they are in fact suited to one another. Many are assured by average-sized friends that their relationship will be stable and secure, because they are the same height. Tim and I knew the absurdity of that belief.

I have yet to read a book counseling couples on things to look for when building a relationship which says size is a significant factor. How many couples do you know who were assured their marriage would work simply because of their proximity in height?

Yet many Little People have been pressured into believing that their marriage will work, because they have their height in common. This is supposed to make them understand, love, and communicate with each other? Height does none of these things. All height gives you in common is to know what it's like to be short. It teaches nothing about living together 'happily ever after.'

Experience has proven that many marriages founded on this basis have resulted in very poor matches, between people with nothing in common. Disappointment and heartache are an inevitable outcome. Tim and I resisted being pushed together and the attempts made us very angry. Sadly, many Little People are more concerned about finding a mate and do not realize the mistake they are making. They have been brainwashed into believing the public view, that Little People go together like peas in a pod.

The reverse side of the coin is the belief that Little People do not go well with average-sized persons. John Strudwick at three feet eight inches and nineteen years talked of his efforts to get a date with a girl on the college campus. One girl said to him, *"Why don't you go out with someone your own size?"* He didn't buy that. He explained his philosophy to a newspaper reporter this way:

"Everybody's the same to me. I don't go around asking if a girl is five feet two inches and I don't expect them to ask how tall I am. If it clicks between me and a girl, that's all that matters." [1]

Many Little People have a different reaction than John's and will only seek a spouse among those their own size. Those Little People who venture outside the group for a marriage partner are tainted with entering a 'mixed marriage.' Other Little People are perplexed and ask, *"Why? How could you marry an average-sized person?"* The answer is too simple for some to accept --- love!

Adrian tells of a day she attended her first meeting of the Little People of America, Inc., (LPA). She was standing and talking with a group of Little People, who started out as very open and friendly. They noticed her wedding ring and asked if her husband was present. She gladly pointed to Derek. He was the good looking tall guy across the room. Their reaction took Adrian by surprise. She was immediately given the cold shoulder treatment. Adrian perceived their displeasure, but never understood the reason for it. Did they think she had married above her station, or was she seen as a traitor?

The experience is not an isolated one. Laura and Ronald were hap-

---

1   Tom Teide, *"Wesley Looks up to its Little Man,"* Wilmington Delaware, Evening Journal (October 17, 1973).

pily married for many years before they knew they had a 'mixed marriage.' Until then most people had accepted them at face value. It
wasn't until they became members of LPA that Ronald learned of his
indiscretion --- he had married an average-sized woman! Laura was
disturbed by people's reactions and said, *"LPA was the last place I expected to hear, Why did you? I couldn't, marriage is difficult enough!"*
She paralleled dwarf members struggling for acceptance in society,
with her own struggle for acceptance within LPA.[1]

Similarly, an average-sized person entering marriage with a Little
Person experiences horror from those of their size. Adrian tells of the
time she and Derek were together at the nightclub where she was resident singer. The news of their recent engagement spread through the
audience. When Adrian was in a bathroom cubicle, she overheard the
conversation of two women at the hand-basin. *"What does he see in
her? And he's so good looking!"* Adrian did not miss the chance to put
them in their place. She immediately walked into the room to wash her
hands. Her presence was enough for their tongues to stop wagging, but
nothing could be done to improve their attitude.

Another Little Person tells that, *"From a distance people will react
to an average-sized spouse as though they are a child molester."*
Today Laura laughs about an incident, when she walked into a restaurant with Ronald and their son Norman, who is also a dwarf.
However at the time, instead of laughter she was shocked to over-hear
the comment of another customer: *"Who does she think she is, Snow
White?"*

From my knowledge of these couples, their attraction to each other
is based in reality, not fiction. They understand that the value of people
is not measured by a yard stick. The basis for their marriages is the
same as for any couple. Their marriages are no different, neither do
they expect to be treated differently.

The limited view people have about relationships and Little People
is distressing for everyone concerned. Tim and I would like to be freed
from these stereotypes. We are willing to 'size-up' a prospective marriage partner, but will not eliminate someone because they are too tall

---

1   For a discussion of marriage between short and average-sized people,
     and the reaction of Little People across the United States, see Joan
     Ablon's *"Little People in America: the Social Dimensions of Dwarfism"*
     (1984), Praeger Press.

or too short. Our suitability cannot be reflected in the looking glass.

Reasons for short-statured people meeting

It takes a lot of strength to break free from stereotypes, but it is worth the effort made. Fortunately, we don't have to fight the battle alone. In organizations of Little People, we can come together for mutual support and combine our forces. Even though our meeting compounds the public reaction, this accentuated public response shows all the more need for us to meet. It is not until we come together, that we realize the extremity of people's views.

In an organization, Tim and I could learn more about the possibility of achieving equality and breaking down the barriers of prejudice and misunderstanding. As individuals, we may have successfully broken through barriers on one occasion, only to find that in another situation we are faced again with the same barrier. However, if we join together with other Little People, we have a better chance of not only knocking barriers down, but also of making sure they stay down.

By working together, we will certainly attract more attention, but this is an occasion to take pleasure in the attention. As individuals, we attract attention, as a group we invite it. We should take advantage of the ready made audience waiting with their pens and cameras. We can let it roll.[1] The audience cannot wriggle out of recognition of what we are saying, because every way they turn there is another Little Person waiting to reinforce what someone else has said. There is strength in numbers. Our message can have a great impact if we simply choose to stand together. There is great value in coming together.

"Two can accomplish much more than twice as much as one,
for the result can be much better.
And one standing alone can be attacked and defeated,
but two standing back to back can conquer:
three is even better,
for a triple braided cord is not easily broken." [2]

As Little People, our results will be better and we may even con-

---

1   See Chapter 9, *"Attention Gives Opportunity."*
2   Ecclesiasties 4:12.

quer if we stand and fight our battles together. We each face the limitations society has placed in our path; if we also share our energies to
fight discrimination, we have a good chance of removing the barriers.

The energies of the group are channeled toward two primary exter-
nal objectives: helping the average-sized public to appreciate our
equality and place in society; and helping the parents of Little People
to overcome the limitations society places in the path of their child.
The goals are equally important and are worked on simultaneously.

As Little People, we face society 'square on' and by our activities
demonstrate our equality. As Paul Miller, a Little Person, has said,
"We are not asking for a hand-out, we are asking for a fair shake." [1]

Parents can be helped to reject the limitations society has placed on
their dwarf child if they are encouraged by a membership that represents people from every walk of life and all manner of occupations.
Their hope for the child's future is restored as they realize what Little
People can accomplish. The parents soon learn that the sky is the only
limit to our reach and when looking down from above it makes no difference whether you are short or tall. One member put it this way, *"To
measure your stature from head top to ground is often misleading if
you're lying down."* [2]

The goal is to eliminate the horror stories that surface from time to
time about the reaction of parents to the arrival of a Little Person in the
family. Some parents have gone so far as to hide their child in a closet,
to be sure they are not seen by anyone. Although these accounts are
rarely heard today, one story told is one too many. Little People set
goals, come together to accomplish them and as a bonus share in the
discovery of new freedoms. As two members said after attending their
first convention, *"It is like coming home, everyone is your own size ---
It is like being in a whole different world, like being normal."* [3] There
is respite from physical barriers and differences, from 'being on stage,'

---

1   Michael Malamut, *"A Fine Line Divides Special Treatment and What
      Harvard Could Learn From Hofstra,"* the Harvard Law Record, Vol.
      80, No. 5 (March 15, 1985).

2   Leonard Sawisch, Ph.D., President of the Mid-Michigan chapter of the
      Little People of America, Inc., and President of the Little People of
      America Foundation.

3   Comments of Edna Troyer and Jay Knox, Northcoast Breeze, chapter
      newsletter of the Northcoast chapter of the Little People of America, Inc.
      (September, 1984).

and 'time out' from routine struggles. A national meeting provides the opportunity to be in the majority. This unusual situation means the environment is to the order of Little People, whether by design or nature. For once, it is the needs of the average-sized person's present which need special consideration.

The environment is only temporary, as the meeting will end in a few days and there will not be another for months or maybe even a whole year. However, it is often just the water stop people need to keep fit for their daily activities in the average-sized world. It doesn't matter how well-adjusted Tim and I become; we get tired of being 'on stage;' we tire of all the questions and looks and fun making at our expense and we tire of having to behave in a manner that will enhance the publics' view of Little People. It's great to be relieved of that task for a week and to feel free to react however we please. We earn 'time out' from the physical battles of keeping up with fast walkers, being overcome by peoples' smelly bottoms in elevators, from the risk of being trampled on or burnt in the face by cigarettes every time we venture across a crowded room, from stifling the feelings of frustration when people continually speak to us in language suitable for children, from constantly angling our head upwards to see and from straining our ears to hear what people up there are saying. It is more than relief, it is sheer bliss to be able to communicate eye-to-eye and even cheek to cheek on the dance floor.

I found it interesting to notice that when this distance was first removed and I was at the same level as other people, I was very self-conscious. Few people had communicated with me that close before. It took some getting used to, but helped me learn confidence at all levels.

At meetings of Little People, the physical environment is often reordered. For once, we don't have to fit in. We recreate the environment to fit us. As a majority, we have the upper-hand. Venues chosen for meetings are on the basis of their accessible features. Light switches, door handles, elevator buttons, bathroom faucets are all within reach. Where no such venue or feature is to be found, stools are placed in strategic positions, such as at the reception counter, elevator and in the bathroom.

Other materials and equipment are set at convenient heights. Domestic staff place towels at a level we can reach and the microphone at meetings is lowered. One hotel manager even attempted to locate telephone books to increase the enjoyment of Little People at the banquet tables. He did not expect our fingers to do the walking, rather our butts to do the rising.

The average-sized minority may experience physical discomfort and inconvenience at a convention as many things are out of their reach. They must be seated when coming to the microphone and crouch down if they want people to hear what they are saying. After a week-long meeting, the stiffness of their neck and knees reminds them of their differences.

The trade in places does us all good. For once, Tim and I learn the power and temptation of the majority to dominate and dictate. Although it is technically our meeting, we have the opportunity to learn consideration and respect for the minority group --- the average-sized. Unfortunately, we don't always demonstrate that sensitivity.

This was apparent the day the chair-person of a meeting asked that all average-sized persons move to the back of the room, so as not to block the view of Little People. The intention was well-meant, but the direction fell like a lead balloon. There was a striking resemblance to the edict that all blacks should ride in the back of the bus!

After appreciating the discriminatory impact, the segregation of short and tall and the splitting up of families with both short and tall members, the request was withdrawn and integrated seating was resumed. The meeting was an opportunity for Little People to learn tolerance and integration of those who are different.

As a result of the reversal, the average-sized minority become more aware of our circumstances. As average-sized parents, siblings, or friends of Little People they learn a lot about the interests, needs, and expectations of Little People. Often they are more willing to advocate with Little People for the removal of discriminatory barriers.

Some of the freedoms found are not limited to the experience of being in the group. They are merely learned in the group and implemented later in the home environment. Frequently members exchange information on clothing, automobile pedal extensions and various other modifications.[1]

Little People share so much, but often miss the opportunity to share it with each other. Tim and I passed-up the opportunity we had, but

---

1   See Chapter 7, *"Doing Things Differently."*

there's no need for our mistake to be perpetuated. By sharing, we not only benefit as individuals but also help society to understand the goal of Little People to be accepted as equal.

Chapter Nine

ATTENTION GIVES OPPORTUNITY

Answering people's questions

I walked into the room and everyone stopped talking. The party was well underway and all eyes turned to see who was arriving late. The silence was unusual, however, as other late arrivals had slipped in unnoticed. In fact, I could have taken advantage of the attention everyone was paying to me by giving a speech to answer the many questions people's eyes darted at me.

Their questions were easy to anticipate. *"How tall are you; How old are you; Why didn't you grow; Do you work; Can you drive; Are you married; Will your children be small like you; Are you the only short one in your family?"* I had a question of my own to add. *"Do I really have to answer all these questions?"*

Instead of responding sharply to their arrowed curiosity, I smiled. Besides, smiling was as good as slapping them in the face, as it had the effect of bringing them to their senses. It worked, and the hum of conversation resumed as people began to feel the awkwardness of the silence. My opportunity for speech making had passed.

This situation was nothing unusual. Whenever I am among strangers, I automatically attract attention. You might wonder if I always have the grace to smile, and how other Little People react in similar situations. Well, there are many ways of dealing with all this attention, and each Little Person develops his or her own style. The reaction may even depend on how the Little Person feels on the particular day.

We have the choice of either answering the question to satisfy the inquirer's curiosity, or of ignoring it by walking on. Some Little People see no reason to stop and answer questions, and will continue as though the question was never asked. However, most of the Little People I know are willing to stop and talk. We see it both as an opportunity to educate and to make friends. David Hornstein, four feet seven inches and an attorney in Washington D. C., advised one teen-age Little Person to take advantage of the opportunity. His advice went like this:

"Most people strive to be noticed. Don't pass it up. It is a motivator. You will do well while you're being noticed." [1]

Although I'd prefer to ignore the questions, I frequently will stop to satisfy peoples' curiosity. I have concluded it is in my best interest to answer most of the time. When people say, *"I have never seen anyone as small as you,"* I know I am the inquirer's first contact with a Little Person. Their questions will mainly be asked because of a sincere interest. They have no malice or intention to offend. If I don't answer them, they will go on their way in ignorance. I will be powerless to affect their attitude toward me and I, or some other Little Person, may eventually be put down by their obstructive behavior. [2] A response can dispel their many misconceptions.

One of the most common questions from adult and child alike is: *"How old are you?"* I am now reaching the age when I prefer not to answer that question. It is not an acceptable query in polite society and I don't always feel inclined to reveal such a vital statistic. Yet, a response is often deserved and to answer removes any excuse a person has for mistaking me for and treating me like a child.

The question will often come from a young child, especially when they see me driving a car. There is total confusion when I step out and greet the child eye to eye. I can easily imagine the child's thoughts:

"What's going on here; you have to be a grown up like mommy and daddy to drive. Why are you driving when you're not a grown up; or are you? There is definitely something different about you."

I can anticipate the question forming as the child struggles to understand the apparent contradiction. It's been drummed into the child's head his or her entire life: *"If you're good and eat all your vegetables,*

---

1   Excerpt from a letter of encouragement written in 1967 to Cathy, a teen-age Little Person.

2   For further discussion of the disabling effect of attitudes, see Chapter 6, *"Attitudes Disable."*

you will grow up to be big and tall like mommy and daddy." The child
is genuinely perplexed to meet someone who can do what mommy and
daddy do, but is no bigger than he or she is. Inevitably the child blurts
out the question, *"How old are you?"*

I have determined that the child is not so much interested in my actual age, as to confirm whether or not I am an adult. I feel obliged to
answer. The mental picture of the child asking for the car keys each
morning to drive to school, or of a female's daily check in the mirror
for the development of breasts is enough to persuade me that the child
should not be put through such anguish.

As often as not, the parent will almost pull the child's arm out of
the socket in an attempt to get the child away from me and to stifle the
question. Ed Lang, a former editor of LPA Today, the national
newsletter of the Little People of America, Inc., has said in response to
this phenomenon: *"I have observed many children walking around
with one arm longer than the other."* Of course he jokes, but the point
is well made.

I don't believe a child should be made to suffer for making an effort to understand. What better time to answer the question and who is
best able to answer the question? It is important for a child to understand early, so that next time they meet a dwarf, the confusion will be
avoided. Also, it helps me if children perceive me as an adult. Then
they will stop inviting me to play with them in their sand-pit! At the
least, they will understand why I am not so thrilled about the idea of
taking up bucket and spade.

With young children, I can get my message across without divulg-
ing my age. It seems to go over better when I relate my age to that of
their parent. When it's appropriate, I will tell them I am as old as their
mommy or daddy.

Occasionally I have been curious about the child's perception of
my age. This has led me to ask the child to tell me how old they think I
am. Their response, more often than not, has been quite shocking and
extremely hurtful to my vanity. I have since stopped opening myself up
to such wild guesses, having no reason to be aged prematurely. Adults
will also ask how old I am. However, I am not as keen to answer their
question. Somehow I feel they should know better than to ask. Even
so, I will sometimes answer in the hope that they will stop treating me
like a child. I'll tell them my age, if I think it will help them to accept

me as a peer.

On days when I feel very private and decide not to disclose my age, I can still accomplish my goal of acceptance by comparing my age with that of the adult asking the question. I will assess whether I'm older or younger. I'm more likely to tell them exactly, if the exchange of personal data is mutual. Although tempted to say, *"It's none of your business,"* I seldom do. I want people to understand that size does not denote age! To answer settles the question.

After the age question is answered, people often want to know why I didn't grow. Little People have many different answers to this question. This is hardly surprising, as there are many different types of dwarfism. To complicate matters even further, it is virtually impossible for a person to pin-point the reason why their dwarfism occurred. The medical experts may be able to diagnose the dwarfism type, but in most cases they have yet to discover the actual cause of dwarfism. However, every day Little People are expected to tell people why they are short. Some of the responses given are far more amusing than educational:

> *"I may be small, but my brain grows as fast as yours."*
> *"I was born this way, what's your excuse?"*
> *"I took a shower and shrank."*
> *"My mother puts me in the dryer every night."*
> *"It must be the cigarettes which stunted my growth."*
> *"I didn't eat all my vegetables."*

As no serious answer can be totally satisfactory, I agree with the light-hearted approach. However, when you're dealing with children you have to be very careful. They will take your answer very seriously. One Little Person responded to the question of a curious child on the beach, by telling him that before he went in swimming he was six foot two inches and when he came out he was only four feet. The next day, the mother tracked down the adult male dwarf quite perturbed. Her son was so concerned about the 'short story' that she had not been able to get him near the bath-tub, let alone the ocean! Only after the dwarf retracted the story would the boy consider taking a bath.

When a person does press for a more serious response, some Little People will tell the person the medical name for their dwarfism type. As a result, the inquirer is often so impressed with the individual's knowledge of such big long words as: Achondroplasia, Diastrophic, Hypo-pituitary, and Spondylo-Epiphyseal-Dysplasia, that they will not dare question any further. They certainly will not notice that they still haven't been told why the Little Person didn't grow. One young boy of six has been taught by his parents to answer the question straight, *"I'm a dwarf."* Most inquirers are satisfied with that.

I was not so straight with a young girl who asked me why I didn't grow. I was tired of not having an answer, and responded to her question by asking what color her eyes were. She told me they were blue, so I asked her how come they weren't green. She shrugged her shoulders. I finished up by telling her, neither do I know why I didn't grow. It just happened. This riddle did nothing to help her understanding, and should have been saved for someone older, but that day I was not in the mood for a glib response.

Some inquirers need to be handled seriously, especially when it's obvious that their understanding is limited. For others, it is difficult to keep a straight face. Questions like this one: *"Are you real, or are you a puppet?"* [1] How could you answer that one with no strings attached?

There is no limit to the number of questions people will ask, but there are definite limits to how many answers people will get. Some people don't even deserve the time of day. I will usually ignore those who are just out to make fun at my expense. Also those under the influence of alcohol are best avoided.

One evening when shopping with my aunt, I was confronted three times by three different drunks. The first lurched toward me and the fumes of alcohol reeking from him left no doubt that he was drunk. We disappeared so fast that he was left wondering if he'd seen an apparition.

A second drunk discovered me as we were about to enter a store. We slipped inside hoping to lose him, but he was not so inebriated as to be incapable of following us. We stood at the counter discussing our purchase with the sales assistant when the man stumbled in. His alcoholic aroma was quite offensive in such close quarters and the assistant, quick to see he was hassling us, suggested we might like to go to the lower level where our purchase item could be found. We descended

---

1   *"Words : That's Life,"* People Weekly, Special Anniversary Edition (March 5, 1984).

quickly and left her at the top of the stairs to prevent his pursuit. She was successful.

The third drunk appeared after our shopping was completed. He turned up when we went to make a phone call to arrange for the ride home. My aunt went into the booth while I waited outside. It was not long before drunk number three made his discovery. Fortunately, my aunt didn't talk long and when she came out of the phone booth we managed to escape him. We were well practiced by then.

Some days, I just don't have the time to answer questions. The person may see me in my working hours, perhaps when I'm hurrying to an appointment. In that instance, I consider the person waiting and paying for my time has priority. I will politely excuse myself. To do so answers the question not even asked: *"Are you able to work?"*

There are times, when in spite of all this rhetoric, I won't even answer the genuine questions of polite people, simply because I can't be bothered. On those days I'm tired and disenchanted with my unpaid 'appointment' to public relations and my wish for privacy over-rules any obligation to give out information. Questions are shelved with a smile and I move on. After all, a public-relations volunteer cannot be on duty twenty-four hours a day, three hundred and sixty five days of the year!

How to educate those making fun of me

When some people see me, they don't want to ask questions. All they're interested in doing is making fun of me. For years, I would just ignore them until I realized that their behavior gave me an opportunity to educate. They are waiting for my reaction so I might as well give it to them. I have two choices. I can worsen their understanding by sneering and scowling, making rude gestures with my face and fingers, or returning a nasty retort. Many Little People believe this is all ignorant people deserve. I don't agree. I have heard my girl-friends say to people, *"Take a picture it lasts longer,"* and have let that pass, but when I noticed passengers in my car making rude gestures to people staring at us from passing cars, I put a stop to it.

For me to respond with like behavior demonstrates a lack of self-control, and indicates to the person concerned that their behavior is acceptable, because I am prepared to act in the same way. It encourages them to continue. Worst of all, I reinforce their judgment of me as an object of ridicule.

I am not threatened by other peoples' view of me, and do not accept their judgment. I have no need to defend myself to them, and don't need their acceptance to be able to accept myself. If they cannot accept me as a person of value, it is their problem, not mine.

I agree with Carol Lynn, a woman with a disability, who wrote:

"The measure of our self-esteem is the way we react to peoples' responses to us ... The more internal our defenses are, the less threatened we are by encounters from the outside. Self-esteem means one likes oneself enough 'to be' at all times, without punishing oneself for being unacceptable to a passer-by." [1]

My second choice is to respond positively. This way means there is a chance for me to improve the person's attitude. I often begin this approach by smiling. It's amazing how much of an impression that can make. Maybe the situation won't develop beyond 'a grin and bear it' encounter, but more often than not, the smile can really turn things around. To some it is like a slap in the face, as it was when I came into the crowded room late. The people suddenly become aware I am not an inanimate object; I am a person with feelings and they realize that their behavior has been inappropriate. It is enough to make them stop.

However, in some circumstances, a smile could be interpreted as approval of the behavior. In those cases, I find it is better to indicate disgust. At these times, I won't hesitate to show hurt and a lack of desire to be near the person. If possible, I will deliberately move out of the person's range, making it clear why I am moving. Sometimes, I will speak to my friend in a voice loud enough for the person making fun of me to over-hear. I may say something like this: *"Some people never grow up,"* or *"Some people have no manners."* No one likes to be accused of being immature or a slob, especially not in front of witnesses.

Children especially love to mimic my walk or descent of stairs. I used to think there wasn't much I could do about this until it occurred

---

1   *"Defense and Self Esteem,"* Achievement, the National Voice of the Disabled (May, 1981).

to me that the interest shown could be used as an awareness tool. It's true, I do walk and descend stairs in a unique way, so much so, that it catches the child's imagination. I decided to catch the child's reason as well.

Now I may stop and watch a child trying to mimic my walk or descent of stairs. I want to see if they have got it right. Most have not. Instead of my getting offended and telling the child off, I point out to them where they have gone wrong. I explain that the reason I walk differently and go down stairs differently is because I can't bend my knees. I invite the child to try again, this time with stiff legs. Most will fail the test by bending their legs.

The children soon realize how difficult it is for me to walk or descend stairs, and begin to understand the reason why I look so awkward. The situation is no longer something to laugh about, not even for them. I can actually see the look in the child's eye changing. As their understanding increases, their desire to make fun decreases. I hold out some hope that in the future they will be more responsive to the equal access rights of people with disabilities.[1]

Judith, a Little Person from California, successfully dealt with a taunting group of young boys. She had arrived at the supermarket to do her shopping and was greeted by boys who began laughing and poking fun at her. Their behavior was horrible, but Judith instead of abusing or avoiding them decided to take them on.

She went over to the boys and straight out asked why they were making fun of her. She didn't wait for an answer and carefully explained that what they were doing was very nasty and they had hurt her feelings very much. The boys were stunned into silence.

When the boys didn't shoot one more smart word after her as she walked into the store, Judith thought that was the end of the incident. However, Judith was wrong. The boys followed her into the store, and she prepared herself for another bad shopping experience. However, this time instead of taunting Judith, the boys came over and apologized for being so rude. Judith was gracious enough to accept their apology, and took the opportunity to make them her friends. In fact, the boys became her devoted servants throughout the shopping expedition, and did

---

1   For further discussion of physical barriers, see Chapter 5, *"At Your Physical Pleasure."*

everything they could to help her. They willingly reached items off high shelves, and fetched and carried items to her shopping basket. All because Judith took the time to show the youngsters how obnoxious their behavior was.

Of course not all children will be so responsive and fortunately not all find pleasure in ridicule. Some will show extra special concern, such as the twelve year old girl I met one day. She came up to me and embraced me with these reassuring words: *"Don't you worry, you'll grow one day!"*

Awkwardness of first encounters

Fortunately, most people do not set out to give me a hard time when they meet me for the first time. Yet, inadvertently some will still offend. They have no idea where to look or what to say. Even worse, there was one woman teller in a bank who did not even know how to speak to me. She would adopt a very patronizing tone, one only used in conversation with young children, and would season it with endearments thrown in for good measure.

Some people are totally tongue-tied when left to make conversation with a Little Person. They just don't know what to talk about. Others are able to speak, but feel it's important to avoid making any reference to the fact I am short.

On such an occasion, I was introduced to a woman by two acquaintances that I had known at least five years earlier. One of these people had been in my law school class. We had not seen each other since finishing law school and had to go more than half way around the world to meet again by chance. The woman following the story with great interest forgot all about her resolution and just had to say: *"Isn't it a small world?"*

I did not give her choice of words a second thought, but the next day I learned from the person who introduced us that the woman had nearly passed out with embarrassment. She thought I would be offended. There was no need for her to worry, because if she hadn't said it I would have. Reference to my size is not taboo and there is no need for anyone to pretend I am not short.

I am always hoping that people will learn that no special skills are needed in order to have conversation with a Little Person. Any subject is acceptable. The art of making conversation is the same for us as with anyone --- a pursuit of mutual interest and endeavor.

Other people don't know what stance they should take. Should they stand up-right, bend over, or crouch down? The indecision causes them greater discomfort as they attempt all three positions consecutively. I am the only one who can relieve their anxiety. I will usually save them from the rigors of behaving like a yo-yo.

I can't say what people should do when talking with other Little People, because Little People each have their own preference. Some prefer to talk with average-sized people face-to-face, and will either invite the other person to sit, or won't be offended if the person crouches; others will not want any concession to their size, and will prefer the person to converse without any stooping. The best thing is to ask the individual Little Person what makes him or her most comfortable. Now if you're asking me, I'll tell you I prefer to be face-to-face. If you don't ask, I'll even suggest that we go and sit down somewhere so that we can talk more comfortably.

Some people are thrown totally off balance when they encounter a Little Person. They find it hard to believe anyone could be so short. A clerk at the New Zealand Department of Internal Affairs[1] had this problem. I applied for a passport and showed my height as one meter and eight centimeters. The clerk called to query the height. How could it be correct? At first, I agreed there might be a mistake. (It was about the time of New Zealand's conversion to metrics and I was not sure that my conversion was accurate). She said, *"Do you realize that 1.08 meters means you are only three feet six inches tall?"* [2] I replied, *"Oh yes, I did do it right."* She decided she had done it all wrong by questioning my calculation.

Others will know my height before we meet and at the time of meeting will still be surprised. One person actually said, *"You're even smaller than I expected you to be."* This person even knew what it was like to be short, since he was not much more than a Zaccheus himself. Yet he was still amazed. The first thing he wanted to do was pat me on the head! Fortunately for him he withstood the temptation.

---

1   The American equivalent would be the State Department.

2   A more recent measurement has revealed that in actuality my height is three feet four inches.

Some people are visibly uncomfortable in my presence. Many of them feel sorry for me. Some will imagine that I have suffered under the wheels of a bus, or been stricken with a dreaded disease. With a few, you can almost hear their sigh of relief. They are so grateful that none of their children have been so 'afflicted.' Often these same people are fearful and are anxious to learn about the 'hereditary risk,' for the sake of their children or grandchildren. *"What if it should happen to one of their own?"* Those not so sophisticated may even be fearful for themselves, believing their diet may put them at risk to join me, or that the so-called 'disease' I carry is contagious. Others have guilt written all over their faces. How come they were the lucky ones fortunate enough to escape, while I was chosen to endure such perceived agony? A few, believe that I have brought my condition on myself. They feel no guilt, believing that I deserve my 'plight.' I have been plagued as a punishment for my misdeeds.

Dispelling ignorance and misconceptions

I feel responsible to dispel their ignorance, as such misconceptions leave these people helpless to communicate with me. I need to take the first step toward shaping a relationship. I cannot bear those looks of pity and don't like to have people avoid me because of their insecurity.

I agree with Doctor Harold Yuker who has said:

"The way people see themselves is very often a major factor in the way other people see them. I am quite convinced that the percentage of time you think of yourself as disabled, influences the percentage of time other people think of you as disabled. Self-concept is critical and it influences others." [1]

I also like the way David Hornstein put it. I trust his judgment which at the time of writing to another Little Person was tested by sixty-seven years of experience.

---

[1]   Harold Yuker, PH.D., J. Richard Block, *"Challenging Barriers to Change : Attitudes Towards the Disabled,"* National Centre on Employment of the Handicapped, Human Resources Centre, Albertson, New York 11507.

"Whoever you meet, look them straight in the eye, talk up clearly, act like you are glad to see them. You can't be brazen and you can't be aggressive. You must let the world know that you have self-respect. If you do, you will get it back. I maintain a studied effort to make everybody comfortable in my company. I think I do this at the outset by showing very plainly that I am not sensitive about my looks. I find that I am accepted as just another one of the crowd." [1]

When I meet with people if I am comfortable and able to interact without feeling self-conscious, people are able to relax and respond to me in the same way they would to anybody else. They will be free to express their concerns and will be able to let go of many of their preconceived notions.

Humor is a great way to 'break the ice' and alert people that I'm not self-conscious about my size. In fact, to refer to my size in a humorous way can be very effective. David Hornstein, often invited as a guest speaker, has eased the tension by beginning his speech this way: *"The only reason I'm here tonight is because they wanted a short speaker."* [2] He says this helps the audience to relax and adjust to his size. He finds he is then eliminated as a distraction and people are ready to listen to his message.

However, sometimes Little People can so much revel in the humor of the situation that their jokes go over the heads of the people they are talking to. This was very apparent one evening when I was having a meal with three Little People, one of whom, namely Leonard Sawisch, was a great humorist.

After the meal, we retired to the hotel lounge for a drink. The music was good and we were in the mood to dance. However, the musicians were surprised to see us dancing, as they were playing quiet after dinner music. The singer apologized to us, as she felt the music was inappropriate. One of our party assured her that she would not hear any complaints from us as we were celebrating. She replied by saying she wasn't aware of the day having any special significance, and asked the reason for our party. To be told it was National Gnome Sighting Week, left her holding the winning ticket --- she had just

---

1   Excerpt from a letter of encouragement written in 1967 to Cathy, a
     teen-age Little Person.
2   ibid.

sighted the four of us! She didn't know if my friend was joking or not. If she had known Leonard was a member of the local comedian's club, and had remembered it was April 1st she would have known it was okay to laugh.

At the same time, humor can take a twist that doesn't enhance the image of Little People. This is the case when a person constantly refers to and is joking about his or her height. It not only becomes boring, but also indicates that they are not fully comfortable with themselves. It damages the chance for equal and meaningful relationships. Some tell jokes at their own expense in an effort to make people laugh. They may get the laughs, but at the same time they can lose self-respect.

The only way I can hope to get through to a person who feels sorry for me is to convince them that their feelings of sympathy are misguided. Unless I can do this, the persons feelings of sorrow prevent them from relating to me as an equal. In order to reach these people, I have to talk with the person about my life. It doesn't mean as much if they hear it from a doctor or friend or relative. I am the best person to show there is no need for pity, and that my life is rewarding and meaningful. I am living proof that a Little Person is not in the midst of a tragic existence, nor even enduring with courage. I know both fulfillment and happiness, independence and direction, and have friends and family who love me. If there is any tragedy, it lies in the fact that people cling to their beliefs that if they were me, life would not be worth living.

Making a favorable impression

What I say is not my only way of making statements. The way I present myself is just as important. It is this unspoken communication that can make or break my ability to get through to people.

No way do I want my aroma to be so strong that people have to step back from me. Good hygiene habits --- familiarity with soap, deodorant, shampoo, toothpaste and clothes detergent will take care of body odor. Of course, subtlety saves people from gasping at the strength of my perfume. I'd rather people savor the experience of meeting me, than swoon from it.

My wardrobe should not speak too loudly. I'm not advertising anything, so there is no need to be outrageous. Yet I must be creative, as recognized name brands don't make clothes in my size. My mirror tells how well a style, which looks great on the tall slender model, will look on me. The advice is good. To ignore it means dressing to suit the fashion of the day, and I'd rather dress to suit myself.

So I make myself look good, but must remember that what comes out of my mouth is still important. Bad manners and over- bearing behavior can turn people right off. If demanding, a waiter or clerk may still smile and even accede to my requests, (but only because the customer is always right), but those who over-hear will not be impressed. Few would put me down publicly, for fear of what others might think of them for being nasty to this 'poor Little Person.' My whims may even be patronized, but I ruin any chance of being accepted as an equal.[1] If I expect to participate fully in society, my behavior must be socially appropriate.

Everyone wants to be popular and to have lots of friends. Little People are no exception. Some Little People make it by allowing themselves to be used as mascots. The only problem with this is that the mascot image doesn't let people see who the Little Person really is, and the friends and fun are based on a fantasy. The moment's laugh is too great a price to pay for sacrificing the individual's personality. I regret the one and only time I allowed myself to be used as a mascot.

It was at a National Student Christian Conference and each University was responsible to contribute an item to the mid-week concert. Tradition called for a time of great hilarity. Our group met to discuss our effort and we were totally void of ideas. We were desperate to come up with some funny skit. Finally, someone had a brilliant idea, or so it seemed at the time.

Our group was to be introduced as a choir, but would then destroy any concept people had of choirs and their function. However, the joke was so badly prepared and so poorly received that I can't even remember what the choir did! All I remember is that it was far from hilarious.

The narrator attempted to create a buzz of excitement in anticipation of the arrival of the conductor, who was being flown in by 'mini-package tour.' As the Little Person, I was the 'mini' part of the tour flying in on a 'packaged' deal --- air-borne in the back-pack of a male

---

1   For a discussion of equality and patronization, see Chapter 6, *"Attitudes Disable."*

transporter. My carrier knelt down, landing the pack on stage and out I stepped!

The audience was stunned into silence. They didn't know whether to laugh or cry. They did neither. I could hear their silent questions, *"Why is she doing this to herself?"*

I am grateful they didn't think it was funny, otherwise my realization that it is not amusing to allow yourself to be paraded as a joke, would not have been so dramatic. I will never forget the sinking sick feeling of our joke falling flat on its face, and even worse, knowing I had allowed myself to be used. A mascot surely gets people's attention, but is no help in getting people to take you seriously.

Getting people to forget size differences

Exposure to me not of me is a most effective way of communicating. Those who know me often say, *"I don't even think of you as a Little Person."* They accept me for myself and forget about our size difference. Don't get me wrong, it's not that I want people to forget I'm short. No, it's just that it makes me happy when my height becomes so insignificant that people don't think to treat me differently because of it.

It's interesting to listen to Little People still in the closed community of a school campus. Many report that their size does not create any difficulty for them. They talk about their friends and say that they go about the routines of school life without any hassles.

Some could conclude that these youngsters are fortunate enough to be growing up in an age when people are more tolerant and attitudes toward Little People are improving. Maybe that's the case, but I don't think that is what's happening. There are too many Little People living in the same generation who experience attitudinal barriers.

Yet at the same time as I question the advanced ability of society as a whole to accept Little People as equals, I don't have trouble accepting the account of the school kids. I believe that their school life may be hassle free. However, I believe their positive experience is the result of their environment. The school gives an opportunity for the development of close interpersonal relationships, and in the natural development of friendships between average-size and Little People, the average-size kids forget the differences between them and their friend who is a dwarf.

Outside of the school and in the broader community, the size of a Little Person is still very obvious. People have yet to know and understand us. The only way this will be possible is if I am willing to expose myself to the community. Unless people get to know me, or another Little Person, as an individual they will find it difficult to understand that Little People are viable members of the community.

Yet it's not that easy to get started. It seems like a vicious circle. People won't accept me until they know me, and won't know me until they accept me. Where do I begin?

No doubt the first step will have to come from me. Somehow I must insist on being included in the natural processes of daily living at work, school and play. After that, all I have to do is be myself. It won't be long before people see how much like them I really am.

I read about the experience of an average-sized person on the set during the filming of the 1981 movie, *"Under the Rainbow,"* which had a cast of dozens of Little People. The person observed that the first time you were in the midst of 'all those Little People,' you would stare shamelessly and uncontrollably. However, after a few days, the 'dwarfs' didn't seem so small anymore. To distinguish between the actor of two feet ten inches, and the one of six feet was by reference to the cleft one had on his chin.[1]

It is ironic that the long term goal of acceptance and integration is achieved by being integrated. People find it hard to conclude Little People are helpless and miserable when they see us participating and having a good time. We are not limited to an evening of television made special by a bar of chocolate. Perhaps this was the initial belief of one of my sister's boyfriend, when he invited me to go out with them and promised to show me a good time.

The invitation came one afternoon when he was at our place working on a friend's car. I was in the house with the record player going. The music was good and I took a break from work to dance. He came into the house and saw me. He was impressed. I know it was not at my dancing ability, but more at the fact that I was dancing. He reserved a dance with me, but we held it for a week when I joined my sister and her boyfriend at their favorite disco.

---

1   Joe Morgenstern, *"Growing Up Little,"* Rolling Stone (April 16, 1981).

Our trio was made more interesting, as Deborah had her leg in plaster, and was using crutches. We took a seat at a table with a full view of the circular dance podium. It was raised about eight inches and no one could dance up there without being noticed.

Deborah pulled me up the step and we were swinging. Deborah caused a sensation by dancing on one leg, supporting herself with the crutches. Together we were sensational. People were watching, but then didn't they always? I took advantage of the attention by showing them how much I could dance and enjoy myself. One guy got the message loud and clear.

Later he asked me to teach him how to dance. I agreed to dance with him, but not to give a lesson. That was just as well, because he was an expert. I enjoyed dancing with this bearded gentleman in the three piece blue suit. He was very charming. Afterwards, he properly escorted me back to my seat and returned to his own table.

It was great for him and everyone watching to see. If I had not gotten up and danced with Deborah, he would never have asked me, and everyone would have continued to feel sorry for the 'poor Little Person' who has to sit back and be a decoration.

Deborah's boyfriend kept reporting to me how everyone was coming up to him and saying how terrific it was that I was dancing. He didn't have to tell me, I could see by the look on their faces. I danced my way to an increase in their awareness. They could see Little People can and do have a good time.

Media

Sheer numbers make it impossible to reach everyone personally. However, I can still open myself to many people through a vehicle often misused --- the media. Little People do not have to seek it out; the media is attracted to us.[1] Yet, we don't complain because through headlines such as *"Short is pretty good: Children with dwarfism learn to stand tall in world proportioned for others;"* [2] *"Life-loving Little Folk Bring Tidings of Hope;"* [3] *"What's so bad about being little?"* [4] we get the chance to tell people what we are really like,[5] and to demonstrate that life can be good.

Regretfully, it is not a case of any publicity is good. Some can do a lot of harm. Headlines such as: *"His size dwarfs other abilities,"* [6] have no hope of improving the public's understanding of Little People.

Good publicity may be hard to come by, but it is imperative that every effort be made to achieve it. I have found that positive press is possible provided certain ground rules are observed.

Telephone interviews should be avoided wherever possible. They are simply too risky. I learned all the reasons for not conducting such interviews the hard way. It happened when I had very little experience with the media, and allowed a reporter to interview me over the telephone. It resulted in a dreadful article.

The cutsy play on words, *"Angela may be short of stature but she's got a giant sense of humor,"* was one of the many things wrong with the article. In addition, the reporter incorporated her own preconceived ideas, misquoted what I actually said, presented what I did say with the wrong emphasis or completely out of context, and made straight out errors. The resulting article also represented dwarfism as synonymous with problems, and encouraged the reader to feel guilty. The article had absolutely no redeeming features.

It was almost inevitable that the article would be bad. I had not been expecting the reporter's call and was not prepared for the interview. I was immediately at a disadvantage. In addition, I had no way of

---

1   See Chapter 8, *"Shared."*
2   Darla Loose, Dayton Daily News (March 20, 1979).
3   The New Zealand Herald (October 20, 1984).
4   John Hicks, Sentinel Star, Orlando, Florida (May 11, 1980).
5   For further discussion on the use of the media by Little People as an organized group, see Chapter 8, *"Shared."*
6   Patricia McGowan, The Post and Evening Times, Florida (January 10, 1982).

assessing where the reporter was coming from, or of knowing how well what I was saying was being understood. Once the article was in print, I discovered that the reporter had understood very little.

It is also important to know the reputation of the newspaper. Little People need to be protected from sensationalism and erroneous reporting. Some newspapers are outrageous with their reports. One paper wrote these headlines about a doctor: *"He turns Dwarfs into Giants."* [1] The rational, educated person would hopefully recognize the tactics of such newspapers and dismiss the claim, but after reading the article some Little People and their parents come looking for the miracle cure.

It is very important to be prepared for an interview. Many times the reporter will have zero knowledge on matters concerning Little People, and will not even know what questions to ask. The reporter will either get stuck on things which are irrelevant, or ask very open questions. In both situations, preparation is imperative. I believe an open question is easier to deal with, because you can take it in the direction you want. However, you can only do this if you know what you want to say.

In preparation for an interview I will anticipate the questions most likely to be asked. Some I will be ready to answer; some I may refuse to answer knowing that reporters do not have me on the witness stand in a court-room and cannot force me to answer; and others I will turn completely around.

A common approach is for a reporter to say: *"Since life for you must be very difficult, tell me about your problems."* This is one of the questions I will turn around before giving an answer. The statement reveals two of the reporter's presumptions: first, that Little People experience great difficulty; and second, that we have many problems. I see the question as being loaded. If the person being interviewed responds to the invitation to discuss their problems, the opportunity to challenge the underlying premise that the lives of Little People are difficult and problem filled is lost.

To avoid a totally negative article, both of these presumptions must be refuted. Little People do not want to be viewed as a pack of sniveling creatures looking for sympathy. Yet this is exactly the impression

---

1   The Globe (June 1, 1982).

that will be left in the public's mind if the reporter's approach to the interview is accepted.

It is necessary to be on the alert for the reporter who only wants to know about problems, and to be especially watchful for those who do not bother to take a note when told about the ability and success of Little People. The article of such a reporter is guaranteed to have a tragic emphasis. The reference to the positive aspects of the persons life will be blanked out and not reported in the article.

Sometimes you can get your message across to a reporter, but a final blow is struck by the newspaper editor who titles the article with a headline which highlights the negative. To avoid this you have to impress the reporter enough that they can strongly advocate for a favorable headline. The alternative is for Little People to continue to be plagued by headlines such as: *"Problems of Dwarfs Grow as They Get More Mature;"* [1] *"Little People Have Big Problems;"* [2] *"Little People Have Big Woes."* [3] If such headlines continue unchecked, it will be no wonder that people will believe that the lives of Little People are miserable.

I find that it's better to discuss what Little People can do, not what we can't do. The only way to accomplish this is to turn the question around to something like this: *"It may be that our lives appear difficult, but that is a common misconception. Little People are as capable and accomplished as any other group in society. What people perceive as difficulties and problems, we have long since overcome. Our size often means we find a different way of doing things,*[4] *but it doesn't mean that we are incapable or that our life experience is full of problems."*

I am willing to admit that we have problems, but I want to be sure that the reporter does not selectively report only the negative side of my experience. For this reason, I am only willing to discuss a problem if the discussion increases the likelihood of effecting change, or of im-

---

1   Frederick Burger, the Miami Herald (December 30, 1979).

2   Mary O. Stone, News Record and Press, Gatlinburg, Indiana (December 27, 1982).

3   Bob Becker, the Plain Dealer, Cleveland (October 7, 1984).

4   For further discussion, see Chapter 7, *"Doing Things Differently."*

proving people's understanding.

For example, I am perfectly willing to talk about problems relating to limitations of attitude, not limitations of size. I want people to understand that my size is not my primary problem, rather it is the attitudinal barriers which other people erect in my path which limits my activity.[1] I may mention some physical limitations, so that people will understand why I am requesting physical accommodations in public facilities. None of the problems mentioned will be to encourage a sense of pity, but rather to encourage society to accept Little People as equals. The goal of my interview is to encourage people to cooperate with Little People so that we can lead lives as full as other people. Some Little People have succeeded in achieving such articles, as these headlines demonstrate: *"Problems of Dwarfs in an Oversized World Gain More Attention: 'Little People of America' Fight Job Bias, Social Ostracism, Out-of-Reach Public Facilities;"* [2] and *"These Little People Meet Full-Sized Problems Head-On."* [3]

When I decide whether to do an interview, I try to keep it clear in my mind that my objective is to educate the public and to improve the quality of life for Little People generally. Unfortunately, some Little People will accept interviews to advance their own interests, and are not in the least bit concerned to use the opportunity to educate the public. An organization needs to be discerning in selecting persons to speak to the media.[4]

Those not selected, but who seek out the press will inevitably have their say at some time or another. Yet I'm sure the public is able to discern between public and self-interest speakers. Somehow the glory

---

1   For a discussion of the disabling effects of attitudes, see Chapter 6, *"Attitudes Disable."*

2   Joann S. Lublin, the Wall Street Journal (September 12, 1973).

3   Bob Arndorfer, Gainesville Sun, Florida (July 25, 1976).

4   For a discussion of Little People organizations, see Chapter 8, *"Shared."*

seekers stand out like sore thumbs, whether they be short or tall.

In preparation for the interview, it is important to consider what the public needs to know about Little People and if necessary to go beyond what the reporter is asking. For example, I believe that *"the similarities between average-sized and Little People should be emphasized, not the differences. To dwell on the differences will only reinforce our separateness."* [1] Some newspaper editors show they have grasped this concept well when they use headlines such as: *"Don't be Afraid -- We Are Like You;"* [2] *"We're not different -- just smaller;"* [3] and *"Small Victory: Adopting a Child Feat for Dwarfs."* [4]

The public also needs to know that Little People are individuals. It is so easy for people to lose us to an abstraction, such as 'the Little People.' We do not want to perpetuate the misconception that Little People are all alike. We are not. [5]

I can easily fall into this trap by just giving my own opinion to a question asked. If I give my opinion and just leave it at that, the reader is likely to conclude that all Little People feel the same way on that issue, when in fact there are a variety of opinions among Little People. For instance, it would be wrong for me to suggest that Little People only have one answer to these questions: *"How old are you? Why didn't you grow? If you had the choice would you choose to be two feet taller? Do you wish you had never been born? Do you think you have the same chance of dating and marriage as any other person? Would you prefer to marry an average-sized or Little Person?"* As many different questions as you can think of, so will Little People have different answers.

Phil Donahue appreciated this first hand in August 1984, when he interviewed a number of members of the Little People of America, Inc.

1   Harold Yuker, PH.D., J. Richard Block, *"Challenging Barriers to Change : Attitudes Towards the Disabled,"* National Centre on Employment of the Handicapped, Human Resources Centre, Albertson, New York 11507.

2   Judy Oppenheimer, the County Advertiser, Maryland (September 29, 1982).

3   Warren Barton, Evening Standard, New Zealand (November 2, 1985).

4   Steve Rothman, The Post, Florida (March 3, 1984).

5   For further discussion of how people regard Little People as being all alike, see Chapter 8, *"Shared."*

The difference of opinion was most dramatically shown by the variant responses to the issue of whether Little People would have their own children knowing that there was a chance that their children would also be dwarfs.[1]

Harry McDonald, an engineer, Little Person and panelist, described his feelings at the time he realized his son was going to be a dwarf:

"When Brendan was born I saw him coming out of the delivery room and my first reaction was like father like son --- I went home and I was really depressed because of the fact that I knew what life was, I've lived it. I've gone through the name-calling, the prejudices so to speak, and it was really depressing to know that I did this to him."

By contrast, Leonard Sawisch, a psychologist, Little Person and panelist, was hoping to have a dwarf child. He said:

"When I was a young kid I had vowed that if there was a chance that my children would be like me that I'd never have children. Then I went through a whole coming out process where I began to ask myself, well, what's wrong with being a dwarf. Then after I began to realize that there was nothing wrong with being a dwarf, then why wouldn't I want to have children like me?"

Leonard's wife Lenette, also a dwarf, by Leonard's description was much more liberal; she was not worried either way. It didn't matter to Lenette whether their child was born a dwarf or average-sized.

As a participant in this Phil Donahue Show, I put in my two cents' worth by saying:

"Not everybody who is a Little Person decides to have their own children and many of our members adopt. So, when a dwarf child is born to an average couple --- if they don't want that child many little people will step into adopt him or her. So they (little people) don't have their own children, but they are willing to raise children who are rejected."

Dr. Charles I. Scott, Jr., a geneticist and panelist, spoke of his experience counseling dwarf couples about their chances of having a dwarf child. He said:

"If I counsel someone that they have a seventy-five percent chance

1   Donahue Transcript #08094, Multimedia Entertainment, Inc.

*to have a dwarf child, any of you, most of you wouldn't want that. Be-
cause you have automatically assumed that 'normal' is what
everybody wants, but that's a matter of perception. Many Little People
come and they find out they have a twenty-five percent chance to have
an average sized kid and they don't want that chance. They would
prefer to adopt and they feel they can be just as good a parent as
anyone else. --- They don't want the average size baby because of their
own feelings and prejudices about raising a child who can look down
on the top of your head at age six. So, many of them, --- choose to
adopt instead."*

This issue plainly demonstrates the variant opinions of Little
People about having children. Some Little People are like Harry and
hope that the fifty/fifty odds will favor them with an average-sized
child; others are like Lenette and have no preference one way or the
other; some are like Leonard and actually hope for a dwarf child; and
others will adopt children because they do not want to take the risk of
having a dwarf child, while others will adopt because they do not want
to raise an average-sized child. Yet, in spite of the diversity of opinions
represented by the Donahue panelists, the responses still do not exhaust
the opinions on the subject. Some Little People choose to remain child-
less. Other Little People would be happy to have a dwarf child, but do
not have the financial resources to cover the projected medical expenses for a child needing frequent and expensive medical care. Some
dwarf women would be happy to have their own child, but lack the
physical health, or ability to bear a child.

Now if I was asked in an interview what attitude Little People have
to producing children, it would be so wrong for me to just give my
own opinion. I feel obliged to point out the various approaches Little
People have taken. My reason for doing an interview is not so that the
world will know what I think about the issue being discussed, but to increase the average person's understanding about Little People in
general. I want them to see us as ordinary people; I want them to
respond to us as individuals. When confronted with the diversity of
opinion among the members of the Little People of America, Inc., Phil
Donahue summed the situation up very nicely when he said: *"Little
People (of America) doesn't expect its membership to march as*

wooden soldiers. There's all kinds of options out there." [1]

Whenever I do an interview I like to stress the equality of Little People. I want people to know that Little People have the same rights as other citizens, and are entitled to be integrated into society. We do not need to be looked after, and in fact are willing and able to contribute to the needs of others. We are not sympathy riders. We are ready to make our contribution to society.

When working with a reporter, I also consider it important to point out the 'four letter words' in my dictionary.[2] They are offensive, not because of the number of letters, but because they are demeaning and indicate negative attitudes. *"Sticks and stones will break my bones but names will really hurt me."* [3]

The hurt has nothing to do with my being a sensitive person who has not learned to ignore the comments of ignorant people. No, I am hurt because the words used label me in away which makes it difficult if not impossible for people to accept me as an equal. Words such as: *" defect, victim, burden, afflicted, unfortunate, restricted, abnormal."* The only way I suffer any of these descriptions is by the mouth of people who insist on using these words to describe me.

If a reporter wants to describe me, I prefer it if they use my name. If it is appropriate, I'll allow them to describe my condition, but no way should the description of my condition also be used as a description of me. I am by medical description a Larsen's syndrome type dwarf, I am not a *" victim of dwarfism."* To call me a victim or use any other label encourages the notion that I need pity. I do not. One of my defenses against pity is to refuse the label which evokes feelings of sympathy.

I am very dogmatic about this, because often the first introduction people have to me is through the media. The image portrayed will be what sticks in their mind when they meet me. It is hard if not impossible to change that image.

---

1   Donahue Transcript #08094, Multimedia Entertainment, Inc.

2   United Cerebral Palsy USA, *" Four Letter Words in the Dictionary of the Disabled."*

3   Robert Ruffener, *"Producing a Public Relations Program for Disabled Adults."*

Usually, it doesn't really matter what a person thinks of you, but when that person has the power to make a decision which will affect you, it matters a lot. The employer, apartment manager, or dean of the school I want to attend will find it very difficult to favorably consider my application when all they can remember is the article about the *"pitiful victim afflicted with dwarfism."* They will not see my ability and will refuse my application.

Fund-raising tactics

Many fund-raisers of charitable organizations for persons with disabilities appreciate the power of the emotion to prompt people to dip their hands into their pockets to give. As a result, they will primarily portray their beneficiaries as helpless and dependent. It serves as an invitation to a 'pity party' for the viewer, and a swelling of the coffers for the organization. Although a very effective means of raising funds, it also lowers the dignity and the view others have of people with disabilities.

The cost of this type of fund-raising is too great. I do not want people to empty their pockets to salve their conscience and keep me at a distance. I prefer to see a hand extended to welcome me into the world. I do not belong to an 'alien race' and have my rightful place as a contributing member of the community. I do not need someone to say to me, *" You can come into this movie at half-price because you are one of 'the afflicted.'"* I want to pay full price. What's more the theater will have no need to offer me charity, if I am given the opportunity to work and earn enough to pay my own way.

I do not give the media license to redraw my image, even under the pretext that it is for my benefit. The picture in peoples' minds will be impossible for me to erase. I am not persuaded by the view that it is a matter of throwing my philosophy out the window for the day, in order to get the money the organization needs to help its members tomorrow. It simply doesn't work out that way, because once the organization has the money, the people will not be free to use it. The media will already have drawn an indelible image in people's minds. No people with disabilities, Little People included, can afford to lose their philosophy for one moment! Whenever we lose it, we ensure the perpetuation of the cycle of paternalism and dependency.[1]

This doesn't mean that Little People are without needs. Of course, that's not true. We have needs just like anybody else, and because of our stature we have particular needs that other people don't have. But to have need in a particular matter, doesn't mean we have to be portrayed as needy in every situation.

In presenting our needs to the public, it is important that we strike a balance. One way of doing this is to also speak of our abilities. Only then will people see that when the particular need is fulfilled, we will be capable of pursuing our goals, and making a contribution to the community.

In striking the balance, it is also important to clarify where the need really is. It is best not to present the person as being needy. I prefer to show the need as being in the circumstances. The need arises because of the lack of funds to pay for medical expenses and research, to equip a building with a lift or ramp, or to purchase a motor vehicle. Then, when the need is acknowledged, the individual Little Person is not placed in a compromised position.

There is no need to present the Little Person in a pitiful light to get the necessary funds. Instead, the Little Person may be presented positively, and at the same time motivate people to give. This method of fund-raising does not destroy the chance of Little People being accepted as equals. I can and must hold onto my philosophy of working toward a positive portrayal of Little People in the media and in fund-raising appeals.

---

1   For further discussion, see Chapter 6, *"Attitudes Disable."*

Chapter Ten

THE RISE AND FALL
OF
DWARF THROWING
Australian report

In February 1985, while I was living in Cleveland, Ohio, I was surprised to receive a phone call from a New York Daily News reporter. It wasn't so much a surprise that a reporter should call, but what she said was incredible. The reporter explained that she was responding to a United Press International (UPI) news release from Sydney, Australia about the *"sport"* of dwarf throwing. Someone had said that I was from New Zealand and she figured I would have heard about the *"sport"* from someone at home.

I didn't take the time to explain that New Zealand and Australia are two countries separated by 1200 miles of ocean, and that what goes on in Australia is not exactly local news in New Zealand. Rather, I found that my nationalistic pride was temporarily over ridden by my pride in being a dwarf. My attention focused on the horror of what the reporter was saying. Although I had nothing to add to the news release, I had no trouble finding words to decry the practice of dwarf throwing.

The whole thing was astounding. Were the customers at the Penthouse Night-club in Surfers Paradise, Queensland really being entertained by bouncers competing to see who could throw a dwarf the furthest? As hard as it was to believe, that's exactly what she was saying. The news was so disturbing, and the reporter so obviously ready for my critical comment, that I decided to break my golden rule of never making statements to the press over the telephone.[1] This was a story that should not be printed without presenting the view-point of someone opposed to the practice.

So what could be wrong with the practice of dwarf throwing? According to the UPI release, Robbie Randall, the Australian dwarf of four feet, considered the contest a fun thing and wasn't remotely worried about his safety. For protection, he wore a crash helmet and body padding and was thrown into a landing zone of mattresses. Well, the apparent consent of Robbie Randall and the precautions taken to prevent his injury did nothing to persuade me that dwarf throwing was okay, not even for those who enjoyed the excitement!

I denounced the practice as both degrading and dehumanizing and refused to label it as *"sport."* How could it be a sport when a dwarf was the object of the competition rather than a part of it? It sounded as absurd as replacing the javelin, or shot-put with a person. It most definitely could not be a sport for the dwarf being thrown. What's more, the dwarf could hardly accept any award for winning the competition. That would be as crazy as awarding a prize to the javelin or shot-put, instead of the thrower.

Of course, once off the phone, I thought of many more reasons why this depraved practice could not be regarded as a sport. I later read in newspaper accounts of dwarf throwing that I was not the only one to regard the practice of using a dwarf as a human missile to be a *"spectacle which dehumanizes and degrades dwarfs to the point of being a mere object."* [2] A reporter of the Chicago- Sun Times also questioned that the practice was a game when he described it as an *"alleged sport."* [3]

For sure, there is nothing sporting about throwing someone into the air, watching the person thump onto the ground, and then measuring how far he or she has flown. I decided the only way to be sporting about any of this nonsense was to do something to make sure this was the first and last to be heard of the practice. Surely, other people would agree that such competitions were not even fit for barroom or night-

---

1   For a discussion of the recommended practice of not giving telephone interviews, see Chapter 9, *"Attention Gives Opportunity."*

2   1985 Press Release of the Association for Research into Restricted Growth, the English organization for short statured persons.

3   Kup's Column (November 12, 1985).

club antics. I hoped that after this initial Australian fling, the dwarf would come to his senses, and the bouncers would return to tossing inanimate objects.

My disbelief and dismay at the news of dwarf tossing was soon to turn to anger. It was only one month later that I read the column of Mike Royko, a Chicago based columnist and humorist, who not only reported on the Australian event, but actually questioned what all the fuss was about.[1] He professed to not understanding why both dwarf and average-sized people in Australia saw the competition as an example of *"man's inhumanity to little man."* [2] After conceding that his view may amount to insensitivity, Royko fanned my anger even further.

Royko makes light of the "sport"

Royko went on to say, *"the incident in Australia made me wonder if dwarf-tossing might catch on here in Chicago."*[3] To make it worse, Royko didn't just settle for letting the idea roll around in his head. No, he actually spoke to several Chicago tavern owners to see if they would be willing to host such a contest at their establishments.

Royko did not conclude his column by saying that dwarf throwing in Chicago taverns wasn't such a great idea until after he had titillated the humor of his readers with the reactions of Chicago area tavern owners. Royko collected their points of view when he interviewed the Chicago tavern keepers who went in for unusual forms of entertainment, such as lip-syncing and ugly face contests.

In reporting both negative and positive reactions, Royko outdid himself by selecting responses designed to make light of the issue. A

---

1   *"Great dwarf toss,"* the Plain Dealer (of Cleveland); *"Will dwarf-throwing catch on in our bars? Small chance,"* the Pittsburgh Press; and in many other newspapers around the country (March 7, 1985).

2   ibid.

3   ibid.

bar owner who regularly organized amateur non-talent Olympics, was willing to approve dwarf throwing as a new event, because it was okay to juggle cats, so why not agree to throw dwarfs.[1]

Another owner even expressed charitable concern for abused dwarfs and an apparent willingness to host a competition for their benefit. However, his charitable motives soon emerged as twisted when he went on to suggest using the basket-ball hoop at one of his bars to have a competition for *"dwarf slam-dunking."* [2] What happened to his understanding for abused dwarfs? The very people who would need the funds being raised by the competition would be the ones being dunked in the baskets!

A Greek tavern owner unwilling to sponsor an event gave this reason for not scheduling such a contest:

"Eees too dangerous. Maybe somebody get keeled --- I don't mean the dwarf get keeled --- what if dwarf heet a regular customer and keel him. How do I tell his wife what happen? And what do the wife tell her keeds? Hey, keeds, I got bad news. Your daddy get keeled by a flying dwarf." [3]

No laughing matter

However, despite Royko's obvious amusement, Little People do not regard dwarf-throwing as a laughing matter. Royko was soon to learn this for himself. As the column is nationally syndicated, many members of the Little People of America Inc. were far from amused when they read his column. In a flood of letters and phone calls, Royko discovered that Little People are not willing to be made sport of, and object to being treated as the play-thing of society.

The very idea of dwarf-throwing smacks of the high-school day pranks of the dwarf being stuffed upside down in the garbage can. It was hard enough teaching immature teen-agers that it's no joke to have such short arms that you can't lift yourself out of the can; the idea of dwarf throwing contests, obviously suggests that many of those teen-

---

1   *"Great dwarf toss,"* the Plain Dealer (of Cleveland); *"Will dwarf-throwing catch on in our bars? Small chance,"* the Pittsburgh Press; and in many other newspapers around the country (March 7, 1985).
2   ibid.
3   ibid.

agers never learned the lesson. However, one thing is for certain, Little People have long since become tired of being ridiculed, made fun of, and being the butt of people's jokes. The promotion of dwarf-throwing as a *"sport"* has convinced many Little People that they will not be canned, dunked, or thrown again.

Craig McCulloh, a Chapter President of the Little People of America Inc. (LPA) from 1984-1986, demonstrated the intensity of many people's feelings when he wrote: *"It's amazing how one's literary skills can be enhanced when rage and anger increases one's blood pressure beyond the boiling point."* [1] Yet neither Craig, myself, nor other members of LPA were satisfied to sit, bubble, and boil. We knew we had a cause to fight for. We knew that our dignity and the public perception of Little People was on the line. We knew that as advocates for ourselves and for one another, we had to do something to preserve our dignity and to ensure that people would take us seriously.

Even in the twentieth century, we find ourselves still working to dispel the public perception of Little People as only being fit for the circus and *"midget"* wrestling. As one opponent of dwarf throwing said,

"We are still seen as dwarf and "midget" caricatures, and fair game as objects for mirth and ridicule ... Because of the images created by freak-shows, the circus, and the Snow White genre of fairy tales, small people are still regarded as clowning stereotypes, alien, and somehow excluded from social acceptability." [2]

In recent years, there has been cause for many Little People to believe that we have progressed beyond these days. Many Little People have been accepted into the mainstream of society, and have been treated with greater sensitivity. Few Little People are willing to sit back and see years of progress fly out the window and plummet into a pile of padded mattresses.

Little People knew that advocacy was the only hope for overcom-

---

1   *"Dwarf Tossing Contest Halted in Chicago,"* LPA Today, Vol. 23, No. 1 (Jan-Feb 1986).

2   1985 Press Release of the Association for Research into Restricted Growth, the English organization for short statured persons.

ing this assault. Indeed as Robert Van Etten, the national President of the Little People of America Inc. from 1984-1986 said:

"If we are to come anything close to ring side spectacles, it should be to fight for equality and justice. The prize really worth having is acceptance and self-respect." [1]

Little People of America, Inc. was fortunate to have Craig McCulloh emerge as the leader in the advocacy battle against dwarf throwing. As Craig said: *"Royko had to be called onto the carpet for his actions."* [2] Craig began with a letter to Royko himself in which he expressed his outrage and deep concern over the insensitive, distasteful, offensive, and irresponsible column Royko had written.[3] Craig went onto say:

"It is one thing to report and inform people of the news as it happens, ... However, for you to attempt to describe and equate the incident as being humorous and for you to explore, hint or even suggest the possibility of these particular contests taking place in this country illustrates a sick mentality and displays total ignorance, the type of ignorance and mentality which we in the Little People of America, Inc. have fought against over the past 25 years." [4]

Not satisfied with censuring Royko for his shabby journalism, Craig turned on two of the editors of newspapers who had printed Royko's syndicated column.[5] In his letters to these editors, Craig not only expressed similar sentiments as those stated in his letter to Royko, but also expressed his objection to their editorial decision to print Royko's column about dwarf throwing in the first place. (Craig was fully aware that newspapers have the editorial discretion to not use all the syndicated columns they receive).

---

1   *"The President's Golden Column,"* LPA Today, Jan-Feb 1986, Vol. 23, No. 1

2   *"Dwarf Tossing Contest Halted in Chicago,"* LPA Today, Vol. 23, No. 1 (Jan-Feb 1986).

3   Craig McCulloh's letter was addressed to Mike Royko at the Chicago Tribune (March 21, 1985).

4   ibid.

5   The York Dispatch in York Pennsylvania, and the Pittsburgh Press of Pittsburgh, Pennsylvania.

European outcry

In the summer of 1985, the Little People of America, Inc. realized that the need for advocacy action was not just a domestic issue. A letter from the English organization for Little People, known as the Association for Research into Restricted Growth, informed the American organization that dwarf throwing had spread to the United Kingdom. Pam Rutt, the Acting Chairperson, also enclosed a newspaper article which described the traveling *"Throw the Dwarf"* show as being a great success in clubs and pubs around the country.[1] According to the article, for the first six weeks, Lennie the Giant, the English counterpart of the Australian flying dwarf, was the only dwarf being thrown. However, the promoter, looking to give Lennie a rest from being launched into the air four times a night, was reported to be canvassing the dwarf population for further volunteers.

The promoter promised that those selected as the dwarf missile would avert any injury by training to fall in professional stunt man fashion by landing on mattresses, and by only being thrown by the club's doorman. The restriction to the doorman was to protect the dwarf from inebriated members of the audience who might take it into their heads to try out as a thrower in the dwarf tossing team. However, later reports showed that the promoter opened the competition up for thrower volunteers from a hard-drinking crowd.[2] According to the Wall Street Journal, on the night of a Fall 1985 contest in Edenbridge England, the contest was won by a postal clerk.[3]

As if that didn't sound bad enough, Pam Rutt, went on to say that things were getting worse. Pam reported that she had recently learned that the English promoter of dwarf throwing, Danny Bamford, had just returned from dwarf throwing tours in Canada and Finland and was planning a tour to United States military bases in West Germany and to

1   Steve Absalom, *"Beware! Dwarfs are flying tonight,"* The Stage and
      Television Today (May 16, 1985).
2   Paul Hemp, *"In Europe, Outcry Is Loud Over a Sport Called
      Dwarf-Tossing,"* The Wall Street Journal (November 1, 1985).
3   ibid.

Australia for the International Dwarf Throwing Contest. According to the Wall Street Journal, the promoter was also planning a contest in Italy.[1]

The English and Europeans, well aware of the power of advocacy, were quick to take action. The English organization had already issued a press release condemning the practice and reporting the outrage of Little People around the world. The release included India's statement which described dwarf throwing as *"grossly uncivilized."* In October 1985, the Netherlands organization for Little People[2] noted that the negative image shaping of dwarf throwing went far beyond the boundaries of Australia and Great Britain and issued a statement to seventeen countries known at that time to have organizations for people of short stature.[3] In this statement, the Netherlands called for solidarity in the protest against dwarf throwing.

In response to the protests in England and Europe, newspapers began reporting on objections to dwarf throwing. In one such article, a closing challenge to the humanity of society read: *"Does a sickening accident have to take place before people realize that dwarf throwing belongs to the Coliseum in ancient Rome, not the supposed 'caring' society of the twentieth century?"* [4]

Not content with newspaper articles, and letters to the editor's of newspapers, the European protesters were successful in gaining a resolution from the European Parliament condemning the practice.[5] They also used every medium available in an effort to ban the practice. Pam Rutt engaged in a radio debate with the English promoter, and with whom she described as ignorant members of the public. Pam also

---

1   Paul Hemp, *"In Europe Outcry is Loud Over a Sport Called Dwarf Tossing,"* The Wall Street Journal (November 1, 1985).

2   BVKM: Belangenvereniging voor kleine mensen.

3   Australia, Belgium, Canada, Costa Rica, Eire, France, Great Britain, India, Israel, Malaysia, New Zealand, Norway, South Africa, Sweden, Switzerland, the United States of America and West Germany. For specific information on any one of these organizations, write to the International Coordinator, Miss Pam Rutt, 24 Pinchfield, Maple Cross, Rickmansworth, Herts WD2 2TP, England.

4   Pam Rutt, Acting Chairperson of the Association for Research into Restricted Growth, *"Dwarfs' denied any shred of human dignity': A degrading spectacle,"* letter to the Editor, the Stage and Television Today (May 16, 1985).

5   Pam Rutt, letter to Robert and Angela Van Etten (December 6, 1985).

publicized a phone-in protest campaign through a daily newspaper. Although neither the protests nor the Resolution of the European Parliament were successful in stopping the English promoter continuing with his plans for dwarf throwing competitions, they were enough of an irritation that the promoter stopped answering his telephone. More importantly, the promoter began to have difficulty finding venues for the contests.

Contest planned in Chicago

As much as the appetite of the Little People of America, Inc. (LPA) for advocacy was intensified by these overseas accounts of dwarf throwing and their efforts to get it banned, it wasn't until LPA learned that dwarf throwing was about to happen in its own back yard that the organization was ready to take corporate action as group advocates. The first public word of a scheduled United States event came in October 1985 from the nationally syndicated columnist, now infamous among Little People, Mike Royko. His daring at publishing a second column on the topic caused his reputation to parallel that of Randy Newman who in 1978 achieved notoriety with his so-called satirical song called *"Short People."* Newman's lyrics were less than flattering when he described short people as having grubby little fingers, dirty little minds, and no reason to live.

Craig McCulloh wrote for LPA Today, the national newsletter of the Little People of America, Inc. (LPA): *"As soon as I read this column, real anger along with a touch of frustration set into me. This jerk wrote another column, and those letters apparently did not get our message across."* [1] Joseph White, a Chapter President for the Central Florida Minigators of LPA, shared Craig's opinion. In Joe's letter to the Editor of the Orlando Sentinel Star of Florida, published under the headline *"Dwarf-tossing leaps to American shores,"* [2] Joe wondered about Mike Royko's obsession with dwarf tossing.

Personally, I'm not so sure that Royko was obsessed with dwarf

---

1   *"Dwarf Tossing Contest Halted in Chicago,"* LPA Today, Vol. 23, No. 1 (Jan-Feb 1986).

2   Submitted to the Editor on October 3, 1985.

tossing, although I do believe he was responsible for setting the stage for an event in Chicago. Despite Royko's prediction that the contest would never take place in Chicago, his reporting of the time, place, and prizes for the planned contest surely did arouse further interest. On the day of the event, the Chicago West-side bar scheduled to host the contest was packed to the doors with fans hoping to see the dwarf throwing competitions take place.[1]

My belief is that if Royko had any obsession, it wasn't with dwarf throwing itself, but rather to find out whether people living in the United States would have any interest in such boorish behavior. The issue of dwarf tossing merely provided Royko with a means to an end. It didn't matter to him that in the process of his research, he was advancing an uncivilized interest in freak entertainment and was risking the physical safety of Little People in general.

Oddly enough, those promoting dwarf throwing claim it's okay, because nobody gets hurt. But even if it's true that nobody has been hurt to date, that's not the same as saying it's not dangerous and someone won't get hurt in the future. In fact, the risk of the dwarf being thrown getting hurt is not only high, but higher than it would be if it was an average-sized person being thrown. That's because most Little People have potential or existing orthopedic complications which may or do affect the stability of their necks, spines, or joints.

Under the stress of everyday living, many Little People undergo surgery at some point in their lives. For Little People to allow themselves to be thrown in a contest is an invitation to disaster. Even if the dwarf bounces back after the throw, there is no telling what long term damage has been done to the body. Every time a dwarf acts as a missile, there is no doubt that he or she is preparing for a future in which there is a potential for dependence on wheels for mobility. Just as likely is the possibility that the dwarf will have no future at all!

Even Royko raises the issue of increased danger, when he suggests a way to throw a dwarf even further.[2] He notes that the distance a dwarf is thrown is limited by the fact that the current rules call for the

---

1   Tom Fitzpatrick, *"Bears dwarf pub's event,"* the Chicago Sun-Times (November 18, 1985).

2   *"Great dwarf toss,"* the Plain Dealer (of Cleveland); *"Will dwarf-throwing catch on in our bars? Small chance,"* the Pittsburgh Press; and in many other newspapers around the country (March 7, 1985).

dwarf to wear a harness which the tosser uses to make an underhanded throw. He comments that had the thrower been able to hold the dwarf by the ankles and spin a few times before releasing him, the dwarf would probably have been thrown into the next tavern. What if somebody took to Royko's set of rules? It's hard to imagine that a dwarf could live through that version of the game and bounce back to bow before a cheering crowd. Besides, as Royko himself said: *"Yeah, it's probably not a good idea after all. It would be just a matter of time before somebody wanted to play catch."* [1]

Actually the problem isn't just limited to the dwarf being thrown in the bar. The Little Person objecting to the practice can't even dismiss the issue by saying: *"If the dwarf being thrown is silly enough to take the chance, why should I worry about it?"* The Little Person out on the street is genuinely concerned that dwarf throwing will degenerate from the bar-room toss of the consenting dwarf to the back alley toss of the non- consenting dwarf.[2]

The fear of being attacked by thugs, drunks, and school bullies looking for fun and ignorant of both the social and physical consequences for the dwarf is very real. The upside down trick in the garbage-can truly begins to look like child's play by comparison. There's no way in the world dwarf throwing can be said to be okay because nobody gets hurt. Like Russian roulette, it's just a matter of time.

When the Chicago bar scheduled a dwarf throwing competition, Royko's curiosity could have been satisfied. He had discovered that there were Americans who pride themselves in advanced technology and enlightened thinking, who are also willing to reduce themselves to uncivilized patterns of behavior. However, Royko was not so easily satisfied. Having learned that Americans are still interested in freak

---

[1]   *"Great dwarf toss,"* the Plain Dealer (of Cleveland); *"Will dwarf throwing catch on in our bars? Small chance,"* the Pittsburgh Press; and in many other newspapers around the country (March 7, 1985).

[2]   This view was expressed at a chapter meeting by the members of the Mid-Hudson Valley Chapter of the Little People of America, Inc. (November 16, 1985).

entertainment, he now wanted to know if those opposing such spectacles had the power to put an end to it. In his October 1985 column,[1] his reporting of the protests in Australia and England and his projection that the contest would never take place in Chicago rang more like a challenge to those opposing the event to exercise their influence to get dwarf throwing stopped.

I'm sure Royko was delighted at the emphatic responses to his two columns. With his first column, he aroused the interest of those eager to participate in dwarf throwing; in the second, he aroused the ire of those ready to have it stopped. To him the real sport was not to observe the specter of dwarf throwing itself, but to see which group in society would win out.

Well, whatever Royko's game was, he turned out not to be the only player. After November 4, 1985, media attention to the dwarf throwing issue did not just wear the Royko label. Royko lost his front runner position when the Wall Street Journal ran a front page article reporting the loud European outcry *"Over the Sport Called Dwarf-Tossing."*[2] The Journal must have picked up the story when they discovered that such a contest was scheduled in Chicago, Illinois sometime in November 1985.

The time for pondering Royko's true position on the subject of dwarf throwing had passed. Whether Royko was for or against such contests was now irrelevant. The fact of the matter remained that an actual event had been scheduled for November in Chicago. It was a waste of energy to direct anger at Royko personally. Now the Little People of America, Inc. had to do something about getting the event canceled.

Up until now, the response of Little People in America to the dwarf throwing issue had been a matter of self and individual advocacy. As self advocates, Little People objected to the practice on their own behalf; as individual advocates, people had objected to the practice on be-

---

1   *"Why dwarf tossing just won't fly,"* the Delaware County Daily Times; *"Dwarf-tossing leaps to American shores"* the Orlando Sentinel Star; and in many other newspapers around the country (October 3, 1985).

2   Paul Hemp, *"In Europe, Outcry Is Loud Over a Sport Called Dwarf-Tossing,"* The Wall Street Journal (November 1, 1985).

half of someone else. For example, the Chicago mother of a dwarf child filed a complaint with the State Attorney General's Office on behalf of her daughter. Also, many individuals phoned and wrote to newspapers to express their protest. Indeed, in his October 1985 column, Royko admitted receiving many letters from *"dwarfs, friends, and relatives of dwarfs, and people who were none of the above but enjoy a good crusade."* [1]

On November 6, 1985, I joined the ranks of both the self and individual advocates. After reading the Wall Street Journal article, I wrote a letter to the Editor of the Journal to record a protest on behalf of myself and other Little People. On November 22, 1985 I was delighted to see my letter printed, with very little editing, under the headline *"Small Minds Look Down on Dwarfs."* It was great to see that the essence of my protest had been understood. My letter as printed read as follows:

"After reading the Nov. 1 page-one article about dwarf tossing, I feel compelled to add my sentiments to the European outcry about the spectacle. Like Lenny, I am a dwarf. However, unlike Lenny I do not enjoy being thrown around. I can't imagine how Lenny could agree to becoming a human projectile, or understand why the public would derive any pleasure from watching a man be thrown like a lifeless object. I wish someone could tell me that the Journal had mistakenly printed this from a book of seventeenth century history."

"However, at 32 years of age, I have lived enough to know that it is not unusual for dwarfs of the twentieth century to be treated as objects of ridicule, disrespect, and discrimination. We are laughed at by groups of children on the street; we are treated like children, instead of being given the respect that our adult years and appearance command; we are refused jobs, despite having prepared ourselves with a college education."

"Yet dwarfs, who in the U. S. mostly prefer to be called Little People, have the same aspirations and abilities as other people. Our small bodies do not reflect the size of our minds, or talent. Our

---

1   *"Why dwarf tossing just won't fly,"* the Delaware County Daily Times; *"Dwarf-tossing leaps to American shores"* the Orlando Sentinel Star; and in many other newspapers around the country (October 3, 1985).

similarities to the average-sized population far outnumber the superficial differences of our appearance."

"I'd like to see two things happen: first, that the public join in the outcry against the depraved practice of dwarf-tossing; and second, that the public put a stop to the practice of throwing dwarfs into the endless arena of ridicule, disrespect and discrimination. I know which one will take the longest."

How the Chicago contest was halted

With a dwarf toss planned in Chicago, the time had come for the Little People of America, Inc. (LPA) to exercise group advocacy. Robert Van Etten, LPA's national President from 1984-1986, raised the issue in his monthly newsletter to the approximately 80 elected and appointed officials of the organization. He posed a series of questions to stimulate discussion and to promote action among the members.

One of those questions was whether a media campaign should be launched to register the protest of the members of the organization. However, it soon became apparent that a media campaign was already off the ground. Within a few days of the Wall Street Journal article,[1] Steve Bratman, a CBS reporter, called to interview Robert Van Etten, President of Little People of America, Inc.[2] for a thirty second radio spot he was preparing for syndication to CBS radio stations around the country.

Certainly after three articles on the subject of dwarf throwing had been publicized nation-wide,[3] it was high time the Little People of America, Inc. got into gear as an organization to rebut the promotion of dwarf throwing as harmless fun. To date, the critical comments had only come from individuals speaking or writing on behalf of themsel-

---

1   Paul Hemp, *"In Europe, Outcry Is Loud Over a Sport Called Dwarf-Tossing,"* The Wall Street Journal (November 1, 1985).

2   Van Etten was President from 1980-1982, 1984-1986.

3   Royko, *"Great dwarf toss,"* the Plain Dealer of Cleveland (March 7, 1985); Royko, *"Will dwarf-throwing catch on in our bars? Small chance,"* the Pittsburgh Press (March 7, 1985); Royko, *"Why dwarf tossing just won't fly,"* the Delaware County Daily Times (October 3, 1985); Royko, *"Dwarf-tossing leaps to American shores,"* the Orlando Sentinel Star (October 3, 1985); and Paul Hemp, *"In Europe, Outcry Is Loud Over a Sport Called Dwarf-Tossing,"* The Wall Street Journal (November 1, 1985).

ves or others. No one had been authorized to speak as a representative of the organization.

After responding to CBS, Robert Van Etten decided that LPA's appeal for media exposure should be concentrated in Chicago because the dwarf tossing event was going to happen in Chicago, and Chicago was the citadel of Royko, the one held responsible by many Little People for promoting the contest. It was important to appeal to the Chicago community to attract public support for the plan of the Little People of America, Inc. to have the event canceled.

So how best to counter Royko's October column advertising the event? Find a reputable reporter from a competing newspaper willing to present the perspective of the Little People of America, Inc. After some inquiry, the organization was pleased to discover Irv Kupcinet of the Chicago-Sun Times. Kup, as he is called in Chicago, reported in a November 1985 column:

" ... a ridiculous "sport" called dwarf throwing ... is coming to Chicago ... the owner of a Public House is planning to introduce the demeaning endeavor on Sunday ... We've had two calls from two dwarfs associated with the Little People of America, 3-foot-4 Robert Van Etten of Rochester, N.Y. and 4-foot-10 Craig McCulloh of Harrisburg, Pa., both employed in normal jobs."

"THE TWO LEADERS of the Little People of America are justifiably incensed over the alleged sport and will seek means to halt the game as an appalling form of exploitation. Unfortunately, the participating dwarfs do so willingly and are paid for sailing through the air ... We recommend a much more appropriate game on Sunday -- watch the Bears throw the Dallas Cowboys for distance." [1]

Beth Loyless, the Membership Coordinator of the Little People of America, Inc., 1984-1986, and a resident of the Chicago metropolitan area, became the organization's spokesperson for local radio and television. Although this resulted in Beth becoming the target of snide

---

1   Kup's Column (November 12, 1985); the game between the Chicago Bears and the Dallas Cowboys was a crucial foot-ball game in the 1985 United States Super Bowl series which the Chicago Bears went on to win.

remarks from announcers of the radio station advertising the contest, as Craig McCulloh put it: *"the real clincher is that she was being heard and the public was listening. She was delivering our shared message that this contest was dehumanizing and morally wrong."* [1]

As much as the media was useful to stir up public support for our cause, the media coverage alone would not achieve the results we were looking for --- cancellation of the contest. Craig McCulloh took the reins of the group advocacy effort at this point, and successfully located a number of organizations in the Chicago area who were sensitive and understanding to our situation.

Craig did not limit his search to the Little People of Chicago. As an assistant to a Pennsylvania State Representative, Craig understood the dynamics of gaining community support. Craig reached out to a variety of groups in the city, including disability organizations who advocate for the rights of handicapped people, to the significant Irish Catholic community known to reside in Chicago, to the politicians, and to the legal community concerned to protect the civil rights of citizens. His approach was very successful. The community organizations contacted were very receptive to our cause and were instrumental in putting pressure on both the tavern owner planning the contest, and on the political nerve centers in Chicago. Of major significance is the fact that the Attorney General's Office became involved. This was in response to the complaint filed by the parent of a Chicago dwarf child. The attorney assigned to the case from the Attorney General's Office and Division of Disability Advocacy, felt that there were a limited number of legal arguments which could be made in the short time which remained before the contest was to take place. For this reason, she engaged in creative negotiations with Creswell, the bar owner.

The strategy paid off. When Creswell was called into the Attorney General's Office to discuss the planned dwarf throwing contest and was confronted with the news that many Little People, their families, and respectable citizens of the Chicago community were appalled by the prospect of such an event occurring in their city, he agreed to can-

---

1   *"Dwarf Tossing Contest Halted in Chicago,"* LPA Today, Vol. 23, No. 1 (Jan-Feb 1986).

cel the contest. According to Royko's report of his interview with the bar owner after his agreement to cancel, *"all Creswell wanted to do was have a little fun. Get a little publicity. Give the customers a good time. He didn't want to offend anyone."* [1] During the attorney's meeting with Creswell, it became very clear to the bar owner that he was not going to succeed with any of his objectives. Rather than risk the bad publicity, he opted to cancel the contest.

Certainly Creswell's announced plans for the contest had already stirred up bad press for his bar. It had to be bad for business when the Chicago Mayor, Harold Washington, came down hard on dwarf throwing in a press statement which declared the contest as *"degrading and mean-spirited,*[2] *a danger to its participants and repugnant to everyone truly committed to eliminating prejudice against any group."* [3]

Actually, the Mayor's Office did much more than issue a press statement. They also took Creswell to court. As a result, a temporary restraining order was issued prohibiting Creswell from holding the dwarf throwing contest unless he obtained the license which the city required for public amusement events. The court order was issued on the Friday afternoon before the planned Sunday event, which left Creswell with no time to apply for the necessary license.

As a result of the advocacy efforts of Craig McCulloh, the Chicago groups he contacted, Beth Loyless, and other Chicago members of the Little People of America, Inc. it was a delight to pick up newspaper with headlines which read *"Dwarf-toss event canceled here"* [4] and *"Dwarf Toss Banned."* [5] It was just as satisfying to find dwarf tossing

---

1   *"So where do you go to get a dwarf-tossing license?"* the Syracuse Herald-Journal; *"Dwarf-tossing cut short,"* the Pittsburgh Press; and in many other newspapers around the country (November 1985).

2   Jim Quinlan, *"Dwarf-toss event canceled here,"* the Chicago Sun Times (November 18, 1985); and *"Dwarf Toss Banned,"* Union Sun - and Journal of Lockport New York (November 1985).

3   *"So where do you go to get a dwarf-tossing license?"* the Syracuse Herald-Journal; *"Dwarf-tossing cut short,"* the Pittsburgh Press; and in many other newspapers around the country (November 1985).

4   Jim Quinlan of the Chicago Sun Times (November 18, 1985).

5   Union Sun - and Journal of Lockport New York (November 1985).

depicted as a 1985 Dubious Achievement in Entertainment and Sports in the January 1986 issue of Esquire.

Winning the battle but not the war

In celebrating the victory of the cancellation of the Chicago contest, Craig McCulloh warned:

"We have won the battle... However, I must caution that we have not won the war. We must continue to utilize the power of advocacy, as it can work, as long as human decency prevails." [1]

In December 1985, Craig continued the warning with what turned out to be prophetic accuracy:

"Such immoral contests could and may very well occur in ... Philadelphia (Pennsylvania), Rochester, New York, or Anytown U. S. of A." [2]

Only a few months later, members of three Little People of America chapters were faced with the prospect of dwarf throwing competitions in their home towns. The Liberty Chapter in Philadelphia, Pennsylvania was threatened with a 'Dwarf Chucking Contest' in a local cafe;[3] the New York Finger Lakes Chapter in Rochester, New York was disturbed to see an advertisement placed in the personal column of a local newspaper by a three-feet-five-inch dwarf looking for a 400 pound tossing agent able to throw the dwarf at least one hundred yards;[4] and the Mohawk Valley Chapter of Albany, New York, coming in under Craig's prediction of Anytown U. S. of A., were subjected to derogatory remarks by a local radio station.[5]

---

1   *"Dwarf Tossing Contest Halted in Chicago,"* LPA Today, Vol. 23, No. 1 (Jan-Feb 1986).

2   Pennsylvania Dutch Chapter Newsletter of the Little People of America, Inc. (December 1985).

3   Harry McDonald, *"The Power of Advocacy,"* Newsletter of District 2 of the Little People of America, Inc. (January-April, 1986).

4   Advertisement in the personal column of Downtown: The Unbound Magazine, Rochester, New York (April 1, 1986).

5   MaryAnne Panarese, President of the Mohawk Valley Chapter of the Little People of America, Inc., Mohawk Valley Chapter Newsletter (April, 1986).

Nixing the contest planned in Philadelphia

In Philadelphia, the contest was being promoted by John DeBella, the disc jockey host of the *"Morning Zoo"* program on WMMR, a local FM radio station. DeBella learned very quickly that the Little People of the Liberty Chapter were not willing to stand by and see any Little Person be chucked one single inch. The only throwing that would be tolerated by Little People in Philadelphia was of their corporate weight against DeBella to get the planned contest canceled.

Harry McDonald, the Director of District 2 from 1983-1986, headed the advocacy response in Philadelphia. After the successful efforts in Chicago, Harry knew just what steps to take. Within hours, he had the support of both the Mayor's Office, and the Human Relations Commission.

Even though the Commission offered reasonable hope that they could stop the contest by using a local ordinance which prohibited the denial of access into public buildings of handicapped or minority groups, Harry knew not to bank on their success. The Commission readily admitted that to use the ordinance to prohibit a dwarf throwing competition was indeed a broad interpretation of the law. The Commission could not guarantee that a court would agree that a dwarf was being denied access to the bar because the fear of being thrown would prevent a Little Person from entering the bar at the time of the contest.

Harry decided not to risk sitting around to wait for a judge's interpretation of the ordinance. Instead, he called in Craig McCulloh of Harrisburg, Pennsylvania to mobilize a community protest. Craig, who now had the advantage of working in his home state, used the same strategies applied to get dwarf throwing stopped in Chicago.

In Philadelphia, Craig was instrumental in gaining the support of local organizations.[1] While Craig was working on gathering community support, Harry began looking for media exposure. He knew the importance of turning the proposed contest into a public relations

---

1   The United Cerebral Palsy Association, the Disabled Veteran's Organization, two members of the City Council, the State Attorney General's Office, and the Pennsylvania Liquor Control Board.

nightmare for the Heart Throbs Cafe, said to be hosting the event. For this reason, Harry selected Terry Ruggles of WCAU-TV, an affiliate of CBS, who he had a fair idea would be sympathetic to the cause. His assumption was based on the meaningful interview Terry conducted about Harry and the Liberty Chapter of the Little People of America, Inc. a couple of years earlier. Harry also remembered Terry's invitation to call on his services anytime Harry had a good cause to promote. Obviously, this was the time to seek out Terry's services. Harry's hopes were well placed, because only a couple of hours after making contact with Terry Ruggles both Terry and a camera crew met with Harry to film for that night's 5 and 11 o'clock news programs.

At the same time as Harry and Craig were working on media and community support, other chapter members were busy getting newspaper coverage, and making protest calls to both the radio station and the Heart Throbs Cafe. One chapter member even contacted the area's Congressman in Washington, D.C. No stone was left unturned.

The United Cerebral Palsy (UCP) organization was responsible for turning over one of the most important stones. They contacted the owner of the building who was landlord to the Heart Throbs Cafe. UCP was indignant that the owner would tolerate such degrading spectacles from one of its tenants. The owner was quite disturbed to hear of the contest planned and went to the cafe to see what was going on. The result? The owners of the Heart Throbs Cafe demanded an on-the-air apology from DeBella himself. It appeared that the Cafe was also a target of DeBella's humor, as the management claimed to know nothing of the event.

Whoever was the target of DeBella's joke, it was all over within a few hours. The Liberty Chapter, together with the ground swell of support mobilized in the city of Philadelphia, had forcefully countered the radio station's promotion of the dwarf throwing contest. Only one day after the promotion of the contest began, DeBella was on the air saying that no such contest would take place. It was victory within 24 hours! The advocacy efforts of the Little People of America, Inc. had won out once again.

In fact, the public reaction in Philadelphia was so great that DeBella was forced to give the on-the-air apology demanded by the Heart Throbs Cafe. The closest DeBella was capable of coming to an apology, however, was to say that the whole thing was a joke. According to him, the station never intended chucking a dwarf. In a revelation of his bizarre humor, he went on to explain that in the past they had threatened to blow up a cow, but had never actually done so. In this case, he said they only planned to throw a dwarf palm tree or some other small object to show how silly the whole thing was. But if that was really true, why had DeBella previously announced on the radio that the station had the crash helmet and harness and were ready to pay the dwarf eight dollars per throw? Obviously a dwarf palm tree would have no need for payment or any such protective equipment.

Whether DeBella ever intended to go ahead with the dwarf chucking contest is anybody's guess. Although it should be noted for the record that the radio station's general manager made a statement to the press saying that the station never planned to actually hold the contest.[1] Whatever the station's or DeBella's plans were, the closing remarks of DeBella in his so-called *"apology"* demonstrate that any reason he may have had to cancel the contest did not include concern for the interests of Little People. DeBella finished up by suggesting that those who had objected to the holding of the contest should *"open up their little minds."*

Action in up-state New York

The members of the Mohawk Valley Chapter of the Little People of America, Inc. were faced with equally derisive remarks from WROW a radio station in Albany, New York.[2] Even though the station was not actually promoting a contest, the members felt it was important to intercept any such remarks before any proposal for a dwarf throwing contest gained support. A letter of protest was written to the station expressing the concern of the chapter members.[3]

---

1   *"WMMR Host Apologizes for Dwarf 'Joke,'"* City and Region section in Philadelphia newspaper (March 13, 1986).
2   Chapter newsletter, MaryAnne Panarese (April, 1986).
3   MaryAnne Panarese, Letter to the WROW radio station (March 9, 1986).

The New York Finger Lakes Chapter of the Little People of America, Inc. had an easier time dealing with the advertisement placed in the personal column of Downtown: The Unbound Magazine circulated in Rochester, New York. It was pretty obvious that whoever placed the ad, either did not have all their facts together, or was making a total farce out of the idea of dwarf throwing. Anyone who knows anything about dwarf throwing knows that the unofficial record for throwing a dwarf is only 30 feet.[1] It would actually be impossible for someone to toss a dwarf 100 yards. As David Kelly, the President of the New York Finger Lakes Chapter (1985-1987) said, *"even the best quarterback can't throw a football one hundred yards; how could anyone throw a dwarf that far?"* Perhaps the publication date of *"April First"* indicates that the person placing the ad had a sense of humor as sick as DeBella's. However, the local little people would not so easily be made fools of.

Although there was no need for the group to take action in response to an April fools joke, the chapter members were encouraged by a local radio station's response to the advertisement. The disc jockey had never even heard of dwarf throwing, and couldn't believe that such a thing would ever happen. In light of the fact that Rochester's newspaper, the Democrat and Chronicle, exercised it's editorial discretion against printing Royko's three columns on the subject, it wasn't surprising that the disc jockey hadn't heard about dwarf throwing. However, of greater significance was the announcer's reaction. The chapter members had good reason to celebrate that nobody was promoting dwarf throwing in Rochester, New York. Human decency must surely prevail in the Rochester community.

Why the "sport" should be outlawed

In all the United States cities in which the promotion of dwarf throwing had been proposed, the power of advocacy and creative negotiation was sufficient to get the contests canceled. But what if

1   *"Why dwarf tossing just won't fly,"* the Delaware County Daily Times;
"Dwarf-tossing leaps to American shores" the Orlando Sentinel Star;
and in many other newspapers around the country (October 3, 1985).

Chicago's Creswell had not cared about the bad press, and had followed Royko's advice and gone ahead and obtained the appropriate license?[1] How would the Mayor's Office in Chicago and the Little People of America, Inc. have stopped him then?

There is no doubt, that as powerful as advocacy can be, it does have limitations. Not all will be like Creswell of Chicago or DeBella of Philadelphia and agree to cancel the contest. Rather, some will be like Bamford of Britain who blatantly refuse to give up plans and appear to revel in the bad publicity.

When negotiation and advocacy don't prompt an appropriate response, as in the case of Bamford, it is necessary to make the offensive activity unlawful. That may be the only way to challenge the discriminatory behavior. Legislation will be the only means to avert the action.

However, it's one thing to say a law is needed to get dwarf throwing stopped, and quite another to get it enacted. In the case of dwarf throwing, a direct conflict between the rights of two groups of people is immediately apparent. Robert Van Etten, posed this conflict to the elected and appointed officials of the Little People of America, Inc., for resolution on November 4, 1985. He presented the conflict this way:

"Should the desire of the individual dwarf who agrees to be thrown be overruled for the sake of the general dwarf population whose image suffers as a result? Does not the brutality and danger to the dwarf being thrown suggest we should take legal steps to have the sport outlawed?"

Indeed those dwarfs being thrown regarded it as a job. According to Royko,

"the Australian said it beat his regular job of acting in children's

---

1   *"So where do you go to get a dwarf-tossing license?,"* the Syracuse Herald-Journal; *"Dwarf-tossing cut short,"* the Pittsburgh Press; and in many other newspapers around the country (November 1985).

shows. He said he preferred flying across a bar-room to performing before a horde of runny-nosed kids. And the tiny Englishman, who is known as Lennie the Giant, said being tossed wasn't nearly as degrading as working on an assembly line." [1]

Danny Bamford, the promoter who organizes dwarf throwing contests in England, says dwarf throwing *"allows the little fellow to show he can go out and be someone."* [2] But if that's really the case, why does Bamford advise *"the little fellow"* not to give his family name? What sort of recognition will Lennie the Giant ever receive if nobody ever gets to know who he is?

Of course, that's not to say it's the sort of recognition any self-respecting dwarf would be looking for anyway. Just take a look at the audience who revel in this sort of spectacle. According to the Wall Street Journal account of a performance in a run-down section of a town south of London, Lennie the Giant seemed out of place in the seedy milieu where the audience was described as a hard-drinking crowd. [3]

Even if members of the Little People of America, Inc. could accept that an individual dwarf has the right to make a living as a dwarf tossee, it is questionable just how good a living that would be. In England, Lennie was reported to be making only seventy two dollars a night, [4] and he doesn't even get to work every night. And what about the future? The dwarf is totally subject to the changing whims of a bar

---

1   *"Why dwarf tossing just won't fly,"* the Delaware County Daily Times; *"Dwarf-tossing leaps to American shores"* the Orlando Sentinel Star; and in many other newspapers around the country (October 3, 1985).

2   Paul Hemp, *"In Europe, Outcry Is Loud Over a Sport Called Dwarf-Tossing,"* The Wall Street Journal (November 1, 1985).

3   ibid.

4   ibid.

drinking crowd. In Australia, no more contests are planned, as according to the manager of the bar holding the first competition, the novelty has warn off.[1]

Regardless of whether dwarf tossing is a viable employment option, many Little People reject Royko's statement that a consenting adult dwarf who chooses to be tossed has such a right.[2] Such competitions fall into the category of freak show entertainment, which present a clash between the right of the dwarf tossee to earn a living in such contests, and the right of the remaining dwarf population to earn a living in respectable occupations in which they will not be regarded as carnival acts nor treated as subhuman objects.

In appropriate cases, the State may be called upon to decide that the interests of the individual must bow to the competing interests of the public. The State will act when it is necessary to protect the public welfare, health, morals, and safety of the public in general. In my view, dwarf throwing is a case where the State must intervene to promote the interests of people in general, including Little People. To do this, the State must remove the right of the individual dwarf to be tossed.

In fact, the State has a legitimate economic interest in fostering enlightened public understanding and attitudes towards the true nature and problems of Little People. To allow such entertainment to con-

---

1   Paul Hemp, *"In Europe, Outcry Is Loud Over a Sport Called Dwarf-Tossing,"* The Wall Street Journal (November 1, 1985). According to later reports, one further contest took place in Brisbane, Australia on November 11, 1986. However, subsequent contests planned for Sydney and Melbourne Australia, in the international test match series between England and Australia, were canceled in response to public protest, People Magazine of Australia (December 22, 1986), and the Time's Union, Rochester, New York (November 13, 1986).

2   *"So where do you go to get a dwarf-tossing license?,"* the Syracuse Herald-Journal; *"Dwarf-tossing cut short,"* the Pittsburgh Press; and in many other newspapers around the country (November 1985).

tinue, tends to generate the public concept of Little People as freaks which logically tends to make it more difficult for Little People to obtain the regular employment they are otherwise capable of engaging in. If nothing is done to change this concept, the State will be burdened with the responsibility of supporting many unemployed Little People.[1]

There is another very good reason for the State to override an individual's decision to participate in dwarf tossing. The danger of the activity causes the State to determine that its interest in preserving life, overrides the individual's freedom to risk his or her own life and safety. Stunt work and dare-devil feats are common activities which have caused many States to enact laws prohibiting certain feats. Dwarf tossing most certainly falls into this category.

It is well known that any dare-devil who lives through the experience of going over Niagara Falls is met with both arrest and criminal penalties. Dwarfs who allow themselves to be tossed and those who do the tossing should be met with similar penalties. This is the best way of protecting the individual who consents to being thrown to his or her own injury or death. It should also diminish the likelihood of the non-consenting dwarf being harmed by pranksters and bullies.

Many view legislation with trepidation and have little confidence in its ability to change people's attitudes. They do not believe you can legislate away stigma; that may be true. But where the majority of the people believe discriminatory behavior is a breach of individual rights and should be made unlawful, then it is possible through legislation to protect the individual from the few who continue to discriminate. The stigma may remain, but its effect can be removed. For example, Bamford's support of dwarf throwing may continue, but the law will prevent his sponsoring any further events.

However, for legislation to be effective, the majority of the people must believe in it. If they don't, it won't be long before it becomes un-

---

1   This argument was presented to a Florida court, in World Fair Freaks & Attractions, Inc. v Hodges (1972, Fla) 267 So 2d 817, 62 ALR 3d 1232, by the state in an attempt to prohibit the commercial exhibition of any crippled or physically distorted, malformed or disfigured person in any place where admission fees were charged. In this case, one of the persons being exhibited was a dwarf. However, the court did not uphold the state's interest in preventing such exhibitions; rather it declared the statute as unconstitutional because of the failure to provide reasonable standards to be followed in the statutes application.

workable. People would do their best to find loop-holes and remove teeth from any enforcement provisions. Unless people generally agree that dwarf throwing is inappropriate entertainment, any enforcement will be ineffectual, and the practice will continue unchecked.

Some have resisted the introduction of civil-rights legislation on the premise that education is enough. However, it is naive to believe that the opponents of various laws do not know what they are doing when they supposedly forget to put in the curb-cut, or to lower the elevator buttons, or in Bamford's case, promote the throwing of dwarfs. All the education in the world would never change the mind of someone like Bamford. The Europeans surely did try!

Even if a person genuinely does forget to recognize the rights of Little People, the effect is no less adverse. It is irrelevant whether the action is deliberate or accidental. The fact remains; when the rights of Little People are violated, we are treated as less than equal.

Many complain there is already too much legislation and regulation. Nobody can debate that, but there is no excuse for not having legislation which is necessary to correct an injustice. The answer is to re-evaluate existing legislation, to prune what is redundant, and to add what is needed for the protection of Little People in society.

I do not believe it is a question of legislation or education. The two go hand in hand. To support legislation and not education ignores the problem of compliance. It's not much use having a law if people don't understand or want to obey it. The effect will be that people will do their best to circumvent the law. To support education and not legislation, presumes all people will be tuned into the education program, and all will be convinced. This will not happen. Too many violations will fall between the cracks, and too many Little People will suffer at the hands of discrimination.

We need education and legislation operating at the same time to ensure understanding of the reason for the law, to create support for it, and to obtain compliance from those who would escape it if they could. Even if the legislation is never used in enforcement proceedings, the threat of that expense is always a deterrent in the mind of the person asked to comply with the law. Often a person will accede to a request to avoid costly and timely legal proceedings. However, in the case of someone like Bamford who will proceed with his plans regardless, the law would be a tool ready to put a stop to dwarf tossing long before it ever got off the ground.

INDEX

WHY PEOPLE SHOULD READ THIS BOOK:

DWARFS WILL IDENTIFY with the experiences of the author and will be encouraged to accept themselves as individuals of value and to defend their right to a place alongside, not beneath, others in the community.

PARENTS WILL OVERCOME their disappointment and despair at the birth of a dwarf child, and will understand that in return for loving, disciplining, and developing independence and self-esteem in their child, they will be rewarded with a truly whole person fully prepared to meet the world's challenges.

RELATIVES WILL APPRECIATE their role in relating to both the parents and the dwarf in the family.

EDUCATORS WILL LEARN that dwarf children are denied an equal education unless they are integrated into regular classrooms, and are treated according to their age, not their size.

PROFESSIONALS WILL SEE the dynamics of the life experience and expectations of the dwarfs and families they counsel.

DISABLED PEOPLE WILL RECOGNIZE the similarity between the dwarf experience and their own in maintaining self-respect in the face of public ridicule and rejection, and in achieving a positive public reaction through education and integration.

ALL PEOPLE WILL ACCEPT the reality and equality of dwarfs in society by breaking through the barriers which prevent meaningful interaction.

ORDER FORM

Adaptive Living
P.O. Box 60857
Rochester, NY 14606
(716) 458-5455

Please send me:

Dwarfs Don't Live in Doll Houses
by Angela Muir Van Etten

FIRST BOOK ORDERED

First Order X (Book Cost + Shipping & Handling) = Total

___1___ X ($ 15.95   + $ 1.25   ) = $ 17 . 20

ADDITIONAL BOOKS ORDERED

(# Ordered) X (Book Cost + Shipping & Handling) = Total

(___) X ($ 15.95 + $ 0.25   ) = $ ___ . ___

If you are a New York state resident, please add $ 1.12 per book $ ___ . ___

TOTAL AMOUNT ENCLOSED $ ___ . ___

The book(s) should be shipped to:

Name:_____

Address:_____

City:_____State:_____ZIP:_____

Phone number: area code (_____) - _____ - _____

If you are ordering more than 10 books write for discount information.

WHY PEOPLE SHOULD READ THIS BOOK:

DWARFS WILL IDENTIFY with the experiences of the author and will be encouraged to accept themselves as individuals of value and to defend their right to a place alongside, not beneath, others in the community.

PARENTS WILL OVERCOME their disappointment and despair at the birth of a dwarf child, and will understand that in return for loving, disciplining, and developing independence and self-esteem in their child, they will be rewarded with a truly whole person fully prepared to meet the world's challenges.

RELATIVES WILL APPRECIATE their role in relating to both the parents and the dwarf in the family.

EDUCATORS WILL LEARN that dwarf children are denied an equal education unless they are integrated into regular classrooms, and are treated according to their age, not their size.

PROFESSIONALS WILL SEE the dynamics of the life experience and expectations of the dwarfs and families they counsel.

DISABLED PEOPLE WILL RECOGNIZE the similarity between the dwarf experience and their own in maintaining self-respect in the face of public ridicule and rejection, and in achieving a positive public reaction through education and integration.

ALL PEOPLE WILL ACCEPT the reality and equality of dwarfs in society by breaking through the barriers which prevent meaningful interaction.

ORDER FORM

Adaptive Living
P.O. Box 60857
Rochester, NY 14606
(716) 458-5455

Please send me:
Dwarfs Don't Live in Doll Houses
by Angela Muir Van Etten

FIRST BOOK ORDERED

First Order X (Book Cost + Shipping & Handling) =   Total

____1____ X ($ 15.95   + $ 1.25   ) = $ 17 . 20

ADDITIONAL BOOKS ORDERED

(# Ordered) X (Book Cost + Shipping & Handling) =   Total

(____) X ($ 15.95 + $ 0.25   ) = $ ____ . ____

If you are a New York state resident, please add $ 1.12 per book $ ____ . ____

TOTAL AMOUNT ENCLOSED $ _____ . ____

The book(s) should be shipped to:

Name:_____

Address:_____

City:_____State:_____ZIP:_____

Phone number: area code (____) - _____ - _____

If you are ordering more than 10 books write for discount information.

WHY PEOPLE SHOULD READ THIS BOOK:

DWARFS WILL IDENTIFY with the experiences of the author and will be encouraged to accept themselves as individuals of value and to defend their right to a place alongside, not beneath, others in the community.

PARENTS WILL OVERCOME their disappointment and despair at the birth of a dwarf child, and will understand that in return for loving, disciplining, and developing independence and self-esteem in their child, they will be rewarded with a truly whole person fully prepared to meet the world's challenges.

RELATIVES WILL APPRECIATE their role in relating to both the parents and the dwarf in the family.

EDUCATORS WILL LEARN that dwarf children are denied an equal education unless they are integrated into regular classrooms, and are treated according to their age, not their size.

PROFESSIONALS WILL SEE the dynamics of the life experience and expectations of the dwarfs and families they counsel.

DISABLED PEOPLE WILL RECOGNIZE the similarity between the dwarf experience and their own in maintaining self-respect in the face of public ridicule and rejection, and in achieving a positive public reaction through education and integration.

ALL PEOPLE WILL ACCEPT the reality and equality of dwarfs in society by breaking through the barriers which prevent meaningful interaction.

ORDER FORM

Adaptive Living
P.O. Box 60857
Rochester, NY 14606
(716) 458-5455

Please send me:
Dwarfs Don't Live in Doll Houses
by Angela Muir Van Etten

FIRST BOOK ORDERED

First Order X (Book Cost + Shipping & Handling) =   Total

_____1_____ X ($ 15.95   + $ 1.25   ) = $ 17 . 20

ADDITIONAL   BOOKS   ORDERED

(# Ordered) X (Book Cost + Shipping & Handling) =   Total

(_____) X ($ 15.95 + $ 0.25   ) = $ ____ . ___

If you are a New York state resident, please add $ 1.12 per book $ _____ . ___

TOTAL AMOUNT ENCLOSED $ _____ . ____

The book(s) should be shipped to:

Name:_____

Address:_____

City:_____State:_____ZIP:_____

Phone number: area code (_____) - _____ - _____

If you are ordering more than 10 books write for discount information.

WHY PEOPLE SHOULD READ THIS BOOK:

DWARFS WILL IDENTIFY with the experiences of the author and will be encouraged to accept themselves as individuals of value and to defend their right to a place alongside, not beneath, others in the community.

PARENTS WILL OVERCOME their disappointment and despair at the birth of a dwarf child, and will understand that in return for loving, disciplining, and developing independence and self-esteem in their child, they will be rewarded with a truly whole person fully prepared to meet the world's challenges.

RELATIVES WILL APPRECIATE their role in relating to both the parents and the dwarf in the family.

EDUCATORS WILL LEARN that dwarf children are denied an equal education unless they are integrated into regular classrooms, and are treated according to their age, not their size.

PROFESSIONALS WILL SEE the dynamics of the life experience and expectations of the dwarfs and families they counsel.

DISABLED PEOPLE WILL RECOGNIZE the similarity between the dwarf experience and their own in maintaining self-respect in the face of public ridicule and rejection, and in achieving a positive public reaction through education and integration.

ALL PEOPLE WILL ACCEPT the reality and equality of dwarfs in society by breaking through the barriers which prevent meaningful interaction.

ORDER FORM

Adaptive Living
P.O. Box 60857
Rochester, NY 14606
(716) 458-5455

Please send me:
Dwarfs Don't Live in Doll Houses
by Angela Muir Van Etten

FIRST BOOK ORDERED

First Order X (Book Cost + Shipping & Handling) = Total

___1___ X ($ 15.95   + $ 1.25   ) = $ 17 . 20

ADDITIONAL BOOKS ORDERED

(# Ordered) X (Book Cost + Shipping & Handling) = Total

(___) X ($ 15.95 + $ 0.25   ) = $ ___ . ___

If you are a New York state resident, please add $ 1.12 per book $ ___ . ___

TOTAL AMOUNT ENCLOSED $ ___ . ___

The book(s) should be shipped to:

Name:_____

Address:_____

City:_____State:_____ZIP:_____

Phone number: area code (____) - _____ - _____

If you are ordering more than 10 books write for discount information.